Jesus Talks to You

Presented to:

....

On the Occasion of:

....

From:

....

Date:

....

Jesus Talks to You

365 Daily Devotions for Experiencing GOD's Love

ROBERT BARRY

Royal Light
Media

Jesus Talks to You

Paperback is available at:
amazon.com
JesusTalksToYou.com

eBook is available at:
amazon.com (Kindle)
barnesandnoble.com (Nook)

Published by: Royal Light Media
www.JesusTalksToYou.com

SPECIAL SALES
Paperback is available at special quantity discounts when purchased in bulk by churches, organizations, schools, corporations, and non-profits.
For information, please send Email: JesusTalksToYou@aol.com

Paperback
ISBN-13: 978-0692271803
ISBN-10: 0692271805

Printed in the United States of America

Jesus Talks to You

As high as the myriad galaxies are above the earth, so are my ways, my thoughts, my knowledge, and my powers higher than your ways, your understanding, and powers. As high as the heavens are above the earth, so is the depth, the richness, the fullness, and the glory of my love above any love that you have ever experienced.

I am the Most High God; yet I dwell with the one who has a humble heart. I am opening my heart and sharing these truths with you, that you might understand and more readily receive my love. I am your God, and I deeply desire that you experience the riches of my love.

I have the power to give to you abundant life. Only through me can you experience this abundant life. As many as receive me and my love, I give the power and the right to be my child. I inhabit eternity and will cherish and rejoice exceedingly—through the eternal ages—with each child who has received me into their heart. The value of each child of mine transcends all the jewels of the world.

My loving heart greatly delights, exults, and knows no bounds in my relationship with my children. Come and let me love you, care for you, and guide you through this journey of life. I am the Way; I am the Truth; I am the Life. Trust me without doubting. Give me your heart. Come, take my hand; I will lead you into a most glorious life now and through eternity.

Jesus Talks to You

I am the One who created the stars as well as all the intricate life forms of earth. When I make all things new, you will reign with me in the new heavens and new earth that I have prepared for you. It is not the stars or the intricate flowers of creation that I will cherish and rejoice with throughout eternity. It is you, with whom I will live, delight in, and celebrate with forever.

There are no words, in any language, that are able to express properly the glory and majesty that you will experience forever in the kingdom of heaven. The most spectacular sunsets that you have ever experienced, the most magnificent music you have ever heard, the most beautiful and fragrant floral displays your eyes have feasted upon, the majesty of earth's grandest mountain ranges, the wonders of the highest waterfalls, and the brilliant glories of a thousand galaxies all pale in comparison to the glory you will experience—for all eternity!

Jesus Talks to You

Consider My Everlasting Love

I loved you before you received me as your Savior. While you were yet in a life of sin, I loved you. When I created your inmost being and fashioned you in your mother's womb, I knew you and your whole life story—and I loved you. When the Father sent me to the agony of the cross at Calvary to die for your sins, I loved you. During the rise and fall of kingdoms and nations, you were on my mind—and I loved you. When Adam and Eve walked in the midst of the paradise of Eden, I knew exactly where you would be born in their family line. And yes, I loved you then. When I was creating innumerable galaxies and the earth, with its spectacular mountains, oceans, animals, and floral wonders, you were loved. During the eons of eternity, amid the majesty and glory of the kingdom of heaven, where millions of angelic beings rejoiced with me and the Father—where spectacular sights and sounds indescribably surpass all that would be found on the earth that I would create—I loved you with an everlasting love!

NASA

Jesus Talks to You

Introduction by Robert Barry

It was the summer of 1970. I had traveled across Canada and the United States, searching for deeper meaning to life amid the emptiness and hopelessness that prevailed in so many lives. My spiritual training afforded me little in the knowledge of God; I was raised in a Jewish family, with three years of Hebrew school training and yearly acknowledgment of my heritage through holy day feasts. The truths of the God of Abraham, Isaac, and Jacob took a backseat to worldly pursuits.

Up until one glorious day in 1970, I had never even understood that there was a man named Jesus—the One who millions personally knew as their Savior. That he fulfilled a multitude of prophecies, walked on the water, healed thousands miraculously, died for mankind's sins, and rose from the dead were truths that were totally foreign to me.

After meeting some Christians at a small music event, I stayed with them for a couple of days. I witnessed God's love in their midst—there was a pure love one to another. While they were praying one evening, I decided to try praying with them and began to speak to Jesus, as well.

As I prayed for the first time ever to Jesus, his mighty love and Holy Spirit changed my life—radically. I knew at that moment that he loved me beyond any love on earth; I was filled with his love and saw this same love shining from every one of the believers present—and started hugging them. I shouted out, "I love everyone!" It was a miracle. It was as if I had been in a cave my whole life to that point, never seeing real life outside the cave. Jesus, the Messiah, had rolled the stone away from the cave door, and suddenly I was beholding the glory of creation for the first time. I was now filled with God's wondrous love; I was free!

I went out on the streets of the city that same hour, sharing about the love of Jesus—that had just absolutely changed my heart and life. I began to read the Bible the next day, and Jesus began talking to me through his Word. Thus a most wondrous life began—living for my risen Savior.

Called to reach those who needed the Savior, I labored in missionary work for much of the next decade, establishing and strengthening Christian outreaches in a number of urban centers. The Lord God blessed the work, with many being saved—with quite a number of them continuing on with the Lord for a lifetime of service in Christ. I have worked a full time job (every year but one since I met Christ to this day) to support myself, and ministered the Word of God in the evenings and weekends. I have also served as a deacon, assistant pastor, and pastor, having been ordained as a minister in 1984.

I have studied the Holy Scriptures daily since 1970, and affirm the life-changing power of God's Word. Our God has established the 66 books of the Bible as being the very foundation that we are to stand upon spiritually. The Word of God is pure, perfectly inspired, and infallible. The Bible is the final authority of all we believe regarding our faith and how we should live this short life while in this world, as we await the glorious appearing of our great God and Savior, Jesus Christ, the Messiah.

The daily messages of this book, that our Lord has blessed me with to share with you, are the result of many hundreds of hours in prayer and fellowship with our King. These messages, guided by the rich love of Jesus, are shared for your edification, encouragement, and consolation. I consider these messages to be Holy Spirit-inspired, Holy-Spirit anointed, and originating from true revelation. Although they are deeply established in and in concord with the infallible, divine revelation that is the Bible, they do not carry inherent, divine authority and are subject to imperfections. This is similar to the gifted teaching that is so very valuable to our churches today; they are often Holy Spirit-inspired and Holy Spirit-anointed, as well; these teachers provide much edification to believers, but only the Holy Bible is infallible and has divine authority. Though both the Spirit-inspired teaching of our gifted teachers in our churches, and these Spirit-inspired messages in *Jesus Talks to You* bring great blessings, comfort, and the riches of God's love, they need to be assessed and weighed on the basis of the Bible.

A teaching or message is able to be certified as being inspired by the Holy Spirit. True believers who know the Word of God, who are walking in his Spirit, and have Christ reigning in their hearts, will be qualified to confirm with biblically enriched discernment, the validity of prophecies and teachings.

The messages within *Jesus Talks to You* have been imparted by our Lord to me to share with his family of believers—to strengthen, encourage, and comfort the hearts and lives of those who have been born again, as Jesus spoke about in John 3. If you, the reader, do not know Jesus Christ as your personal Savior, perhaps after reading some of *Jesus Talks to You*, your life will be touched in a very special way. He welcomes you to turn your life to him in faith (trust him, and adhere to, and rely fully on Jesus). All have sinned and fallen short of the perfection of God. He paid the price for your sins when he died on the cross. His blood sacrifice will wash away all of your sins when you turn humbly to him and ask for his forgiveness. Invite him into your heart to be your Savior and Lord; he will come in, and by his Spirit will live within you. You will then have reason to greatly rejoice, for you will have been born again and now possess eternal life. (Please see page 249 for more information on receiving new life in Christ.) He loves you with an everlasting love!

Scripture references have been included at the close of each daily devotion to provide further edification and comfort in Christ. I highly encourage you to share the time in these scriptures with Jesus; the message of each day presented will be enhanced and supported by them.

Included throughout the book are some inspirational illustrations created by Gustave Doré (1832-1883), the most renowned illustrator of the 19th century. They depict special highlights and aspects of the life of Jesus during the time he walked the earth, as well as other events in the lives of God's people. They are not as perfect in historical accuracy as a photograph would be if we had them, yet hopefully you will be very blessed and inspired as you experience Doré's realistic style that breathes new life into these biblical events.

Since 1970, when Jesus revealed his reality to me, I have walked with him and served him every day since—filled with the faith, hope, and love that he imparts. Even in times of great sorrow, tribulation, and trials, he has been faithful to guide and comfort me. He truly is the great Shepherd of the sheep.

His sheep hear his voice; I am so very blessed to know him and his most loving voice. Happy are the people that know the joyful sound. He rejoices over you daily; his thoughts toward you are more in number than the sands of the sea. My deep and sincere prayer to our God and Father is, that while reading *Jesus Talks to You,* you will be richly blessed as you hear his song of rejoicing over you. May you be filled with his love and his Spirit, as his gracious plans for your life are made more clearly known to you; may his grace be abundant as you do his will in word and deed, bringing everlasting glory to his name. Amen.

Your brother and fellow servant in the love of Christ Jesus,

Robert Barry

Miraculous Catch of Fish After Jesus' Resurrection—*John 21*

January 1

Jesus Talks to You

When I came to live on the earth, the wondrous miracle of my incarnation heralded the astounding and marvelous truth to all mankind that the God of all creation will dwell with mankind.

I suspended the laws of nature to come to earth. Miraculously, I was born of a virgin by the Holy Spirit—I was fully man, yet fully God—the express image of the invisible God and the brightness of his glory.

The riches of my eternal kingdom were forever in my possession before being born in Bethlehem. But I came to the earth and became poor for your sake, that you, through my poverty, might be rich.

I came here to let you know that it is your heavenly Father's good pleasure to give you his kingdom.

Hebrews 1:1-3 • 2 Corinthians 8:9 • Luke 12:32

January 2

Jesus Talks to You

I know the sorrows of mankind. I came to earth to bear the heavy burden of sin and to turn mourning into joy. I came to heal and bring wholeness to all who would receive me.

In the days ahead, I desire to touch your life by the Holy Spirit. My Spirit will set you free, and if I set you free, you shall be free indeed. I will teach you to be strong in my grace.

Cast your burden upon me and I will sustain you. Take my yoke upon your shoulders and come learn from me, for I am gentle and humble in heart; my yoke is easy to bear and my burden is light. I will give true rest to your soul. You who are weary, trust in me. I shall cause you to soar on high with wings like eagles. You shall run and not be weary; you shall walk and not faint.

John 8:31-2 • Romans 8:2 • John 8:36 • 2 Timothy 2:1 • Isaiah 40:31

Jesus Raises the Daughter of Jairus from the Dead—*Luke 8*

I have called you from heaven to be my child for all eternity. This calling is not according to your works or your own righteousness, but according to my own purpose which was established before time began.

You are saved by grace, not by works. It is a gift; no one deserves eternal life. Forgiveness of sin and life eternal are gifts that I give. Through my shed blood, your debt—because of your sins—has been paid. I purchased you with the highest ransom price that could ever be paid—my life, my blood. I now call you to walk in my grace. Receive the power of a new life, raised in the newness of life, even as I was raised from the dead.

I have written my laws upon your heart—a new heart that I miraculously placed within you. You have wondrously been born again, and you have passed from death into life. I am the resurrection and the life. If you believe in me you shall never die.

You are my workmanship—my poem to the world. Trust me to write a blessed letter of love through your life to all that you meet. May you touch hearts and inspire many to also receive my love and life. I will do a remarkable work in your life. Without me, you can do nothing. With me, all things are possible. Is anything too hard for me? No.

I am the God of miracles. I split the Red Sea, made blind eyes see, healed leprosy, raised the dead, walked on the water, and conquered death itself. Be absolutely assured that I am able to do exceedingly beyond all that you could ever imagine possible in your life.

I will transform your life more and more into my image. Be patient and understand that you will never gain perfection (in the flesh) here on earth; but as you behold my image daily in the Word, you will be changed increasingly into my likeness. On the day of glory, you will be transformed in the twinkling of an eye—to be perfect. You will see me as I am, and be like me. I will say, "Welcome home, my beloved child."

Ephesians 2:10 • Colossians 3:4 • I John 3:1-3 • 2 Timothy 1:9

January 4

I am the same yesterday, today, and forever. I love you with the same love that I shared with mankind when I lived on earth. I embraced the little children and richly blessed them. I washed the disciples feet. I showed great mercy to the woman taken in adultery. I even loved those who crucified me. The greatest love that a man may have is to lay down his life for his friends.

As I have loved you, so love one another. Love has wondrous power. Lives will change when you allow my love to flow through you. Let me reign in your life. I will honor you for the love that you show others. Freely you have received, so freely give. I will add the increase to your life and provide your every need according to my riches in glory.

Hebrews 13:8 • John 15:12-13 • John 12:26 • Philippians 4:13,19

January 5

I am the master jeweler. You are a precious stone, a jewel whose value is priceless! I have proven your value to me by laying down my life for you. Though you were in the miry pit of this world, I sought you out and redeemed you. I have washed you. As the master jeweler, I am cutting facets in you, my jewel. I am polishing you. When my light shines upon and through you, the beauty that I have placed in you will be seen by all. I am the hope of glory that now lives in you. Rejoice in this.

When you received me, you were transferred into my kingdom; all things became new. When you received me, you received power to be my child. You received the Spirit of life which has freed you from the law of sin and death.

You are my crown and joy. You are a royal diadem in my hand.

Malachi 3:17 • John 1:12-13 • Romans 8:2 • Isaiah 62:3 • Colossians 1:27

Sometimes I choose to wait that I might be gracious to you.

When I was told that Lazarus was sick, I told my disciples that this sickness will not end in death. I told them that it is for God's glory, so that I may be glorified through it. I waited two more days, then we returned to Judea.

Lazarus died. When I arrived, both Martha and Mary said, with much sorrow, that if I had been there, their brother would not have died. I said that I am the resurrection and the life; I also said that whoever believes in me will live, even though they die, and whoever lives and believes in me will have eternal life.

The sorrow of Lazarus' sisters and friends was so very great as I approached the tomb. My heart was so deeply moved that I wept.

I had them take the stone away. Martha protested, saying that Lazarus has been dead four days and was decaying. With a loud voice, I said "Lazarus, come forth." Lazarus, after four days, arose from the dead.

Their beloved Lazarus was returned to them. Great glory was given to the God who has all power in heaven and earth. The people marvelled and were astonished; many hearts believed in me that day.

I could have gone to Judea when Lazarus was sick and just healed him. I chose to wait to show my love and power. I came to do my Father's will. His plan was better than what the people would have desired.

Trust me, my child. The trials and problems you face are opportunities for you to trust in my love and my grand plan for your life. I will work all things for your good. In your weakness, my strength will be made perfect. I will deliver you, and your joy and glory in me will be great!

Isaiah 30:18 • John 11:1-45 • Romans 8:28 • 2 Corinthians 1:10
Isaiah 43:2 • Psalm 46:1 • Isaiah 41:10 • Matthew 4:23-4

January 7 *Jesus Talks to You*

When you are thankful to me, my heart is warmed and it rejoices. My thoughts toward you are more in number than the sands of the sea; I continually care for you, so your praise is meaningful to me.

When I healed the ten lepers, only one returned to give thanks and glorify God. When you are like this one who was healed, and you offer thanks, I inhabit your praise and am enthroned on your praise. It is an important part of our fellowship together. I love you so much and desire to be so very close to you. When you are thankful to me, it is a blessed experience for us both.

Whoever offers praise glorifies me. If you desire to bring glory to me and my kingdom, be one who continually gives thanks. This is my will.

Psalm 139:17-18 • Luke 17:12-19 • Thessalonians 5:18 • Psalm 107

January 8 *Jesus Talks to You*

Paul and Silas were thrown into prison after being severely beaten, yet they sang praises unto their God in spite of their pain. They were trusting me. I proceeded to send a violent earthquake, opening the prison doors and loosing the prisoners' chains. After this, the jailer and his family wondrously met me in a personal way, through faith and hearing my Word, receiving salvation and the gift of eternal life.

Centuries earlier, a vast multitude came against Judah and Jerusalem to destroy them. I anointed a prophet and he declared my Word to them. I told them that the battle was mine, not theirs. I told them to not be afraid; they were to stand still and see my salvation on their behalf.

The king and all Judah fell before me and worshiped. They had all their singers going before them as they went out to meet the enemy. They thanked me for my everlasting lovingkindness. I was strong on their behalf; I set ambushments against the enemy, by which they were totally destroyed. I fulfilled my people's trust in me in a very mighty way.

Continually offer up the sacrifice of praise to the God who cherishes you. I will always be mighty on your behalf—though my deliverance will often not be in the timing or the fashion that you desire. When fear strikes, look to me. Even if matters are getting worse, trust me; I have the perfect plan. Stand still and see my salvation. Remember what I did at the Red Sea for the children of Israel. I am able—I have all power.

Absolutely nothing is too hard for me. Be strong in faith and do not lean to your own understanding. From my eternal perspective, your whole life on earth from beginning to end is known by me. I know what is best for you. Trust me for I have a wondrous plan for you.

Remember to put your songs of praise before you every day. I will fight for you in every battle of life. And you will rejoice and thank me even more for the victories and blessings that I have wrought for you.

Acts 16:22-34 • 2 Chronicles 20:1-30 • Hebrews 13:15 • Psalm 92:1-2
Habakkuk 3:17-19 • Psalm 145

January 9

I have called you to be one of my chosen people; you are a royal priest, a citizen of my holy nation, a treasured possession to my heart. I have called you out of darkness and brought you into my glorious light—that you may proclaim the praises of your mighty King.

I am the King of kings. Come reign in life with me. Rejoice in this holy and heavenly calling to which I have called you. I am in you, and you are more than a conqueror through my mighty love.

You are not of this world. As my Father has sent me, so I am sending you. Therefore, as a pilgrim just passing through, do not allow the sinful desires of the flesh to ensnare you. Let me rule in your heart, and your reward will be beyond your greatest dreams—honor for you in the kingdom of heaven and continual blessing and rejoicing in this life.

1 Peter 2:9-12 • 2 Peter 1:3 • Ephesians 1:3-7 • Colossians 1:26-27

January 10 *Jesus Talks to You*

Follow me in all of your ways. Let my attitude and mindset be in you. I took upon myself the form of a servant, though being the God of the universe. I laid aside my mighty power, glory, and majesty; I emptied myself and took on the likeness of men. I took on the greatest need of mankind and became obedient unto death. I became a servant to all.

I took your every sin and the sins of all mankind upon myself, suffering death on the cross. Through my shed blood on the cross, every sin is forgiven when one comes to me in godly sorrow. Every sin you ever committed is blotted out—as if they never existed. Though your sins were as scarlet, they become as white as snow.

Therefore, my Father has highly exalted me to the grandest honor to be known for all eternity. Every knee shall bow and every tongue confess that I am Lord, to the glory of God the Father.

Let me work in you, to help you become a servant of others. I have the power, through the Holy Spirit, to change your heart. Whatever you do to one of my children, you do to me. If you serve me, you will be honored forever by my Father.

Philippians 2:1-13 • John 12:26 • Mark 10:42-45 • Isaiah 1:18

January 11 *Jesus Talks to You*

Come before me each day and honestly share your struggles, your shortcomings, and your sins with me. I know them already. I know your every thought, heart attitude, and fear; but by your being open and honest, I will be able to transform your life by the Holy Spirit. As you seek me in Scripture, I will reveal truths. These truths will set you free. Behold my image in the Word; open your heart and my truth will be grafted into your life. You will be changed from glory to glory to be more like me.

There is no condemnation to you who abide in me. You are walking after the Spirit and not after the flesh. The law of the Spirit of life that is in me has set you free from the law of sin and death.

I am faithful to continue the work that I began in you. You will fall short often, but do not be discouraged. Like a child that is learning to walk, you will sometimes stumble and fall. But seek and you shall find; knock and the door shall be opened. I am willing and able to help you. Come before my throne anytime for help when you need it. My sons and daughters are always welcome to spend time with me.

I am not a God that is far off. I am right here with you now. Your tears, fears, doubts, cares, and worries are important to me. I will answer you. My Word has all truth and you will find comfort, strength, hope, and resolution. I will guide you and bring truths to remembrance by my Spirit. I will speak to your heart and comfort you; receive my peace that surpasses understanding.

Growth does not always come easy. As a tree struggles to grow, its roots finding their way to water, so must you seek me. Through study in my Word, prayer, thankfulness, trust, and faith, your root system will expand. Your waters and sustenance will be sure. Your leaves will grow, and you will bear fruit in due season. Whatever you do shall prosper.

1 John 1:7-9 • Colossians 3:16 • Romans 8:1-2 • 2 Corinthians 3:18
Psalm 1:1-3 • Philippians 1:6

January 12

You cannot perfect yourself. Having begun your faith in me by the power of the Holy Spirit and being given the free gift of eternal life, can you be made perfect by your own works? No. But, you have my perfect righteousness, for I live in you. In me, the Christ, dwells the fullness of the Godhead bodily, and you are complete in me.

You do not need to strive to please me by your good works. What pleases me most is your faith in me—your trusting in the finished work of the cross. I love you, not because of any good works that you might accomplish—though I truly rejoice in the works of love that you do as you are led by my Spirit—but because you are my child. You are my greatest treasure in the universe. I highly value you, richly love you, and desire to be very close to you. As you more fully realize how true this is, you will become more filled with peace, joy, and purpose for living.

When you enter my glorious kingdom, you will be changed in the twinkling of an eye. You will have a glorified body and will reign with me in a world with no sorrow, pain, sin, or death. You will see me as I am and be transformed to be in my likeness. You will know fully even as I have known you.

Galatians 3:3 • Colossians 2:9-10 • Galatians 3:11 • Zephaniah 3:17
1 Corinthians 15:49-57 • Jude 20-21, 24-25

January 13 *Jesus Talks to You*

I am the Lord God of Israel. I am the God of all creation. I have absolute power over heaven and earth. I have shown my power in times past through miracles. I am able to suspend the laws of nature, as I often did when I walked the earth.

One night, the disciples boat was being buffeted by strong winds and waves. Before dawn, I went out to them walking on the Sea of Galilee. Believing I was a ghost, they cried out in fear. I told them to not be afraid. Peter said that if it was me, to have him come to me on the water. I told him to come, and Peter walked on the water to come meet me.

When Peter saw the strong winds and high waves, he was afraid and began to sink. He cried out for me to save him. I reached out and caught him. I told him that he had little faith and asked why he doubted. We climbed into the boat and the wind died down. My disciples in the boat then worshiped me and said, "Truly, you're the Son of God."

When I come to you during turbulent times in your life, do not be afraid. You may even have prayed for deliverance in a situation. Expect me to come to your aid in these times. You need not fear any situation. As I bid Peter to walk on the water, I can have you walk on the waters of this life in amazing ways. Only believe and doubt not.

When I bid you come, and you step out of the boat of your comfort zone, look unto me and not at the winds and the waves that are so boisterous about you. People, events, and circumstances may assail you with doubts and discouragement. But they are no match for my power to uphold and bless your life. Peter walked on the water by my power. Only the God of creation can perform such a miracle.

I can do this for you in your spiritual walk with me. Ask and you shall receive. I am able to do immeasurably more than you can ask or imagine. I am at work in your life. I am God. Believe in me.

Matthew 14:22-33 • Ephesians 3:20-21

January 14 *Jesus Talks to You*

One day I entered a synagogue where there was a man with a shriveled hand. I was moved by his affliction. The Pharisees were watching and wanted to bring charges against me if I healed on the Sabbath. How sad; their religion had no mercy.

I then told the man to stretch out his hand. He stretched it out and I restored it completely, just like his other hand. The hypocritical Pharisees then went out and plotted how they would be able to kill me.

I miraculously healed this man's hand. When I told him to stretch out his withered hand, he did not argue or tell me it could not be done. Like Peter, he took the step of faith and stretched forth his hand.

I can work wonders in your life. Are you willing to stretch forth an area of your life? I can make you whole. A relationship perhaps needs healing; stretch forth your heart and share love. I will give you that love as you step out of the boat of your comfort zone, like Peter. Perhaps you have a special hope for your employment or a life's dream you would like to see fulfilled. Afraid of failure? Remember, Peter did walk on the water—but when he started to sink, I was there to lift him up.

I ask you to come and step out of the boat of your comfort zone. Share my love with a neighbor. Use the talents that I have given you and attempt a work that might glorify my name. May you through the study of my Word and godly counsel expand your horizons in your new stretching forth. The Holy Spirit will enable you and anoint you for the work and bless your relationships. Ask and you shall receive.

Reach out in my love to a family member, a neighbor, or even an enemy. Be not afraid of rejection. What a great reward it is to share love with others. The power of my Word and my love can flow through you and change lives—including yours.

Matthew 12:10-23 • Matthew 7:7-11

January 15 *Jesus Talks to You*

Today is a day to forgive others. Oh, how you have been hurt by others throughout your life. I have seen every instance. I know that it is hard to let it go. People have a hard time forgiving because they feel that they are owed by the one that trespassed against them. They want to be paid back for the pain and the losses.

But you can be free of any resentment and anger. Forgive them. Resentment and anger only holds you captive to its debilitating influences. Forgive and be free. Trust me to repay you with my blessings. Whoever I bless from heaven is blessed indeed. Trespasses that others have perpetrated against you cannot hinder my rich blessings in your life, which I will bestow in my way and in my timing. Forgive others and trust me for the rest. Again, it is a step out of the boat of your comfort zone. It is hard to do at times, but by doing it you will be healed and blessed.

Joseph, who was sold into slavery by his own brothers, suffered greatly. He lost contact with his family for many years. He felt the rejection of his brothers. Besides this suffering that came upon Joseph, there was an intense travesty of justice—a false accusation that sent him to prison. I worked in his heart, and he was able to forgive his brothers. He also forgave his false accuser. He was free to live with an unfettered faith in his God. He was able to rejoice in his life.

I soon honored Joseph's faith and forgiveness. By a miracle from my hand, Joseph became a ruler over the whole land of Egypt. He also saved his whole family from famine and was reunited with them. Joseph's love to his brothers was exemplified when in a most beautiful scene he met with them and shared that he forgave them fully.

My prophets and apostles were to be born through the ancestral line of Jacob (Joseph's father), who came to Egypt and was rescued from famine because of Joseph. I also came to earth through this ancestral line.

Being unforgiving does not hurt the one that caused your pain; it hurts you. It prevents you from growing in grace. I will honor you when you forgive others. I will bless your life as you follow my way.

Genesis 41:38-44 • Matthew 6:14-15 • Matthew 5:44-45 • Luke 7:36-50

January 16 *Jesus Talks to You*

I love you, my beloved child. I am with you and have the power to bless your life in a multitude of ways.

I know the desires of your heart, your hopes, and dreams. There is a deep longing in your heart at times that yearns for fulfillment. It is most important to trust me with your future. Seek my kingdom and my righteousness first, and everything that pertains to your physical and spiritual life will be added to you. If I become to you that which is most essential in your life, I will give you the desires of your heart.

You know the hurts and sorrows of your heart well. I know them better; I have known your every thought and action since you came into this world. I know your physical, emotional, and spiritual makeup in the most precise details. I am the God that heals you physically, emotionally, and spiritually. Today, every day, I am with you and desire to work mightily in your life. I will bless you and perform healing in my own timing.

What is most essential is that you come into an intimate relationship with me. This is where your deepest healing will occur; being transformed daily more into my image. By the Holy Spirit, I will touch those deep areas of your heart and life. It will be nothing short of miraculous, just like all of my mighty miracles. It will happen in you. Come before me each day; open your heart to me in prayer and in the reading of my Word—let me speak to you. Invite the Holy Spirit to fill your life and fully wash you, renewing you each new day.

Your own personal expectations of how and what I should do for you are really not helpful for you to hold on to. Be patient. I will be working in many areas of your life. I am God. My miracle of life will happen in you as it does in a tree. A tree grows and bears fruit in its season—have patience. You will grow and bear fruit, and your fruit will remain for eternity. I will do this through you. Without me you can accomplish nothing; but with me all things are possible.

Be content to get to know me, the living God. What a great and wonderful truth: you know the God who created all things—the One who created you. Trust me; I know what I am doing. I promise that I will be strong on your behalf.

Matthew 19:26 • John 14:23 • Hebrews 11:16 • 2 Corinthians 3:18

January 17 *Jesus Talks to You*

During Israel's wilderness journey, I called Bezaleel, of the tribe of Judah, to be a skilled craftsman. I filled him with my Spirit, with wisdom, knowledge, and a high level of skill in working with gold, silver, brass, stone cutting, and more—to help build a place to honor the God of Israel with worship.

I am calling you to fulfill a special work in my kingdom. Your calling is unique. I am performing a work and transforming your life to bring you into that calling. My purpose for you will often reflect your desires, your skills, and your life's experiences. But these, by no means, can limit the mighty work I can accomplish through you by the anointing of my Spirit. I can give you new skills, and a calling that far surpasses your natural abilities. When on earth, I stated that the same works that I do shall you do also, and greater works, because I was going to the Father. This is still true today.

Look to me for your anointing upon the work that I have called you to. Know this: I often call my children into a very different, yet often wondrous and joyful path than what they might have expected.

Seek me with all your heart, that you might apprehend that for which I have apprehended you. Remember, even as my Father has called me and sent me to earth to fulfill works ordained since before time began, so I send you—to fulfill my calling upon your life, to walk in the works that I have prepared for you before the world began.

Do not worry; as you seek me, I will do the work in your heart and life, working all things for your good. I will bring you into the place I need you to be to fulfill my plan for you. I began the work in you; I will finish it. Just like I did for Bezaleel; I can bestow upon you, by my Spirit, wisdom, understanding, and skill for every endeavor I call you to.

Psalm 90:16-17 • John 14:12-17 • Ephesians 2:10 • Philippians 2:13
2 Thessalonians 2:16-17 • Exodus 31:1-11

January 18 — *Jesus Talks to You*

I love you and desire to give you my peace. My peace is not at all like the peace that the world gives to you. My peace surpasses all understanding!

The disciples and I were in the boat one evening. A fierce gale of wind arose, creating waves that were close to swamping us. I was sleeping, but was awakened by men quite fearful for their lives. I rebuked the winds and told the waves, "Peace! Be still!" The wind fell silent and there was a great calm. I asked my disciples why they were so fearful and asked where their faith was. Awestruck and terrified, they wondered who this was who could command the winds and the waves to obey him.

I am the Son of God, with all power in heaven and earth. My dear son, my treasured daughter—you are so dear to my heart continually—there are fears you have each day, when the winds and waves of life assail you. Come under the shadow of my wings. I will say to those winds and waves, "Peace! Be still!"

The gales and waves of life are at times almost swamping the boat that you are in. This can be terrifying for you. I alone have the power to deliver you. By trusting me and allowing me to do my will in each situation, and not trying to deliver yourself, you will behold my love and care for you. You will be delivered in my timing, and you will have grown in faith while learning more about me and my love for you.

And by the way, I knew that the waves and the winds would be fierce that day with the disciples. I sometimes cause, set up, or allow situations to occur, that you may learn of my power and love. I do this to set you free from any worldly ways of thinking that you may have. I am renewing your mind and transforming you daily.

Allow my peace that passes understanding to reign in your heart today.

Mark 4:35-41 • Isaiah 41:13 • 2 Timothy 1:7 • Hebrews 13:6
Psalm 91 • Isaiah 43:2 • Psalm 23:4-6 • Philippians 4:7

January 19 *Jesus Talks to You*

Your life is hidden in me. When I appear in glory, then you shall also appear with me in glory!

In this world, you will endure much tribulation on your journey to the kingdom of heaven. I have called you to be a servant, seeking to please your Father who is in heaven. You are called to endure hardship as a good soldier. You are called to put on the whole armor of God. If you do not pick up your cross each day and follow me, you are not worthy of me. Be strong in my power; the battle is not fought and won by your strength, but by my Spirit. You can do all things through me.

Take my yoke upon you; learn from me. Yes, I will give rest to your soul, but there is a daily battle. The lust of the flesh, the lust of the eyes, and the pride of life are strong contenders for your affections. Seek me with all of your heart, that you might sow to the Spirit and not to the flesh; you will reap life everlasting and not corruption as you do.

Do not be discouraged in your day of adversity. I am your strength and your shield. You will fall short at times. When you do, turn to me with a repentant heart. I am faithful to forgive you, and I will cleanse you of all unrighteousness. I died for your sins. My blood has been shed that you might have your sins washed away—no more guilt and no more shame. You are righteous in my eyes through my work on the cross!

For the joy that was set before me—that many would receive life everlasting and become my children—I endured the cross. I set my face like a flint. I scorned the shame of the cross and pressed on to do the will of my Father. I conquered sin and death, that you might reign with me today and forever. My Father has honored me; I now sit at the right hand of the throne of my Father.

Look to me always; I am the author and finisher of your faith. Give your whole heart to me, and I will transform your life. Humble yourself and pray daily that you may be led by the Holy Spirit; ask and you will receive. Endure hardships, even as I did; I live in you and will give you grace to overcome. When I appear, you shall appear with me in glory. I will rejoice exceedingly that you have done well and been faithful. Pleasures forevermore shall you enjoy in the paradise of God!

Colossians 3:4 • Matthew 11:28-30 • 2 Timothy 2:3 • Ephesians 6:10-18
1 John 2:15-17 • Galatians 6:8 • Hebrews 12:2-4 • Matthew 25:21

Through mighty miracles and wonders, I brought my people Israel out of Egypt, to bring them to the land that I promised to their ancestors.

During the forty years that the children of Israel were in the wilderness, I humbled and tested them to know what was in their heart, and to see if they would keep my commands. I caused them to hunger, but fed them with manna faithfully. I wanted them to learn that man shall not live by bread alone, but on every word that comes from the mouth of the Lord. I did bless them in many special ways; their clothes did not wear out, and their feet did not swell during those forty years.

At times you will suffer need. These times will try your faith. I am teaching you that I am your provider. If you are financially hurting or lacking employment, look only to me for your provision or the open door. I am your healer, whether it be for a sickness or a broken relationship. I will provide all of your needs according to my riches in glory—which are infinite. Trust me and say from the heart, "Your will be done, Lord."

As a man disciplines his son, so do I discipline you. When you stray, I will need to work with you to get you on the right path. You may suffer consequences for your sin. I allow this so you might learn to walk with me according to my Word. I will be merciful to you, and I will forgive you, when you come to me with a humble, and repentant heart. I will restore your joy and your relationship with me.

Keep my ways and honor my Word. I am bringing you into an abundant life here on earth. My blessings will be very rich, as you abide in me. Continue to be thankful, and rejoice in what I have done in your life. I promise to bring you, and all my children who believe in me, to my heavenly kingdom. There will be no hunger, pain, or tears there. All things will be made new. You shall inherit my kingdom, and I will be your God forever.

Deuteronomy 8:1-10 • Philippians 4:19 • Hebrews 12:11
Revelation 21:1-7

January 21

Jesus Talks to You

I am the vine and you are a branch in me. My Father is the vinedresser. Every branch that bears fruit, he will prune, so that it can bear much fruit. As you grow in me, there will be areas in you life that are not righteous. They are the ways of your flesh. I desire for you to be free from the effects of sin. Those wild branches in your life need to be pruned.

You need to be in my Word to know the truth. I will set you free so that you will continue to bear much fruit.

If you dwell in me and my words dwell in you, ask whatever you wish, and it will be done for you. My Father is glorified when you bear much fruit.

John 15:1-8

January 22

Jesus Talks to You

You are never alone. I am always here with you. You do not need to suffer as much as you do in some situations. Please turn to me, and let me speak to your heart and comfort you.

As you love me and keep my Word, the Holy Spirit, which is in you by faith, will be your Counselor. He is the Comforter. He is the Helper. He will guide you into all truth, and bring all things that I said when on earth to your remembrance. He will provide wisdom and encouragement for your journey.

When on earth, I had deep sorrows and was familiar with grief. I know your hurts and pains; they can be very deep. Let my Spirit comfort you and give you peace. Continue in me and be patient. During your darkest hour, remember that the light of my love will yet shine forth brightly for you and bring you blessing, for you have placed your trust in me.

John 14:26-27 • Isaiah 53:3-8 • 2 Corinthians 1:2-7 • Psalm 27:13-14
Psalm 42:5

January 23 *Jesus Talks to You*

Whenever you are gathered in my name with one or more other believers, I am in your midst. You have been raised up and are now seated in heavenly places with me; I have richly blessed you with all spiritual blessings. You are not of this world anymore. You are a jewel in the kingdom of God.

When you have fellowship with others, I am there and listening. I am writing a book of remembrance for those that revere, honor, and love to think about me.

Matthew 18:20 • Philippians 3:20 • Ephesians 1:3 • Ephesians 2:6
Malachi 3:16-17

January 24 *Jesus Talks to You*

You are being kept by my power through faith. I have saved you and will bring you to my kingdom on that glorious day. This is a wonderful reason for great rejoicing. Think about it; you have eternal life. You will reign forever with me—beginning today.

Yes, rejoice, even though for a little while you may have to endure various trials and temptations. Your faith is more precious to me than gold. These trials will prove the genuineness of your faith. As gold is tried in the fire, so shall your faith be. Your praise to me shall be rich and joyful, as you behold the mighty work that I will continue to do in your life.

My disciples were blessed to have seen me and believed. It is especially a wonder to enjoy your faith; blessed are you who have not seen me in the flesh, and yet you believe. Many prophets and kings have desired to know what you know of me and my Word.

I am able to keep you from falling and to present you sinless and perfect on that day—into my glorious presence with exceeding joy.

1 Peter 1:3-9 • Luke 10:24 • Jude 24-25

January 25

Jesus Talks to You

Today, may this be a day of rejoicing for you; I created this day. All things are upheld by the power of my Word. Be glad for I am with you. My joy is your strength; it is a fruit of my Spirit, which is in you. You live by my faith and you rest in my peace. Today let my joy fill your heart.

David the king, who endured through much hardship and trial, often began his days with joy-filled praise and song. I am enthroned on and inhabit your praise. I rejoice when I see that you trust me to give you the victory for each day. Rejoice, I will guide you. Rejoice by faith, even if you do not feel like it. Whoever offers praise as a sacrifice unto me, honors and glorifies me.

Nehemiah 8:9-11 • Galatians 5:22 • Psalm 145:1-13 • Psalm 50:23

January 26

Jesus Talks to You

My beloved child, do not worry about the things of the day. Do not look to the right or the left, but look to me. Remember Peter, who began to sink as he feared the winds and waves while walking on the water. The world will try to distract you. Your mind may doubt that I am able to accomplish what you have been praying for. I have heard your every prayer and know each dream that you possess. I value them; trust me that I will accomplish what is best in every area of your life. And, if like Peter, you also start to sink, call on me; I will lift you up and save you.

This day, you will walk boldly with me. You represent my kingdom; I have called you to be the light of the world. Your work today is to believe in me. Keep your eyes on me and be led by the Holy Spirit.

Rest in my love. Do not let the small worries rob you of the confidence and rejoicing that is yours today. Seek first my kingdom and my righteousness, and I will take care of all your needs. You are a joint-heir with me of the kingdom of heaven. What an inheritance you have!

Philippians 4:6-7 • Matthew 5:14-16 • Matthew 6:33 • Romans 8:17-18

January 27

Jesus Talks to You

Fear not; I am the Lord your God who will hold your right hand. I will surely help you; I will replace your fears with confidence and hope, as you trust in me and fully lean on me. I have not given you the spirit of fearfulness. I have given you the spirit of love, power, and self-discipline.

You, who are a partaker of the heavenly calling, consider me, the Apostle of your faith. I was faithful to the Father. Though many were against me while I was on earth, I was determined to fulfill the work I was sent here for.

Build yourself up in your most holy faith, praying in the Holy Spirit. Continue in my Word, the Scriptures. Be established upon the foundation of the apostles and prophets—I am the chief Cornerstone.

Isaiah 54:14 • 2 Timothy 1:7 • Hebrews 3:1-6 • Jude 1:20-21
Ephesians 2:19-22

January 28

Jesus Talks to You

Your life is like a mist that appears for a little while and then vanishes. Whatever you are called to do, let it be done with your whole heart. Nothing more can be accomplished on earth once you're in the grave.

Whatever your daily work, it can make a great difference. A job well done helps provide a quality product or service for your fellow man. Let your light shine. You represent me. People are watching you.

Ask me to bless your work and your relationships. Pray for those in your sphere of influence; your earnest, continued prayer for others will avail much. Expect me to answer in very special ways. I will also give you wisdom in the areas that you are praying about. Let me be the Lord of your life. Always be willing, when asked, to share the reason for the hope that you have in me with respect and kindness.

James 4:14 • Matthew 5:16 • 1 Peter 3:15

January 29 *Jesus Talks to You*

I will be returning soon. I will come in my Father's glory and power with his angels. My reward is with me to give to everyone according to what they have done.

Hold on strong to the faith you have in me, so that no one may seize your crown. If you are victorious, you shall inherit all things, and I will be your God, and you will be my child forever.

When I appear, you shall be like me; you shall see me as I am. Let this hope be an anchor to your soul—anchoring you into the Most Holy Place. With this confidence and hope in me, you will purify yourself even as I am pure.

Matthew 16:27 • Revelation 22:12 • Revelation 3:11 • 1 John 3:1-3

January 30 *Jesus Talks to You*

During my work on earth, thousands beheld my miracles and heard the Word of truth that I shared. They wondered who I was; some said that I was John the Baptist; others said that I was Elijah or Jeremiah.

One day I took Peter, James, and John to the top of a high mountain. I was transformed before them. My face shone like the sun and my clothing became white as light. Then Moses and Elijah appeared and spoke with me. A bright cloud overshadowed us; my Father's voice spoke from heaven saying that I was his beloved Son, in whom he was well pleased. He said, "Listen to him."

When the disciples heard my Father's voice, they were filled with fear. I touched them and said to not be afraid. When they looked up, they did not see Moses (my servant & the lawgiver) or Elijah (the prophet). They saw only me, who perfectly fulfilled the law of Moses and fulfilled all the prophecies of the prophets.

Moses, Elijah, and the prophets were men whom I called. They were of this world, as are you and all mankind. I am from heaven. I am the Word of God. I am the Creator of the universe. I am the author of eternal salvation; I am the Savior of the world.

I spoke much about my Father to the disciples. Philip one day asked me to show him the Father. I shared with him that if he has seen me, he has seen the Father. I am in the Father and the Father is in me. I told him that the words that I speak, I do not speak on my own authority, but the Father does his miracles through me, and I speak his words.

I am the Son of God with all power. I will be your friend; one that is closer than a brother. Share your heart with me; I will be strong on your behalf. My Father told the three on the mountain, "Listen to him." I have the words of eternal life. I am the great Shepherd. My sheep hear my voice. I will lead you and guide you now and forever.

Matthew 17:1-8 • 2 Peter 1:16-21 • John 14:6-11 • John 10:27-30

January 31 *Jesus Talks to You*

All the rivers flow into the ocean, and yet the ocean is not full. Mankind is continually trying to fill themselves with that which will never fully satisfy. I offer abundant life here on the earth and the riches of my kingdom forever—the price is free.

I am a sun and shield to you. I will light your path. I will warm your heart. I will guard you from the enemy. I will not withhold any good thing if you walk with me.

If you love me and keep my words, my Father will love you, and we will come and make our special home in your life. Do not let your heart be troubled or afraid. I freely and abundantly give you my peace. It is a peace that is not of this world. Receive this peace from me now.

You will have perfect peace as your trust me wholeheartedly.

Isaiah 55:1-3 • Psalm 103:1-5 • Psalm 84:11 • John 14:27 • Isaiah 26:3

Jesus Blesses the Little Children—*Mark 10*

Darkness at the Crucifixion—*Luke 23*

February 1

Jesus Talks to You

I am your God. Before you were born, I knew every word and action that you would ever say and do. I loved you before you were born; I love you now and forever.

I died for your sins over two thousand years ago. Since you were born, I have worked in your life to bring you into a full knowledge of my love and my free gift of eternal life.

I desire that you are transformed inwardly more and more into my image, as I guide you on my path of life. I will lead you on a path that is not known by the world. The world is ever learning but never coming to the knowledge of the truth. I am the Way, the Truth, and the Life.

Choose my path today. I am the great Shepherd and know what is best for you. If I am for you, nothing or no one can be against you. Seeing that I gave my very life for you, shall I not also give you all things that pertain to life and godliness?

Psalm 139 • Psalm 16:11 • Romans 8:29-32

February 2

Jesus Talks to You

The first man, Adam, who was created in my image, was from the earth, made from the dust of the ground. I am the last Adam, the Christ, and I came from heaven. As you have borne the image of the man of earth, so shall you also bear the image of the Lord of heaven.

By receiving me, you became a partaker of my divine nature. I will continue to give you foretastes of my heavenly kingdom and my love, as you seek me with all of your heart.

Your flesh and blood cannot inherit the kingdom of heaven. You have been created with a corruptible body. But at the last trumpet, the dead shall be raised and be changed into incorruptible. Your mortal body will put on immortality.

I have been victorious, conquering both sin and death. The wages of sin is death; I paid for your sins on the cross. I took the sting of death. I then rose from the dead to give assurance of eternal life to all who believe (trust in, cling to, and rely on me, the Messiah).

Rejoice today in the victory that I have wrought for you, my beloved child. You will be changed to be immortal. You will be changed into my image, and will enjoy the kingdom of heaven for all eternity. It sounds like a dream, but it is more real than anything on the earth.

1 Corinthians 15:47-57

February 3 *Jesus Talks to You*

One day a multitude followed me, because they saw the miracles I performed on those who were diseased. My heart is always moved with people's infirmities, whether they believe in me or not. I healed many that day and taught about my kingdom.

It was evening and the people were hungry. The disciples wanted me to send everyone back to the villages that they might buy food. I asked my disciple Philip about buying bread to feed the people. I said this to test him, for I knew what I was going to do.

Andrew said that a little boy had five barley loaves and two small fish, but felt it was insignificant among such a multitude. I gave thanks and the food was distributed to the crowd. I blessed the food and gave an increase that was able to feed five thousand men; there is nothing too hard for me. Twelve baskets full of fragments were gathered up as well.

I bring streams to the desert, sight to the blind, life from the dead, and provide all the needs of mankind. I am the bread of life. The bread that I provided that day was essential for the well being of each person's physical body. But the true bread I give to every living soul is myself, and whoever eats this bread will live forever. Do not work feverishly for the bread of this world; look to me to give you an endless supply of the bread from heaven—it fully satisfies and endures unto eternal life.

John 6:1-15

At times you may experience loneliness; everyone does. Whether someone has many friends, heads up a business with many employees, or lives an active, event-filled life, loneliness will be experienced sooner or later.

Modern media in its many forms, and the world views expressed every place you look, will seek to lead you away from the spiritual life that is in me. The lust of the eyes, the lust of the flesh, and the pride of life are what prevail in the world. They are like cotton candy. Each tastes good but gives no true sustenance at all.

Relationships are sometimes like this as well. They may not be adding to one's spiritual health, life, and fullness. I created you to know me in a personal way and not to be a God that is far off. You can experience my love and care in ways that will bring you the deepest joy—as well as a peace that surpasses understanding. No relationship on earth can bring you the fulfillment that I can. I created you with a deep need for me to be in the innermost heart of your being.

I am the lover of your soul; I cherish you and care for your every need. Come to me today and everyday. Listen to my words of comfort. Receive and embrace the many promises that fill my Word. I will enrich your life with a friendship that is beyond anything the world knows. When you are feeling lonely, come to me; I created man and relationships. I am not a force or a higher power. I am Jesus, the one who walked the earth. I knew pain, sorrow, and great joy. I will be your best friend.

John 16:33 • Matthew 11:28 • Psalm 27:13-14 • Romans 15:13
2 Corinthians 1:3-4 • Psalm 147:3 • John 14:16-21

All things were created by me, whether in heaven or upon earth, things seen and unseen. The billions of stars, the earth, and all life on it I have spoken into existence by the Word of my power. I hold together every atom in your body and I rule over all circumstances in your life.

There are areas of your life that are not the way that you wish they would be. I desire that you trust me in this. I am working all things together for your good, not just some things—all things. Thankfulness for the many blessings that surround your life will help you experience my peace more fully. Take your eyes off your problems and look only to me. I am the answer to every dilemma and concern. Shall not the one who gave his very life for you also provide for you in times of need?

My ways are not your ways. Endure and be patient; I am developing you in many areas. I will always be merciful to you, even though at times it seems that I am not giving my full attention yo you. At times, I allow situations to be present, that I may prove your faith and purify it.

As gold is refined in the fire, so I am burning away the dross in you. You have prayed for me to work in your life; this is what I am doing, and I use ways that are often hard to understand. But my child, look at the many men and women in my Word who have also endured intense trials. I blessed every one of them in very unique ways, through it all.

You are a treasured living gemstone that is being built into my spiritual house. You are a royal member of my family that is being called to walk in my love and the power of a new life. Trust me when I say that the finished jewel that I am creating you to be is so very wonderful, that you would greatly rejoice if you could see the future I have for you. Rejoice, my child, in the hope of my glory that will be rich in your life. I promise to be faithful to complete the wondrous work that I began in you. Please rest in my immeasurable, unceasing, and eternal love for you.

Colossians 1:16 • Hebrews 11:3 • Romans 8:28,32 • Romans 5:3-5
James 1:2-8 • James 5:11 • Job 23:8-10 • 1 Peter 2:5 • Hebrews 13:21

February 6 *Jesus Talks to You*

A great mystery—a great wonder; I became flesh and tabernacled with mankind. You beheld the glory that I share with my Father, full of grace and truth.

A great mystery—a great wonder; when you received me, I came to live inside you. Most fantastic, would you not agree? Realize how glorious this is. The God of all creation now lives in you. Jesus, the risen Savior, lives in you. I chose to come to earth two thousand years ago; but I also chose you and desire to live and reign in your life.

This mighty and priceless treasure (me) is now living in you, a jar of clay, so that it will be evident that the awesome power in you is from God and not from yourself. Do not be discouraged. Though you encounter trials often and your outer body is gradually dying over time, inwardly you are being renewed by the Holy Spirit day by day.

John 1:1-14 • 2 Corinthians 4:6-18

February 7 *Jesus Talks to You*

My glorious child, and that is just what you are to me—glorious. You will reign with me forever, you who are so dear to my heart. My rejoicing is boundless as I behold you, my child.

I have clothed you with the garments of salvation; and I have covered you with a robe of righteousness. I have adorned you with the finest of jewels, as a bride is readied for her wedding. I am your Husband; I am your Maker. I am your Redeemer, the Holy One of Israel, and the God of all creation.

Rest in my finished work, you who are redeemed by the power of my blood. I am in you. I am your hope of glory. Let my peace rule in your heart today and always. I love you with a love that will last forever!

Isaiah 54:5; 61:10 • Zephaniah 3:17 • Colossians 3:15 • Jeremiah 31:3

How I long to spend more quiet time with you. So often the activities of the day keep you too preoccupied.

Once when I visited the home of Martha, she was overly busy with serving me. Her sister, Mary, was sitting at my feet, listening to my words. Martha asked me if I cared that Mary had left all the work to her. Martha wanted me to tell Mary to help. I told Martha that she was fretting and troubled about many things. I said that there is only one thing that is essential; Mary has chosen what is better, and that will not be taken from her.

To spend time with me, the God of the universe, is the best choice. It cannot get any better. I have the deepest delight when you choose to have special quiet times with me. When you open your heart to me, I can speak to you by my Spirit. I will touch your life deeply during these times. They become part of a rich deep fellowship that you and I share now and forever. Our relationship will grow deeper in love.

I am not a God that is far away. As I was with Mary that day, so am I with you. Intimacy in heart can be experienced with your God. This is the meaning of life on earth. You are not called to have mere religion; you and I can have a rich relationship. We can be very close.

Continue in my Word, that you might get to know my voice more clearly. Man's heart and mind can be quite deceptive, and my voice may be muddled in the midst of all the distractions competing for your attention. But I am a rewarder of all who diligently seek me. You will find me when you seek me wholeheartedly. I will speak to you by my Word and my Spirit (my still small voice); I will reveal myself to you clearly. You will greatly rejoice that you personally know me, the risen Savior.

I will show you the path of life. In my presence is joy unspeakable and everlasting pleasures. Come and enjoy many quiet times with me.

Luke 10:38-42 • Jeremiah 29:13 • Hebrews 11:6 • Psalm 16:7-11

February 9

I love you exceedingly more than you love yourself. Nothing in this world can separate you from my love.

I care immeasurably about all of your physical, spiritual, and emotional needs. You are my child, and with boundless love I will watch over you and take care of you. My heart always goes out to you when I see you in emotional stress or in a dilemma. I am always present to bring you comfort and hope, even in the most trying of situations. Others will fail you, but I love at all times.

My counsel will be perfect, for I know you perfectly, now and forever—my wisdom is infinite. Come into my presence with thanksgiving, knowing that I am the God of all creation. I am able to do exceedingly more than you could ever imagine in the circumstances of your life, as well as transform your heart and mind. I conquered death—I am the resurrection and the life. I will bring you abundant life. Trust wholly in me. Listen to my guidance, and you will have peace like a river.

Romans 8:38-39 • 1 Peter 5:7 • Psalm 33:11 • Psalm 73:24
Psalm 95:1-3 • Hebrews 4:16 • Ephesians 3:20-21

February 10

Jesus Talks to You

I have wonderful plans for you, a future filled with hope and the richest of my blessings.

I am the good Shepherd. Yes, that means you are my sheep. This may be humbling, but it reveals an important truth; without me, you go terribly astray. Even with a well-marked path, you wander directly toward grave dangers—like sheep near rushing waters who can easily be swept away. You cannot see over the hill or around the bend as you journey on. I see all and will give you perfect counsel. I will hold you so very close at times. I will bring you into green pastures and beside still waters.

Jeremiah 29:11-13 • 1 Peter 2:25 • Isaiah 40:11 • Psalm 23

One day, I went into a town called Nain, along with many of my disciples. A widow's only son who had died, was being carried out of the town gate. Many of the town were with her, and she was weeping so sorrowfully. With my heart overflowing with compassion, I gently told her not to cry. I walked over and touched the coffin. I told the young man to arise—he that was dead arose. Sitting up, he began to talk to his mother. Great fear was upon all the people; they glorified God, exclaiming that a great prophet had arisen among them, and that God was visiting his people.

With a love deeper than the sea, with the power that holds the universe together, and with such fathomless mercy that brought me from heaven itself to the cross for all mankind, did I also visit this widow that day.

There are no words to express the rich love that I feel for you. I come to you this day. Trust me. If I have the power to raise the dead, I can surely work in your life situations today. I felt the widow's sorrow, and I also feel everything you are going through. I hold you close to me even now. Feel my love and compassion telling your heart to not fear.

I cannot explain to you now why I allow some circumstances to be in your life. Your whole future is in my hands, and I see it all from now into eternity. What I do in your life will impact you now and forever. I am the master jeweler—you are my priceless gem. As I cut the facets in you, it hurts, but this is needful for what I intend to create of you. Circumstances are often the cutting agents. Broken or troubled relationships, tragedy, closed doors of opportunity, and disappointments cause such a depth of pain and uncertainty, that it is often difficult to even get your bearings emotionally or spiritually. But I am working all things to your good. You have wondered how this can be. I am God; if I can raise the dead, I will also work all things to your good according to my divine plan for your life. My child, you will be richly blessed. Trust me to be faithful to perform all I have promised and always rest in my love.

Luke 7:11-16 • Matthew 5:4 • James 5:10-11 • Romans 5:3-5

I revealed the glory of the holy city, new Jerusalem, to my apostle John. There will be new heavens and a new earth. I will dwell with my people. There shall be no more tears, pain, sorrow, or death. All things will be made new. You and all of my children will inherit the kingdom, and you will reign with me forever. You, whose name is written in the Lamb's book of life, will have the name of new Jerusalem and my new name written upon you.

You will sit down with Abraham, Isaac, Jacob, Moses, David, and Daniel in the golden city. You will enjoy the most fantastic eternal fellowship with them. You will rejoice exceedingly in your friendship with the apostles. They faithfully bore witness of my love and glory to a dark world that desperately needed the true Light.

The glory and blessings of the love you will share forever with loved ones and those you helped come into the faith while on earth, is beyond your ability to comprehend. Untold numbers of the people of God, who were more than conquerors through their faith in me, will be there. They bring with them the richest blessings, as their glorious works follow them into the kingdom. You and all of these will have been changed in the twinkling of an eye, transformed into my image—while enjoying perfect righteousness, love, and joy beyond measure.

Whoever overcomes, I will give the right to eat of the tree of life which is in the midst of the paradise of God. Whoever overcomes, I will give the right to sit with me on my throne, even as I was victorious and sat down with my Father on his throne. And to the overcomer I will also give the morning star.

Come my beloved son. Come daughter of my heart. I have loved you with an eternal love and welcome you home. Come drink of the water of life freely.

Revelation 21:1-7 • Revelation 2:7, 11, 17, 26-28
Revelation 3:5, 12, 21

February 13

Jesus Talks to You

Happy are you that are in my family, for you know the joyful sound. My power and love have touched your heart. I have delivered you from the dominion of darkness and miraculously brought you into my kingdom of light. I took you out of a horrible pit of destruction and set your feet upon the rock—I am the Rock of salvation. I have established your steps to walk my path. I have put a new song in your mouth, even the rich praises of your King. Many will see the glorious work that I have accomplished in your life, and shall put their trust in the God of salvation.

Let this day be one of rejoicing for the miracle of new life. I transferred you from death to life. Be thankful; enter into my presence with songs of praise. Share my love; freely you have received, so freely give, for many need my touch. Let me love them through you; I will do great things through your life. Ask and you shall receive.

Psalm 40:2-3 • Colossians 1:12-13 • Psalm 100:4 • Psalm 71:19
1 Chronicles 16:8-12

February 14

Jesus Talks to You

The glories of my creation that you see with your eyes and hear with your ears are only the beginning of the display of the richness of my love. Sunsets, flowers, waterfalls, oceans, mountains, music, delicious foods, sun, moon, and stars are a small taste of the glory of my love.

My love is not of this world—it is of the kingdom of heaven. My eternal love compelled me to come from heaven to earth for you, my child.

You are never alone; I am here—the lover of your soul. Draw near to me, and I will surely draw near to you. The depth of friendship and love that you and I can share is fathomless. The love that I desire to show you is vastly more rich, full, and glorious than the love the world offers. Come close to me; rest your head on my shoulder and know this day that I love you.

Psalm 63:3 • Psalm 23:5-6 • John 15:9 • Song of Solomon 2:1-16

I am the King of righteousness, and by faith you have received my gift of righteousness. Righteousness was not earned by your good works or by trying to follow me the best that you can. It is not earned by following the Ten Commandments to the best of your ability or staying true to the Golden Rule. Righteousness is absolutely a gift from heaven; it is not from the earth.

You cannot enter the kingdom of heaven still in your sin. Only those who have been redeemed by my blood sacrifice will eat of the tree of life that is in paradise. Only those that have my perfect righteousness shall walk in the holy city, new Jerusalem.

You were separated from me because of your sin; the soul that sins shall die. The prophets foretold of me, the Messiah, the Christ, who would pay the price for all of mankind's sin. I took your sin upon myself. The Father made me to be sin, I who was perfect and knew no sin, so that you might be the righteousness of God in me. In receiving me, your life of sin was crucified with me. It is no longer you that lives, but I am living in you. And the life that you are now living in your body, you live by my faith, the faith of the Son of God.

My pure, holy faith—a most wondrous gift—enables you to be a partaker of my divine nature. As a branch is part of the vine, so are you a part of me. As waters bring nutrients to the vine and branches, so let the living water of my Word strengthen your faith and miraculously bring forth much fruit from you.

Being born again, now a partaker of my divine nature and fully righteous by faith, you are now a citizen of the kingdom of heaven. You may now come to Mount Zion and to the heavenly Jerusalem. You are truly special, and you are immeasurably loved. I joyously anticipate your joining heaven's family celebration for all eternity.

Romans 10:4 • 2 Corinthians 5:21 • Isaiah 53:3-12 • Galatians 2:20
2 Peter 1:4 • Hebrews 12:22-23

February 16

By faith, Moses stretched out his hand over the sea as commanded, and I divided it, so that the children of Israel could walk across on dry ground. By faith, the walls of Jericho fell down, after the children of Israel marched around them for seven days. By faith, Elijah hit the Jordan River with his mantle, and I split the waters so that he crossed over on dry ground. Being full of faith, Stephen, by my blessing, wrought great miracles among the people. By faith, Peter went into the room of the dead disciple, Tabitha, and after praying for her, saw her rise from the dead. By faith, Paul was used by me as I healed a man who was born crippled, making him perfectly whole and able to walk.

When I walked the earth, I healed many by my power. Lepers were cleansed, demons were cast out, the lame walked, blind eyes were made to see, the deaf made to hear, and the dead were raised back to life again. I am able to suspend the laws of nature and perform miracles that no man on earth could do.

All things are possible for you who believe in me. If you have faith the size of a mustard seed, you can say to a mountain to move and it will move. Be strong in the faith which I have placed in you by the Holy Spirit. Be strong in the power of my might. Be led by my Spirit, and I will help you to accomplish the works and share the words that I have planned for you to fulfill and share.

Acts 6:8 • Acts 14:7-10 • Acts 19:11-12 • Hebrews 11:1,6
1 Corinthians 2:5 • Luke 17:6 • Matthew 21:21 • Mark 16:20

February 17

I know your sorrows and heartaches. I am always present and feel the hurts you feel. I am close to you when you have anguished thoughts and a tearful heart.

At times, relationships can be so enriching and blessed. At other times, the demands of change and communication gaps between people can be a cause of much distress. Hopelessness is a common emotion.

I am God, the Creator of man, relationships, and emotions. I understand completely every trial and emotion you experience. When I walked the earth, I was a man of sorrows and well acquainted with grief. You can pour out your complaint or share your confusion and sorrows with me. Cast all of your cares on me, for I deeply care for you. I will heal your broken heart. I will comfort you who are crushed in spirit. I am the God of healing; I am the God of love. Entrust me with your deepest hurts, and allow me to anoint you with the Holy Spirit. Rest in my presence, and let my Word speak gently to your heart. Hope and healing will be yours.

Weeping may endure for a night, but joy comes in the morning. Rest in my love. Be patient; I am working in you and your situations to bring my blessings and comforts to your heart. I am your God forever!

Psalm 34:18 • Psalm 73:26 • Psalm 147:3 • Matthew 5:1-4 • John 14:27
Psalm 31:9-10 • John 11:35 • Psalm 63:1-8 • 2 Corinthians 1:3-4

February 18 *Jesus Talks to You*

I am the great Shepherd of the sheep. I will always protect you. Do not fear what man can do to you. I rule all circumstances in your life; all things will I work for your good.

Three men, Hananiah, Mishael, and Azariah (whose Babylonian names were Shadrach, Meshach, and Abednego) would not bow down and worship the golden image that king Nebuchadnezzar had set up. Just before being thrown into the fiery furnace as punishment for not bowing, they boldly proclaimed that their God is able to deliver them from the blazing furnace and from the hand of the king.

With the furnace heated seven times hotter than usual, the three men bound in their clothing, were thrown into the blazing fire. The astonished king jumped up and asked his counselors if three bound men were thrown into the fire. They said it was true. He exclaimed that he saw four men, unbound and unhurt, walking in the midst of the fire. He added that the fourth looked like the Son of God.

When you are walking with me in a life of faith, I will always be there for you. When you are thrust into a fiery trial (and they will come at times), I will walk in the midst of the fire with you. Fear nothing, for you are more than a conqueror through me.

The three men were unharmed by the flames. The only thing that happened to them, in this fiery trial, was that their bonds were burned off. The king, governors, and advisors all saw that the fire had no power over the three. Their hair was not singed, their clothing looked the same, and not even the smell of smoke clung to them.

The king made a proclamation about how great the God of these men were. He stated that they trusted their God and had refused to serve any other. These three men were then promoted in the province of Babylon.

I will set you free through your fiery trials. Trust me. I rule over all circumstances. My counsel and my deeds will stand forever. Follow my Word and be strong in faith; I will be with you. I will prosper you according to my perfect plan for your life. I will bless your life, my child.

Isaiah 43:2 • 1 Peter 4:12-14 • 1 Peter 3:13-15 • Isaiah 41:10
Deuteronomy 31:6 • Psalm 23:4-6 • Psalm 56:3-4 • Daniel 3

February 19 *Jesus Talks to You*

Be filled with the praises of the Lord your God. I have worked wonders for you continually. I redeemed your life from the pit. I have forgiven all of your iniquities. I am the healer of your sicknesses. I have crowned you with lovingkindness and tender mercies. I open the windows of heaven and provide bread for you daily. I am preparing a place for you in my kingdom and preparing you for that place—transforming your life by my Spirit. Lift up your heart and voice with thanksgiving.

Solomon had just finished building a house for the name of the Lord God of Israel. He offered praise to me, proclaiming that there was no God like me in heaven or earth—the God which keeps his covenant of love with his servants who follow him fully. He desired that I would clothe my servants with salvation and that they would rejoice in my goodness.

When Solomon finished his prayer and praise, I sent a fire from heaven which consumed the burnt offering and the sacrifices. My glory then filled the temple. So wondrous was the sight of the fire coming down from heaven and the glory filling the temple, that all the people bowed down with their faces to the ground. They worshiped their God; they praised me for being good and for my mercy that endures forever.

Offer praise to the King of creation, my son. Give glory from your heart to the Lord of life, my daughter. I will send down my fire of love. I will warm your heart with the glory of my love. I will fill you, my temple, with the Holy Spirit.

Psalm 103 • 2 Chronicles 6:1-15, 40-42 • 2 Chronicles 7:1-3

February 20 *Jesus Talks to You*

My ways are certainly not the world's ways. The prince of this world wreaks havoc in lives and relationships. I came to earth to restore lives, to heal the brokenhearted, and to comfort all that mourn. I came to open the prison doors to the captives who are bound.

I have shown you how to love. I have shown you how to forgive. As I have loved you, so should you also love one another. Be kind to one another, compassionate, and tenderhearted. Forgive others with your whole heart, even as my Father has forgiven you fully and freely, through my sacrifice on the cross.

Ask me to fill you with my love. It is a gift from heaven. Ask and you will receive. With my love, you will be able to show patience and kindness toward others. Unselfishly, you will seek what is best for them.

With my love reigning in your heart, you will bear much fruit in all of your relationships. Love will not easily be made angry. Love hopes, trusts, and perseveres. Love will never fail!

I will give you opportunities in the days ahead to show my love to others. Some people are hard to love; but they need my love. I choose you to walk in the newness of life—you who are raised from the dead life of your past. I live in you. Let my love warm the lives around you. You will greatly rejoice that you did. Love changes lives. Love changed yours!

John 15:13 • Ephesians 4:32 • Colossians 3:12-14 • 1 Corinthians 13:4-7

February 21

I came unto my own, and my own did not receive me. But as many as do receive me, I give the power and the right to be my son or daughter—to be children of the living God.

When I walked the earth, many people wrongfully judged me. Some said that I was a blasphemer, others that I was possessed by a demon, or that I was a drunkard. Others accused me of being a sabbath breaker; I was also proclaimed as a liar or insane by some.

Being rejected hurts—especially when you really love the one who is rejecting you. When you experience this kind of pain, you need to draw near to me; allow me to comfort your heart. I know what you are going through. As Counselor and the Prince of Peace, I have words of comfort that will give you truth, hope, and my love; my love will help you weather any storm. If you are walking with me, the truth will bring comfort if you are being falsely accused or misunderstood. I am living inside of you and will give you hope; know that I love you and will richly bless your life.

Spend time with me in prayer and my Word. My Spirit will bring you peace. I have my way in the whirlwinds of life. I calmed the storm at sea for my disciples. I will say to your storm, "Peace, be still."

Hebrews 13:6 • Isaiah 12:2 • John 14:27

My eyes are watching closely throughout the whole world, to show myself strong on behalf of those whose heart is fully committed to me.

Joshua and Caleb were the only two men of all the children of Israel, who left Egypt as adults, whom I allowed to enter the Promised Land. Why? Because they had a different spirit; they followed me wholeheartedly. They were not supermen; they were ordinary men who had humble hearts and desired all that I had for them. They gave me their hearts and lives.

I do not usually call the great and mighty of this world to be my light bearers. I choose those who are poor in spirit—those who desire to be rich in faith. These are the co-heirs with me of my kingdom. When on earth, I called four fisherman, a tax collector, and other ordinary men. They made many mistakes, but were willing to learn. As time went by, they were filled with the Holy Spirit. By my Spirit, they were willing to do my work in all circumstances. They were all even willing to die for me and the glorious kingdom of heaven, for the love I shared with each of them was so deep that it was much stronger than death itself.

Will you share your heart with me today? Will you let me reign in your life in a deeper way than yesterday? Will you commit to following me wholeheartedly? I have been with you, watching you, and loving you. I desire to be strong on your behalf. Give me your heart, and I will give you the deepest love you could ever know. Trust me with your life and future. I will guide you continuously by my Spirit, my heavenly counsel, and perfect wisdom. It is my Father's good pleasure to give you the kingdom of heaven. Welcome the Holy Spirit to fill you and empower you. You will never be the same. I will bless you in all that you do and say.

Numbers 14:24 • 1 Corinthians 1:26-31 • Zechariah 4:6 • John 16:13
Romans 5:5 • 2 Corinthians 4:17-18 • Psalm 32:8 • Psalm 73:24

As high as the heavens are above the earth, so great is my lovingkindness and mercy to you, my child.

There are times when you feel guilt for the sins you have committed in the past. I see how you hurt, and my heart is toward you, desiring that you might have my freedom and complete healing. Every human being on earth will fall short of perfection every day. No one can stand before the Father based on their own righteousness, even on a person's best day. One's own righteousness is as a filthy rag (strong words, but true).

The wondrous news is that by my death, the debt has been paid for any and all of your sins, past, present, and future. My shed blood has covered every transgression since the day you were born.

I have also covered you with my robe of righteousness. I am God, perfectly righteous and I live in you. You have my righteousness. You cannot be any more righteous. When your Father in heaven looks upon you, he sees me, the Christ; my righteousness has filled your life. There is no sin remembered from the past. He has forgiven all sins and has absolutely forgotten them forever.

Peter denied me three times; this was after having walked with me for over three years. He had seen a multitude of miracles and experienced my eternal love in such rich ways. Oh how bitterly he wept. The guilt and shame broke his heart. No sin could be greater, was the thought coursing through his mind—as his tears flowed.

Very early on the first day of the week some devoted women came to the tomb. By this time the sun had risen; I, the Son of God, had also risen!

Accompanied by a great earthquake, the angel had rolled away the stone. The angel was as bright as lightning, and his clothes as white as snow. He told them to not be afraid and that Jesus of Nazareth, whom they were looking for, who had been crucified, was risen. He said that Jesus was not here and you can see the place where they had lain his body.

My special message, through the angel, also shared a most important note of comfort; tell his disciples *and Peter*, that Jesus is going before you into Galilee, and that they would see him there. A special look of love, a smile from me to Peter, went with my special mention of Peter through the angel. I was telling Peter to receive my forgiveness and comfort (which shortly after this I did richly confirm my love and forgiveness to him). I was saying that my love was unconditional; everyone falls short. This is why I died on the cross.

I now share this comfort with you. The stone has been rolled away. I am alive. Your sins are forgiven. The Sun of Righteousness has risen with healing in his wings. Receive my forgiveness; receive my healing. Leap for joy, and let your songs of praise abound; for I have done great things for you, my righteous child. You are a true jewel of my heart. Enjoy my presence, and the deep love that I have for you today and forever!

Psalm 103:8-14 • Isaiah 61:10 • Mark 16:1-7 • Malachi 4:2
Romans 8:1 • Psalm 71:14-23 • Psalm 95:1-3

February 24 *Jesus Talks to You*

My grace is sufficient for you, for my power is made perfect when you are weak.

Gideon felt that he was too young, weak, and poor. But I spoke to Gideon through the angel telling him that he was a mighty man of valor. Gideon went on, with my guidance and my miracle, to deliver Israel from the hand of the enormous enemy army that was against Israel.

You may feel weak and not special enough for the work of God. But I have called you, my child, to be great in my kingdom (to be great, one needs to be a servant of all). I see you as a mighty one of valor. With my help, you are more than a conqueror.

You have this wondrous treasure, Christ, in you—a clay jar; so that the exceeding greatness of power will be known to come from me and not you. The light of God, the gift of heaven, resides in you, beloved one.

Gideon and his very small army had lamps in clay jars. They stood all around the exceedingly great enemy army, with no chance for victory—except it be for my mighty miraculous power. In their weakness, I was about to show that all things are possible to him who believes.

They broke the clay jars, and the lamps shone brightly as they blew the trumpets and shouted the victory phrase, as I showed them. You can read the whole story in my Word. The enemy was absolutely defeated miraculously. A great victory was wrought that day—a mighty miracle through a weak, lowly person, who used his mustard seed of faith.

O mighty one of valor (that's you), will you go forth with my lamp of love (the Light of the world) in your clay jar? Let your jar be broken so that your light will shine brightly. Blow the trumpet. Proclaim my love. Marvelous blessings and victories will be wrought through you in lives all around you. In your weakness, my strength and glory will be made perfect and wondrous. "God dwells in this one," they shall say. They will know that only God can do the miracle in your life that they behold!

2 Corinthians 12:9 • Philippians 4:13 • Ephesians 3:16-21
Isaiah 40:28-31 • Judges 6 & 7

February 25 *Jesus Talks to You*

Be strong and courageous. Do not be afraid, dismayed, or discouraged, for I the Lord your God will be with you wherever you go. I gave the same advice to Joshua after Moses my servant died.

Joshua now shared the burden of a vast multitude, who for forty years trekked through the desert. I would soon split the Jordan River, and bring the children of Israel into their inheritance—the Promised Land.

Trust me on your journey into my land of promise. I have given you exceedingly great promises of my love: righteousness, guidance, provision, and spiritual fulfillment. I am with you wherever you go.

Joshua 1:1-9 • 1 Peter 5:7 • John 16:33 • 1 Corinthians 15:58

February 26 *Jesus Talks to You*

It was not easy for Joshua and the children of Israel; they had many battles to fight to gain their inheritance. So it is with you, my child.

Take upon you today the whole armor that I provide for the battles ahead. Take the helmet of salvation, the shield of faith, the belt of truth, the breastplate of righteousness, and the sword of the Spirit (my Word). Wear "good news" shoes and a readiness to share my Word of peace.

As you seek me in prayer, remember that I am continually making intercession for you according to the Father's will. Also, the Spirit is helping you in your weakness by pleading for you with groanings too deep for words. You have God, the Creator of the universe, on your side. Nothing and no one can be victorious against you. I see the end from the beginning—and have all power. The battle is not yours; it is mine!

A glorious throne on high, since before time began, is the place of your sanctuary. Come into my presence for help in time of need. My child, I am here to comfort and encourage you. I will be strong on your behalf, and will fight every battle for you.

Ephesians 6:10-18 • Romans 8:26-28 • Jeremiah 17:12 • Revelation 3:21

February 27 *Jesus Talks to You*

My child, I know you perfectly and I love you perfectly. Every heart beat, every breath, and every thought you think are before me. I fashioned your innermost being. I formed you in your mother's womb. I was with you then and am still here with you today. I am God. I love you dearly and will always enjoy sweet communion with you.

Today, rest in my presence knowing how much I care. As much as possible be thankful, even for your hardships. I have allowed these trials in your life. They are producing patience and endurance in you. Endurance in turn produces experience and a confident hope in me. This hope will not disappoint, because by the Holy Spirit I have poured out my love into your heart.

You need not spend your time worrying. Draw near to me and I will draw near to you. Look singlemindedly toward me. In my presence is fullness of joy. With me are hidden all the treasures of wisdom and knowledge. The wonders of sweet communion that you can have with me are readily available to you. Just give me your whole heart and I will truly fill it. I will make known to you the riches and grace of my covenant as you seek me.

The day is coming when you will no longer hunger or thirst. The trials of earth will be no longer. I, the Lamb of God, who gave myself for you, will soon shelter you forever in my presence. I will reign as King of kings upon the throne of heaven. I will be your Shepherd and lead you to springs of living water. I will wipe away every tear from your eyes.

Psalm 139:1-18 • Romans 5:3-5 • Psalm 73:28 • Psalm 16:11
Colossians 2:3 • Psalm 25:14 • Revelation 7:15-17

February 28 *Jesus Talks to You*

The longer that you walk with me, the more you realize that you are not of this world, even as I am not of this world. You are a pilgrim, a temporary resident on earth. In this world you will have suffering and tribulation. But take heart my child; I have conquered the world.

I was tempted fully and never sinned. I know temptation. I know suffering. I will help you. Greater am I who lives in you, than Satan who is in the world. You are truly more than a conqueror through me. By my Spirit, the victory is yours. Let me reign in your life today.

My beloved child, open your heart today to my peace. The peace that I give you is not from this world. It surpasses all understanding. Let my peace be your guide. If you are overanxious, come into my presence. Be filled with thanksgiving, for I have richly blessed you and always will.

John 17:16 • John 16:33 • Romans 8:37-39 • 1 John 4:4 • John 14:27

When facing a daunting task or insurmountable obstacles, look to me. When hope seems to be almost gone, I am waiting to help you. I am the God of the impossible. What is impossible for man is not hard for me.

Remember the man called Legion? He was a wild man living among the tombs; he was often screaming and cutting himself with rocks. He was a demon-possessed man who could not even be chained; he would break the shackles into pieces.

I had great compassion on him and cast the demons out of this man. I gave him complete wholeness and a perfectly sound mind. He went his way and boldly proclaimed in Decapolis the mighty miracle that I had performed in his life. All who heard were amazed!

To most people, his was a hopeless case. Do you know someone like this wild, insane, demon-possessed man? Perhaps you don't, however a neighbor, relative, or employer may seem to be beyond help. Nothing is too hard for me! Look what I did in this wild man's life.

In earnest prayer, bring that difficult person before me. Your little mustard seed of faith and my power combined may work wonders. Please be patient; continue in prayer with thanksgiving for this person, and be willing to show love to this person. As I have loved you, so love this person. It is not hard to love. Acknowledge that the Christ of God is living in you; let me love that person through you, by yielding to the Holy Spirit. Miracles do happen; in my timing, I will be strong on your behalf. I alone can transform that person's life (if they are willing). But perhaps as wondrous as that person coming into the faith, is the miracle of you reflecting the glory of my love to that person!

Mark 5:1-20 • Psalm 34:17 • John 15:7 • James 5:16
Thessalonians 5:17 • 1 John 5:14-15 • Ephesians 6:18

Jesus Healing the Sick—*Matthew 15:30-31*

Sometimes I set up situations that are very contrary to your ways and planning. I desire to work mightily in your heart and life through these situations. I will be glorified and bring you freedom as well.

I told Moses the exact location by the Red Sea where the children of Israel were to encamp. I knew Pharaoh would harden his heart and follow them to this point.

Over four hundred years earlier, I told my friend and faithful servant, Abraham, that I would judge the nation that would be afflicting my people with bitter bondage during these centuries. The time of judgement had arrived. From this time forward, the world for millennia to come would know that I am the Lord God, the mighty Deliverer!

The Egyptians came after the children of Israel. They were trapped and were terrified at the sight of the mighty Egyptian army closing in. They thought they were going to die! I had a much better plan. I had a Promised Land for these people; it was time to get them on their way.

As I instructed Moses, he lifted his hand over the sea, and I divided the waters. The vast multitude crossed over on dry land. Once again, Moses lifted his hand, and I returned the waters, which covered all the chariots, horsemen, and the entire Egyptian army. My people were free of the bondage and fear that they had known for four hundred years!

At times, I will direct your life in a direction that is hard for you to understand. It may be an uncomfortable situation. You may even complain. I know your feelings and confusion at these times. Trust me with all of your heart. Submit to the direction that I show you in prayer, my Word, and by my Spirit. My ways are so very much higher than your ways, and I have your best interests in my view. I will fight for you. I will do wonders as needed, and you will be very blessed and thankful.

Genesis 15:13-14 • Exodus 14 • Deuteronomy 28:1-13 • Romans 15:13
Romans 8:32 • Psalm 28:7 • Proverbs 3:5-6

Buyers and Sellers are Driven Out of the Temple—Luke 19

I often had communion with the Father while I was on the earth. Sometimes I desired to be alone with him before dawn in a quiet place, or I would even spend a whole starry night on a mountain in prayer. The wondrous fellowship that I enjoyed with my Father before the world began was richly a part of my life during my years on earth.

The time was nearing for me to fulfill my mission. I am the perfect Lamb of God, foreordained before I spoke the world into existence to be the sacrifice for the sins of the world. As fully God and yet fully man, my sacrifice would show forth the greatest wonder of the grace of God.

I would soon take upon myself all of the horrendous evils and sins of man. I would become sin for you, I who knew no sin, that you might become the righteousness of God in me. I would be cut off from the glorious presence and eternally rich communion that I had forever known with my Father. I would be separated from my Father for the only time ever.

With loud cries and tears to the one who was able to save me from death, I was heard by my Father. Though great suffering was ahead, I was fully committed to my Father's will—"Yet not what I will, but what you will." In the deep turmoil of my soul, my heart's deep cry was that my strength was being broken in midcourse, and the number of my days were being reduced—as my crucifixion was looming just ahead. I asked the Father to not have me be taken away in the middle of my life!

With the warmth and depth of my Father's love, his response deeply comforted me. His reassurance was that I was the Beginning of the creation of God—that I laid the foundations of the earth and the heavens are the work of my hands. I was told that they will perish and that I would endure. They will wear out like an old garment; like clothing I would change them. He said that I will remain the same, and my years would never end. He said the children of my servants would continue and their descendants would be established before me. The great love that my Father has for me was seen as he comforted me at this time when my soul and heart were so stressed.

I was fully determined to do my Father's will—"Yet not what I will, but what you will." His encouragement was there for me. I then went on to fulfill my purpose on earth. I went to the place called The Skull (Calvary, Golgotha)—my place of extreme suffering and death. For the joy that awaited me forever, I endured my being executed on a cross like a criminal. You are the joy that awaited me! You are the crown of my heart! We shall reign together forever in paradise!

As my Father comforted me in my greatest time of suffering and sorrow, so shall I comfort you when you come to me in your times of need. As my Father honored me with the crown of life and the glory of heaven—that I had with him from everlasting to everlasting—so shall I give you the crown of life for overcoming by faith. You will share the glories and pleasures of paradise with me forever, my beloved child!

Luke 6:12 • Hebrews 5:7 • Mark 14:34-36 • Psalm 102:23-28
Hebrews 1:8-12 • James 1:12

March 3 *Jesus Talks to You*

Come to me, you who are weary and burdened, and I will give true rest to your heart and soul. Come learn from me. I am the Lord God, your Redeemer. I am the one that teaches you to profit. I have only your benefit in mind. I will teach you the ways of my kingdom. I will enrich you with my love and will guide you on the path of life.

Take the time to rest with me, even as I rested and enjoyed my Father's communion while I was on earth. I will restore your soul. Do not be like the man with the dull axe head. He would chop and chop without getting much done. I will sharpen your life (axe) for service to me. Share quiet times with me in prayer and in my Word; my wisdom, guidance, and power will help you be sharpened. Life will be so much better when you seek me first. My wisdom from above is profitable to direct you.

Matthew 11:28-30 • Isaiah 48:17-18 • Psalm 25:4-10 • Psalm 23:3

Long before I was born in Bethlehem, of the ancestral line of Abram and King David, I called Abram to a walk of faith. I told him to leave his country and go to a land that I would show him. I said that I would make a great nation of him, make his name great, and all families of the earth would be blessed in him. By faith, he obeyed my Word and left. He was seventy-five years old. He and his wife Sarai had no children.

About ten years later, my Word came to Abram in a vision encouraging him to not be afraid. I told him that I am his shield and his very great reward. He was wondering about his still being childless (my promise was to make of him a great nation). I brought him outside and told him to look up into the heavens and count the stars, if he is able to number them; I said that is how many descendants you will have. He believed in me with a steadfast trust, and I counted it unto him for righteousness. By my miracle, when Abram was ninety-nine and Sarai was ninety, she conceived; Abram became Abraham, the father of many nations.

I was Abraham's shield and his exceedingly great reward. He did have descendants innumerable. Even the prophets and apostles were his descendants—and I am a descendant, in the flesh, of Abraham. And certainly all who have faith like Abraham (those who believe my Word of promise and salvation through me, the Messiah) are Abraham's spiritual descendants. Truly his reward is great beyond measure; all families of the earth are blessed because of his faith.

I say to you, my child, that I am your sun and your shield. I will give you daily light to walk my path. I will protect you in more ways than I can share. I will give you my grace; I will empower you to walk with me. I will give you my glory; you are a joint-heir with me of the kingdom. I will also bless your words and deeds as you abide in me. You will have everlasting fruit—treasures in heaven. By your faith in me, in my blood sacrifice for your sins, and in my resurrection from the dead, you are like Abraham; your faith will be counted unto you for righteousness.

Genesis 15:1-6 • Psalm 84:11-12 • Romans 4:17-25

March 5 *Jesus Talks to You*

After my crucifixion and resurrection, I appeared to my disciples for forty days. By many infallible proofs and miracles, they were assured that their Lord was truly alive. I spoke with them during this time concerning my kingdom. I commanded them to not leave Jerusalem, for in a few days they would be baptized with the Holy Spirit.

In a wondrous fashion, the promise of the Father, the Holy Spirit, filled the disciples in Jerusalem, and they spoke with other languages. Devout men, who were there from every nation under heaven, heard them speak of the mighty works of God in their own languages.

Peter was now boldly proclaiming spiritual truths of my kingdom. I had endued him with power from above. As I had promised the disciples, there were now rivers of living water flowing from their innermost being. Peter spoke the words that the Spirit gave him to say. The Spirit worked a mighty wonder, for that day three thousand souls that I loved came to believe in me with their heart; they were born again.

This was just the beginning. From that point on, many wonders and signs were performed by the apostles.

Peter was transformed by the power of the Holy Spirit. Ask and you shall receive this transforming power to be bold. Out of your innermost being will flow rivers of living water. I will fill you to overflowing with my love. The fruit of this blessing in your life will be as a tree of life; you will inspire others to desire to know and receive me unto life eternal.

Acts 1:1-12 • Acts 2 • John 7:38-39 • Proverbs 11:30

March 6 *Jesus Talks to You*

Peter and John were truly becoming fishers of men, just as I said they would. As they went into the temple, a man lame from birth was asking them for money. Peter told him that he did not have silver or gold, but what he did have he would give him. He told the lame man to rise up and walk in the name of Jesus Christ of Nazareth. By the power of the Holy Spirit, I gave that man's feet and ankles strength—a miraculous healing.

As the man was walking, leaping, and praising God, the people were amazed at the miracle they had witnessed. The people recognized the one who was now leaping as the one who usually was begging.

Once again, Spirit-filled Peter boldly spoke of my death and resurrection to the multitude gathered. He proclaimed truths of the prophecies of my coming. He explained the need the people had for the God who has fulfilled these prophecies.

While he was still speaking, the religious leaders came and arrested Peter and John, and put them in prison until the next day. The Sadducees were grieved that Peter and John were proclaiming in Jesus the resurrection of the dead. However, a multitude who heard the Word that day became believers.

It was not by Peter's or John's might that the man was healed. It was not fancy words of man's wisdom that touched lives that saved the multitude. The Holy Spirit performed the healing; my Spirit revealed the truth, and convinced the hearts of their need for repentance.

I am the God of wonders. Behold the many miracles that the Father had me work; you will see that every one was beyond what man would perceive as possible—they all are beyond the laws of nature. I am desiring to do miracles in your life. I can heal a broken heart. I can bring love where there was not love. I am able to replace deep sorrow with hope and joy. I will transform your life in so many ways. Rejoice, for people will be amazed when they see that it is Jesus who now lives in you. Count on me; I am able and will do it.

Acts 3 • Acts 4:1-22 • Zechariah 4:6 • 1 Corinthians 2:4-7

While I was living on earth, it was wonderful to be with the people I had created. My love for humanity is everlasting; my sacrifice for all of mankind was my grand purpose and passion for coming into the world.

After ascending back to heaven in full view of my disciples, I sat down at the right hand of the Father. Exactly as told to my disciples before my ascension, the promise of the Holy Spirit was fulfilled on the day of Pentecost; he would now be guiding them. I was working with them and confirming the Word they preached with signs and wonders.

The day after I had healed the lame man (the one Peter and John met at the temple gate), Peter, filled with the Holy Spirit, boldly proclaimed the truth of my death and resurrection, and the power of my name. This time it was the religious leaders who were the hearers. After threatening the two apostles, the chief priests and elders let them go.

They returned to their companions and told of the threats of the leaders. With one heart of faith, the whole company lifted their voice to their Father in heaven. They acknowledged the power and providence of the Father, and humbly implored that he would stretch forth his hand and perform miraculous signs and wonders by the name of his Son, Jesus.

After their prayer, I shook the place they were meeting in and filled them with the Holy Spirit. They spoke my Word with boldness to many. The community of believers were of one heart and mind, sharing all things; no one had lack of anything. I richly blessed them because of their love of God and their love one to another. I also gave amazing power to the apostles as they gave testimony of my resurrection from the dead. I placed my lovingkindness and favor richly upon all their lives.

Like the apostles were, be led by my Spirit. Share my love and Word. Do not fear what man says. Seek me with your whole heart, and I will work mightily on your behalf. You will be richly blessed as you bless others.

Acts 4:1-33 • John 15:7 • John 15:16 • Isaiah 65:24

March 8

Jesus Talks to You

I love you dearly, and my heart goes out to you when you have anxieties and fears. It is very natural to have them, but I desire to set you free and bring you into a new walk with me. Confidence, strength, and peace will fill your life as you draw near to me and let the power of my Word transform you day by day.

When the cares of this life begin to crowd your mind, humbly ask in prayer, with thanksgiving, for your needs to be met by me. I already know every need you have; casting your cares on me in prayer will help you trust that I have heard you, and trust that I will work on your behalf. And I will. After praying about your needs, you will know that it is in my hands. You will not have to try to get things done or get a need met by your own doings. It is better to be patient and let me work in your heart and life as you await my fulfillment of each need. This is an important part of walking with me, the King of kings. I will honor your patience. You will have grown in character by trusting in me, and you will see me work in special, loving, and sometimes wondrous ways.

Philippians 4:6-7 • 1 Peter 5:6-7 • Isaiah 43:1-3 • James 1:5
Matthew 6:31-33

March 9

Jesus Talks to You

The kingdom of heaven is more real than the creation that you see around you. What you see with your eyes are temporary, so focus on that which is unseen—the eternal realm.

The disciples witnessed my ascension back to my eternal kingdom. As they were watching, a cloud took me out of their sight. My two white-robed messengers told them that this same Jesus that they had seen being taken up to heaven shall return in the same way they saw him go.

During my walk on earth, I shared with my disciples that I would be going to prepare a place for them; that is what I have been doing. I am soon returning to come for you and all of my sons and daughters who believe, that you all might be with me where I am. This is a perfect reason for you to rejoice. You will soon be reigning with me as a joint-heir of the kingdom of heaven.

Behold the beauty of this world: towering mountain ranges, mighty rivers, vast wonders of the floral and animal kingdoms, awesome sunsets, wondrous waterfalls, and brilliant star-filled nights; these have displayed a sampling of my majesty for many centuries.

Your eyes have not seen, nor have your ears heard, or any of your senses experienced the exceeding wondrous glories of my soon appearing kingdom. Open your heart to me today; my Spirit will reveal the deep things of my love and heavenly kingdom. Rejoice and be thankful, for all that I promised I will soon fulfill. You will reign with me forever.

Acts 1:9-11 • 2 Corinthians 4:18 • John 14:1-3 • 1 Corinthians 2:9

March 10 *Jesus Talks to You*

I love you with an eternal love whose depth and richness cannot even be fathomed by your mind. My ways and thoughts are exceedingly higher than yours—as the galaxies are high above the earth. I share this to comfort you, even to the depths of your soul. I only desire that you experience the richest blessings in this world and the one to come.

Trust in me, the God of all creation. Nothing is too hard for me. Allow me to work in all situations. My ways are best. Do not rely on your own wisdom; I see the end from the beginning. Always be patient, for I will complete the work that I have begun in your life, and will work out all things for your good. Even times of sorrow and disappointments will I absolutely use for your good.

Give me your whole heart. Let me reign supreme, and I will raise you up to be a great blessing; all that you do will prosper, and the love you share shall be an inspiration to others.

Isaiah 55:8-13 • Proverbs 3:5-6 • Proverbs 10:22 • Romans 8:28

I have chosen you, and I will fulfill my purpose for you. I am the Lord God, who gave my life for you, that you might be one with me and the Father. My plan for all who have received me is to transform them more and more into my image. I chose you, a rough stone dug out of the miry pit of this world; by my glorious miracle power, I am transforming you into a precious and priceless gem.

Many of my beloved eternal gems were once such common and earthly rocks. Behold the former estate of some of the living stones in my glorious temple that I inhabit by my Spirit: Paul was a blasphemer and helped kill Christians; Moses was a murderer; Mary Magdalene was a woman out of whom I cast seven demons; Matthew was a hated tax collector; Peter, Andrew, James, and John were everyday fishermen; David, the shepherd and king, was an adulterer and a murderer. The miracles in these lives were truly magnificent. I will work miracles in your life.

Be strong in your faith; I live in you and my resurrection power is able to transform your heart. I will raise you up in my ways, my wisdom, and my truth. Embrace all of the promises in my Word. By them, you are partakers of my divine nature.

Keep yourself from idols; anything that you put as more important in your life than me is an idol. My commandments are to love the Lord your God with all your heart, soul, mind, and strength, and to love your neighbor, even as you love yourself.

I have saved you and called you to a holy calling, not because of works you have done, but because of my own purpose and grace which was given to you in me, the Christ, before the world began. I will fulfill my plan for you. Throughout the eternal ages, I will show you the exceeding riches of my love and glory. I love you, my priceless gem.

John 15:16 • Psalm 138:8 • Malachi 3:17 • 2 Peter 1:4 • Isaiah 62:3-4
1 Peter 2:9 • 1 Corinthians 6:19-20 • 2 Corinthians 6:16-18
Romans 8:32 • Ephesians 2:1-7 • 2 Timothy 1:9

March 12

Jesus Talks to You

You were once a dried up branch: withered, dying, and bearing bitter fruit. But now you are a branch grafted into the living vine, whose sustenance comes from the very power of the God of all creation. I am the true vine and you are absolutely a part of me—a living branch with my life in you.

I am the Light of the world. I am the Sun of Righteousness. Open your heart to me. Let the glorious light of my love be a transforming power to you. You will grow in grace as you come into my presence each day.

Let your roots be deep in me; let me be the foundation of your life. Just as leaves reach toward the sun, let your leaves reach out in faith to me, the Sun of Righteousness. Let your life flow with thanksgiving to the God who loves you. Your praise is a blessing to me; you are acknowledging the many gifts I bestow upon you daily.

John 15:5 • Ephesians 3:17 • Malachi 4:2 • Colossians 3:12-17

March 13

Jesus Talks to You

Each day, ask me to fill you with my Spirit. Acknowledge me in all your ways, and pray to be led by my Spirit in all you do and say.

As you abide in me, your life will be transformed in wonderful ways. You shall be like a tree planted by streams of water. You shall bear abundant fruit in due season. You shall flourish with the fruit of the Spirit. A love that surpasses knowledge shall flow from your life. Fountains of an inexpressible glorious joy shall well up inside of you. My peace which passes understanding shall guard your heart and mind.

If I am for you, nothing can be against you. Seeing that I gave my life for you, shall I not also provide you with everything that you need? I will.

Psalm 1:3 • Galatians 5:22-23 • Ephesians 3:16-21 • 1 Peter 1:8
Philippians 4:7 • Romans 8:31-32

March 14

You are being built upon the foundation of the apostles and prophets; I am the chief Cornerstone. You are a co-laborer with me—now that I live in you. When you are led by my Spirit and share my love through word and deed, you are building with gold, silver, and precious stones on this glorious foundation. When you are led by the flesh, you are building with wood, hay, and straw. I, the Lord God, am a consuming fire; on the day of the Lord, my fire will test every man's work. If your work upon the foundation was gold, silver, or precious stones, you shall receive your reward. If wood, hay, or straw, it will be burned and you will suffer loss—but you will be saved, yet so as through fire.

Therefore my beloved child, be steadfast, unmovable, always abounding in my work, forasmuch as you know that your labor is not in vain. Build well on the foundation; your rewards in glory shall be phenomenal.

Ephesians 2:20 • 1 Corinthians 3:8-15 • Hebrews 12:29
Galatians 6:9 • 1 Corinthians 15:58 • Hebrews 13:20-21

March 15

After teaching the multitude from Simon's boat by the Sea of Galilee, I told Simon to put out into the deep water and lower his nets for a catch. He answered that they had worked all night and had caught nothing. Nevertheless, upon my request he did so. They enclosed such a large number of fish that their nets began to break. He called his partners, James and John, who were in the other boat, to come and help.

Both boats were filled to the point that they began to sink. Simon and his partners were totally astonished at the miracle. Simon fell down before me and told me to go away, because he was a sinful man. I told him to not be afraid because from now on he would be fishing for men. When the men pulled the boats up on the shore, they forsook all and followed me.

I came into this world to seek and to save that which was lost. I will use my infinite and loving wisdom, and power—and have given my life to the death—to reach every one of my children, that they might come into my kingdom forever. I have all control over nature. I can hold back fish or give such abundance that even the boats start to sink. I called these men with a wondrous miracle that would be especially amazing to them.

These ordinary men followed me from that day on. By my Spirit's power working in their lives, these living stones are now a part of the foundation of my everlasting dwelling place where I live by my Spirit.

Luke 5:1-11 • Luke 19:10 • Revelation 21:14 • Ephesians 2:19-21

March 16 *Jesus Talks to You*

Sometimes I will hold back some blessings in life to get your attention. Perhaps I desire for you to see that these gifts are precisely that—a gift of love from me to you. For you to be thankful from your heart to mine is an important part of our relationship.

Sometimes I am holding back from giving because I want you to know that man shall not live by bread alone, but by every Word that proceeds from my mouth. I desire that you live by faith, and not by sight. I do not want you to love me only because of what I do for you—especially if what I do for you must be according to your plans.

I desire for you to love me for who I am; I certainly love you for who you are and not for what you do for me. You are my beloved child, a treasured member of my family, who will be rejoicing with me forever in a world that is much more real and glorious that this present world. I am the God of the universe who loves you with a love beyond words.

I love you so much, that I want you to experience my life in you. I want you to live by my faith, the faith of the Son of God. Like Abraham, be strong in faith, giving glory to God. He believed the promises of a personal God. He embraced my promises and trusted me.

By my mercy I humbled the fishermen with the sinking ships that day. It was to help free them from serving this world and their own selves, that they might walk with me and forever share the glory I had with the Father since before I spoke the worlds into existence. Blessed were these men for they beheld my miracles. They knew me, the Son of Man, on earth for over three years. But blessed are you who have not seen me in the flesh, and yet you love me from the heart. You, who know the joyful sound of my song in your heart day by day, are rejoicing with joy unspeakable and full of glory.

Trust me always, especially when a prayer is not being answered quickly enough for you, or circumstances are unfavorable—I have all power and will work all things to your good. Humble yourself before my mighty hand and in due time I will exalt you. Be content to know me, and let your relationship with me grow deeper. Ours is an eternal friendship.

You see what I did for those fishermen. If I desire, I could rain down any blessing upon your life at any time. But I desire your love for me to be pure, loving me not for the gifts I give, but because I am the God who loves you. I treasure you just for who you are; you are my child. I will always provide for you according to my riches in glory, beloved one.

Let me be everything to you: Savior, Lord, King, Comforter, Counsellor, best friend, joint-heir of the kingdom, and Everlasting God.

Romans 4:17-25 • John 17 • 1 Peter 1:3-9

March 17 *Jesus Talks to You*

Within the church at Antioch there were certain prophets and teachers. While they were ministering unto me through worship during a time of fasting, my Spirit told them to set apart Barnabas and Saul for the special work that I had called them to do. After prayer and laying on of hands, they were sent forth to fulfill their calling.

Thus began the journeys of Saul (Paul) and Barnabas who I richly used and blessed by my Spirit. My Word, shared by men whose lives had been changed mightily by my Spirit, transformed many lives wherever they journeyed. Paul and Barnabas sought me with their whole hearts daily in prayer, and I blessed them by working signs and miracles through them.

Paul, my instrument in writing many of my New Testament letters to the world, continually was in rich worship and thankfulness for all that I did for him. He daily prayed to do my will, knowing that I would work mightily in his heart and life by my Spirit. Through much tribulation, I transformed his life to the praise of the glory of my grace.

You, my child, like Paul and Barnabas, are chosen and loved. They also were only human—with faults, fears, and emotions. But these men did not dwell on their weaknesses; they gloried in my power. They knew that I was able to do immeasurably more through them, as yielded vessels, than they could ever imagine. Through the faith of men like these, millions of lives have been saved and inspired through the centuries.

Come before my presence and minister unto me, the King of kings. In prayer and worship with your church leaders or others who have dedicated their lives to me, seek me that I might show you the work that I have called you to do. Seek me and my Word with prayer and thanksgiving; I will reveal my will to you. I will anoint you and guide you into a rich ministry of love and care to others. Lives will be changed; by your work of love, you will help many of my children to come home to me. I will fill you with my Spirit and my love.

I will do the work in and through your life. I raised the dead, cleansed the lepers, and made blind eyes see; I can change your heart and life in so many ways. Rest in my love and power. All things are possible to you that believe. Being thankful in all things is a key to your victory.

Acts 13:1-5 • Acts 15:12 • 2 Chronicles 15:7 • Joshua 1:9
Isaiah 43:1-13 • 1 Thessalonians 5:18

By the mighty miracles that I worked while on earth and through my Word that you received, you believe in me. I have delivered you from the bondage of Egypt (sin and this present evil world).

Through mighty miracles, I also freed the children of Israel from their bitter bondage in Egypt. For forty years in the wilderness, I loved them and guided them as I taught them of my ways. I also humbled them, that they might learn that man does not live by bread alone.

At one point, the congregation of Israel had no water to drink and came to Moses, bitterly complaining against him. They did not know me or look to me for their daily provision. I told Moses to take the staff with which he struck the Nile River, whose waters I turned to blood, and strike the rock in Horeb. I told him that water would gush out of the rock for the people to drink. He did what I told him to do, and the congregation had abundance of water.

The children of Israel ate manna that I sent to them for forty years. That bread could not give them eternal life. But I am the bread of life that came down from heaven. The bread that I give for the life of the world is my flesh. Whoever eats this bread will live forever.

The waters they drank from the rock in Horeb only satisfied temporarily. I am the spiritual Rock. By my crucifixion, foreordained before the world began, my body was struck—like the rock in Horeb. True living water flows from me daily for you, that I may impart the newness of life. As I was raised up from the dead by the glory of the Father, so have you been raised by my power; I am the resurrection and the life. On your journey through this wilderness world, drink of me. Drink and you will never thirst again. Drink every day freely of my living water. Drink and live forever, beloved one.

Psalm 78:1-35 • 1 Corinthians 10:1-14 • Revelation 22:17
Isaiah 55:1-3 • John 6:29-35 • John 7:37-39

March 19

Moses the leader, David the king, Elijah the prophet, and Paul the apostle all suffered times of weakness in the midst of their successful lives of service. At times they despaired of life itself. But they all knew to cry out to me for help. They came confidently before my throne of grace to receive mercy and grace in their time of need.

When you are humbled by your weaknesses, allow my power to reside in you. I will provide the strength needed for each day. My power is made perfect when you are weak. My glory will be seen more clearly, when I am seen to be the one who delivered you or blessed you, and that the provision was not by your own hand. I was crucified in weakness, but I live by the power of God. You are weak, but you will live in me by my power working in you and through you.

Colossians 1:11 • Philippians 4:13 • 2 Corinthians 12:9-10
1 Corinthians 10:13 • Isaiah 40:28-31 • 2 Corinthians 13:4

March 20

Jesus Talks to You

Take heed and be on your guard against covetousness, for your life does not consist of the abundance of your possessions. I led a simple life for over thirty years on earth. I greatly enjoyed communion with my Father—delighting in the everlasting fellowship that I have with him. During my ministry I did not even have a place to lay my head. I esteemed the riches of loving others during those years to be of exceeding more value that all the gold, jewels, and possessions on earth.

Be free of the love of money, for I will never leave you or forsake you. You brought nothing into the world, and you certainly are not bringing any possessions from earth to my kingdom of heaven. There truly is great gain in godliness. Store up for yourselves in heaven treasures that are eternal. Let my love fill your life, that you may bring life to the lost.

Luke 12:15 • Hebrews 13:5 • 1 Timothy 6:6-19 • Matthew 6:19-21

March 21

Jesus Talks to You

So many people continue to learn, but they never find true wisdom. My words are pure words, like silver refined in a furnace, purified seven times. My Word, my promises, and my testimonies will bring much wisdom to the soul who embraces them. The wisdom from above is more valuable than all the treasures found in every kingdom that ever existed on earth.

Happy is the one who receives my wisdom. Seek my wisdom as most men would seek after gold and silver. Come daily into my presence, and seek me in the Word and prayer. Call unto me, and I will show you great and hidden things that you have not known.

Solomon had extraordinary wisdom, but a greater than Solomon now lives in you. I will make known to you the deep things of my love and kingdom. Follow my counsel; I will guide you on the path of righteousness. My Father will honor you forever if you serve me while on earth.

Proverbs 2:3-9; 8:10-35 • James 3:17 • Jeremiah 33:3 • John 12:26

March 22

Jesus Talks to You

Is this not most phenomenal—that you may know me personally? I absolutely rejoice in my friendship and love relationship with each of my children. Life is wonderful, and it is my children who always brighten my heart.

I created love and relationships. Mankind has written many books and songs extolling love, relationships, and wondrous emotions. But a relationship with the God who created them is considered by most to be non-existent. Many doubt that I am a personal God, or that I even exist. I proclaim to all today, that I am the living God with all power over all creation. I, who inhabit eternity, also dwell in the hearts of my beloved children who have received me. I came into the world that you might know me in a very personal way. I ate, drank, walked, talked, loved, laughed, and cried just like you. I experienced life to the fullest with my family and friends during my life on earth.

Through my Word and my miracles I instilled faith in my disciples. I bore all sins in my body on the cross. I shed my life's blood in sacrificial love on the cross and through it made payment in full for every person's trespasses. I now can live fully in your life, reigning in your heart and mind.

You can now have a rich love relationship with me, the risen Savior, the King of kings, and the Lord of heaven and earth. The experience of the beauty and depth of my love relationship that I warmly offer to each of my children is far beyond the relationships that one knows without me. As amazing as my myriad of miracles and the love I have shown mankind while I was on earth, so also is how wondrous my relationship will be with you, if you would like.

Jeremiah 31:3 • 1 Peter 1:3 • Ephesians 1:3-7 • Romans 8:37-39
John 3:16 • Ephesians 3:17-19 • Isaiah 54:10

March 23 *Jesus Talks to You*

Forever I will rejoice with you, as I reveal the glories of my everlasting kingdom to you. I am the One who spoke the innumerable galaxies into existence, each with a myriad of stars and celestial wonders. The glories of the universe are beyond anything that man on earth can know. Yet, the wonders of the kingdom of heaven are exceedingly far beyond all the glories of all the galaxies combined.

You shall be changed in the twinkling of an eye. I will transform you into an immortal body, changed to be in my image—that you might experience forever my kingdom that is filled beyond measure with love and peace. The pleasures, the unspeakable joy, and the love that will be shared by you and me are astronomically beyond what could be known by man on earth. My love for you is so rich and immeasurable, that it will take all eternity to share it with you.

Colossians 1:12-17 • Ephesians 2:6-7 • Revelation 22:1-5 • 1 John 3:1-3

The children of Israel had seen the amazing miracles in Egypt that I worked. By my mighty hand, I delivered them from the cruel bondage of Egypt. I then saved the vast multitude by splitting the Red Sea and having them cross on dry ground. There was tremendous rejoicing with song and dance on the other side of the sea; they were finally free of their enemy who perished when I returned the great waters to their place.

As they journeyed three days into the wilderness, they came to a place where they could not drink the water. It was bitter and was named Marah, which means bitter. They murmured against Moses. He cried out to me. I showed him a tree, which he threw into the waters, and they became sweet and drinkable.

After the miracle, I told them that if they would diligently listen to my voice, do what is right, and give ear to my commandments, that I will not bring upon them any of the diseases that I brought upon the Egyptians; for I am the Lord that heals them.

My child, I have set you free from the bondage of Egypt (bondage to sin and the resulting death) by my miracle of love and a mighty hand. You too have rejoiced greatly for what I have done for you, like the children of Israel. As you travel on your journey with me, you also will encounter bitter waters, whether it be experiencing financial hardship, a time of sickness or suffering, a broken relationship, or any trial of your faith.

My cross is the tree, that when thrown into your bitter waters will make it sweet. By the work of my cross, I have brought you from the kingdom of darkness into my kingdom of light. My cross, the tree, has transformed the bitterness of sin and death in your life into the sweetest of living water flowing with forgiveness from my throne to your heart —true life giving drink indeed. By the power of the cross, you now can freely forgive others, bringing sweetness to your relationships.

Throw the tree (the cross) into those bitter waters in your life. I do the impossible; your work is only to believe. I am the Lord God who heals you.

I work all things together for your good. As you place your trust fully in me during any trial of your faith, you will be strengthened by my Holy Spirit. I will give you wisdom from above, open just the right door at just the right time, or I will heal your broken heart or a troubled relationship, according to my will. Seek me first and my righteousness, and all things of the abundant life that I promise you will be yours.

Exodus 15:18-27 • James 1:1-6 • Matthew 6:33

March 25 *Jesus Talks to You*

I have called you, and have chosen you to have the most wondrous treasure within you. My Spirit will fill your life to overflowing, as you give your heart to me in total surrender. By knowing and embracing my many precious promises, you are enabled to share my divine nature. I am the God of all creation, perfectly holy and righteous, and desire to dwell richly in you, a jar of clay. Truly this is a miracle—God dwelling in you.

I am calling you to be holy. Give me every area of your life. Any sin that you might be clinging to is absolutely not worth it. Ask me and I will help you get the victory. I love you vastly beyond what any words could express. Fear not, I know your every sin, every weakness, and I understand you perfectly; I know you exceedingly more than you know yourself. I know what will bring you complete joy and peace. I will greatly help you to be set free so that I might reign in every area of your life. Sin will blind you and make you a slave. My love, glory, and truth is of the kingdom of heaven, and when they replace sin in your life, you will soar like an eagle. Your joy will be complete when you sit daily with me in heavenly places.

My beloved child, look at what my life was like on earth. I know you love the way I showed love and mercy to all. I know you also believe that my miracles and the truths of my teaching were awesome. I desire for the same life that is in me to dwell richly in and shine forth from your life. Let me rule in every area of your heart. Let Christ in you, the hope of glory, be so real in your life.

Press on toward holiness as shown in my Word. I will complete the work that I began in you. I will transform your life in so many wondrous ways. My love and my life will shine more and more from you. You will truly be blessed and a blessing to many. You will rejoice throughout your life while on earth and throughout the endless ages of eternity.

2 Peter 1:1-11 • Romans 12:1-2 • 1 Peter 1:13-23 • Philippians 4:8
Philippians 1:6 • Colossians 1:27

March 26

In the third month after I brought the children of Israel out of Egypt, I called to Moses from the mountain in the desert of Sinai. I told him what to declare to the Israelites. Through Moses, I said that they have seen what I did to the Egyptians, how I carried them on eagles' wings, bringing them to myself. If they would truly obey my voice and keep my covenant, they would be my treasured people above all nations. They would be a kingdom of priests—my holy nation.

I told Moses that I would come down upon Mount Sinai in the sight of all the people. On the morning of the third day, as I had promised, I came to visit. With thunder and lightning, a thick cloud upon the mountain, and an exceedingly loud trumpet blast, I made my presence known. All the people were trembling with fear. I descended upon Mount Sinai in fire, and the mountain was covered with smoke, as from a furnace. I shook the whole mountain violently. I made the sound of the trumpet blasts louder and louder.

I called Moses to the top of the mountain. I also charged the people, through Moses, that no one was to force their way through the boundaries set up around the mountain, that they might gaze upon me. If they did, many might perish. Moses came to the top of the mountain.

I spoke from heaven out of the midst of the fearsome fire. The people heard my voice and understood what I was saying, but they did not see me. I declared my covenant, the Ten Commandments, which I commanded them to follow, and wrote them on two stone tablets.

I had promised to Abraham that I would make of him a great nation, and would deliver them after four hundred years of bondage. I foretold that they would leave with considerable wealth, which they did. This vast multitude who knew only slavery, had seen the mighty miracles I worked in Egypt. Now I was speaking to them accompanied by a most fearful display; this was just a small touch of my power. They were learning that it truly is a fearful thing to fall into my hands, the hands of the living God. Never had I spoken to a nation, but now I was revealing my holy laws for a nation to live by.

I am holy. My Ten Commandments are holy, and no man can fulfill these commandments in their flesh. Only I fulfilled every law perfectly, when I lived on earth. If you fail any of the commandments, the penalty is death. The soul that sins shall die. But I paid the debt for any and all of your sins by my blood sacrifice on the cross. When I came into your heart, you received me—perfect righteousness. You shall not die; you shall live with me in my everlasting kingdom of heaven.

Exodus 19 • Exodus 20:1-22 • Deuteronomy 4:7-13 • Romans 6:23
John 3:16

March 27 *Jesus Talks to You*

You have not come to a physical mountain that can be touched, like Mount Sinai, with flaming fire, blackness, darkness, tempest, the sound of trumpet blasts, and a voice speaking words; so fearful were the people that they begged for me to not speak to them any more. The whole sight was so terrifying that even Moses was trembling with fear.

You have come to Mount Zion, and unto my city, the heavenly Jerusalem. You have come to countless multitudes of angels in joyful assembly. You are part of my eternal family, whose names are written in heaven. You've come to me, the Messiah, the mediator of the New Covenant.

The law was given through Moses, but grace and truth came through me, Jesus, the Son of God. I called the children of Israel at Mount Sinai to follow commandments and statutes, that they might learn of sin and holiness. You are not called to live under laws, but under my abundant grace. You are called to walk in my Spirit. I have written my laws upon your heart and mind. I fulfilled the law perfectly and I live in you; I am your righteousness. Be filled and led by my Spirit; by my grace and power, you shall truly love your God with all your heart, soul, mind, and strength, and your neighbor as yourself.

I spoke from heaven, a sign to the children of Israel and the world that I am real. The giving of the Ten Commandments was truly a fearful event for the people. But I call you now to come close to me as my dear child. You now hear my voice. I am your Savior and your God, and will speak to you every day as you draw near to me. Through my Word and my Spirit, you will be led forth with peace into green pastures and beside still waters. I am your Shepherd and have only good plans for you. You are always welcome to come into my presence. You are my dear child.

Hebrews 12:18-24 • 1 Peter 2:9 • Philippians 3:20 • Isaiah 51:11
Psalm 23

March 28 *Jesus Talks to You*

When I brought to you the Old Covenant, my Ten Commandments were delivered in a most fearful manner upon Mount Sinai. I am holy, and you needed to know of the great gulf between man's sinful human nature and the God of all creation. From that day until now, no man has been able to keep all of the Ten Commandments without sin. All have fallen drastically short of my perfection.

I came into the world to bring you to myself, by way of a New Covenant, in a most glorious fashion. I became human and lived among you. Mankind actually saw my glory and majesty, the glory as of the only begotten Son of the Father, full of grace and truth. I was not the untouchable, unapproachable Mighty God of Sinai, but man beheld the Word of God made flesh, felt the warmth of my love, heard the words of heaven, were healed by miracles of mercy, and given hope by my precious promises.

Every sin that all human beings had ever committed against the Ten Commandments, against the holy God of heaven and earth, was placed on me the day I was crucified; I bore the punishment of all of mankind's sins. A most remarkable miracle among all the wonders wrought during my life on earth—washing away of all sins, providing eternal forgiveness, and making the way possible for me to live in every man's heart—happened that day. My New Covenant (my new agreement with mankind) was delivered to the world and was signed and sealed by my very own blood; Almighty God became man and shed his blood for you.

My New Covenant is not like the covenant that I made with the children of Israel when I took them by the hand to lead them out of Egypt, for I have placed my laws into your mind and have written them on your heart (not on tables of stone). I will be your God and you shall be my child forever. I will forgive your iniquities, and will never remember them.

As many as receive me, to them I give power to be a child of the living God. If you love me and keep my Word, my Father will love you, and we will come and live inside you. We are not far off as in Sinai; you have been brought into a most wondrous oneness and communion with your God. We desire to make our love deeply and richly known to you. We have come to you in a most personal way. My Holy Spirit is calling you now, and encouraging you to make every effort of the heart and in your life to get to know me, your Savior and God—who cherishes you with a love that is vastly beyond any love you have ever known or could even imagine. I will bless you in a multitude of ways. Open you heart to me and receive my love.

Behold, my beloved child, my royal priest, my chosen jewel; you shall soon reign with me in the new heaven and the new earth. My dwelling will be with you for all eternity. I will be with you and be your God, and you shall be my child, forever. Amen.

John 1:14 • Hebrews 2:9-18 • Jeremiah 31:31-34 • Hebrews 8:7-12 Matthew 26:28 • Ephesians 2:12-13 • John 14:23 • Revelation 21:1-7 Hebrews 13:20-21

March 29

Jesus Talks to You

I am the God of Israel, the Mighty God that brought forth the vast multitude from the bondage of Egypt. By awesome signs and wonders, I was made known to them. I brought them into their land of promise, a land flowing with milk and honey. I gave them a king named David. He brought praise and worship to the people called by my name, and I richly blessed the nation for many years.

Come into my presence today with singing and praise, for I have dealt bountifully with you. I am the One that provides all your needs according to my riches in glory. I fulfill my promises to you, guide you with my counsel, heal your diseases, and forgive your iniquities. I conquered sin and death for you. I give you my Spirit and my love to bring you my truth and comfort every day. Offer the sacrifice of praise today. Be filled with thankfulness always, for my steadfast love to you endures forever.

Psalm 100:1-5 • Hebrews 13:15 • Jude 1:24-25 • Psalm 136:1-26

March 30

Jesus Talks to You

You may face many troubles, sorrows, and trials between now and when you come home to reign with me. But I, the Lord God, will deliver you, comfort you, and always show you the way. I am the Way, the Truth, and the Life. I am the resurrection and the life. Cling tightly to me and remain faithful through these hard times. I will never leave you. Be patient and allow my Spirit to work deeply in your heart during these times.

If you faint in the day of adversity, how small is your strength. Remember, in your struggle against sin and for the truth, you have not yet resisted to the point of shedding your blood. I have won the battle for you. You can do all things through the strength I give you. You are more than a conqueror through me. Trust me wholeheartedly, and know that I will be mighty on your behalf.

John 16:33 • Romans 8:18 • Romans 5:3-5 • James 1:2-4, 12
Revelation 21:4 • Isaiah 61:1-3 • 1 Peter 4:12-13 • Isaiah 35:10

I have come that you might have abundant life. Ask of me, and I will show you great and mighty things which you do not know; my secret is with them that fear me. I will open up your understanding of my Word. I will guide you each day on my glorious path. I will hold your hand; fear not, your battles are not yours, they are mine. I will conquer, for I am the God of all power. There is nothing too hard for me.

Listen to me daily; through the study of my Word, in earnest prayer, and an open heart to my Spirit, you will hear me talking to you—my sheep hear my voice. I will open your understanding to my goodness, my grace, and the way to walk daily with me.

The world, Satan, and the lusts of the flesh will tempt you and desperately try to draw you to fulfill the desires of the flesh. I became fully human, though fully God; I became like you to show you the way. I was tempted in all points just like you, yet without sin. I will always make a way of escape in your times of temptation. Call upon me; I will help you to overcome. You can do all things through me who lives in you.

With each victory over sin you will become more confident in me; you will rejoice that I am transforming your life. Rejoice even now for the many victories of times past. Though you may have fallen short in recent times, fret not; a godly sorrow from within a humble heart receives my forgiveness. I paid the debt for your sins by the blood I shed on the cross. Your sins are forgiven and forgotten. There is no condemnation for you who are in me—for you do not live according to the flesh, but live according to the Spirit.

The path of those who live in me is like a shining light that shines more and more unto the perfect day. Press on, my child, toward the goal of the heavenly prize, which my Father has called you to win, through your faith in me. He that overcomes by faith will receive the crown of life.

Psalm 25:14 • Colossians 3:16 • 1 Corinthians 10:13 • James 1:12-18
James 4:7-10 • Hebrews 2:18 • Hebrews 4:14-16 • Romans 8:1
Proverbs 4:18 • Phil. 3:12-14

Jesus Preaches to the Multitude—*Luke 12*

Jesus and Two Disciples Go to Emmaus—*Luke 24*

The day I rose from the dead, I drew near to two gloomy-countenanced disciples who were on their way to the village Emmaus. I restrained their eyes from recognizing me. I asked one of them, Cleopas, about their intent discussion. He shared all about how Jesus of Nazareth, a prophet mighty in deed and word, had been delivered to be crucified. He went on to share that they had hoped that it was Jesus who would redeem Israel and set them free. He added that certain women of their company amazed them with the news that the body of Jesus was not in the tomb, and angels said that he was living.

Two broken-hearted and confused men were about to hear the best news of their life. I spoke up and said that they were dull in their perception and slow of heart in believing all things which the prophets had spoken. I shared with them that the Messiah, as predicted by the prophets, needed to suffer all that he did and then to enter his glory. I began at Moses, and proceeding through the prophets, I interpreted the scriptures to them of all the things concerning myself.

I was invited to stay as a house guest in Emmaus. As we dined, I broke bread and gave thanks. I opened their eyes, and they instantly recognized me—and I vanished from their sight. With newly invigorated hearts and minds, they returned to Jerusalem that very hour and found the eleven apostles with others that were with them. These two men, with hope and excitement, rehearsed in full all that had happened on the road, and how they recognized me in the breaking of bread.

When your hopes have been dashed, and sorrow has filled your heart, be ready for me to come alongside you, as I did for these two men on their way to Emmaus. I will be there to remind you to believe and embrace my promises. My promises—and I will fulfill them all—can turn your mourning into joy. I love you and want you to be filled with hope, joy, and love.

Luke 24:13-35 • Proverbs 13:12 • Psalm 43:5 • Romans 15:13

The two from Emmaus returned to Jerusalem and shared with the apostles what had just happened regarding the Messiah. I suddenly appeared to the apostles and stood among them with my greeting, "Peace be to you." They were terrified and were thinking they were seeing a spirit. I asked them why they were so troubled. I showed them my hands and my feet, and said that a spirit does not have flesh and bones as you see that I have. They beheld the marks of the nails, and were now amazed and wondered. I asked them if there was anything to eat. They gave me a portion of broiled fish which I ate in their presence.

I shared with them that I had fulfilled what had been written about me in the Law of Moses, the Prophets, and the Psalms. Then I thoroughly opened their minds that they might understand the scriptures concerning me. I then said that the Christ (the Messiah) should suffer and on the third day arise from the dead, and that repentance and forgiveness of sins should be preached to all nations, beginning at Jerusalem. You, having seen these things, are my witnesses. Behold, I will be sending the promise of my Father upon you; stay in the city of Jerusalem until you are clothed with power from on high.

I led them out as far as Bethany. As I lifted up my hands and blessed them, I was parted from them and carried up into heaven. I rejoiced abundantly in heart as my beloved disciples worshiped me and returned to Jerusalem with wondrous joy. And they were continually in the temple, celebrating with praising and blessing their God.

I had redeemed them and had given them the richest hope that anyone could possess. I would be a personal God, the same that I was for the three years I walked with them. I would love them everyday. I would soon send the Comforter, the Holy Spirit, and endue them with power. As my Father had sent me, so I was now sending them. I would fill them with my Spirit and guide them; and soon bring them to glory forever.

Luke 24:36-53 • John 14:26-29

April 3

Jesus Talks to You

My beloved son, my treasured daughter, how I desire to richly bless you in the same ways that I have blessed my early followers. My grace will abundantly be granted to you as you rely on me. I will pour out the Holy Spirit upon you, so that rivers of living water flow from your innermost being. I will bless and anoint your words and works as you seek me with your whole heart. You will touch many lives with my love.

I am the same yesterday, today, and for all eternity. As I performed miracles in thousands of lives then, I have the same power and will do so today. As I filled my disciples with the promise of the Father, the Holy Spirit, and clothed them with power from on high, so shall I do to any today that seek me whole-heartedly and obey me.

How I love you; no words on earth in any language can sufficiently express the depth and richness of my love. For all eternity, I will reveal to you my kindness, goodness, grace, and love.

John 7:38 • Psalm 90:17 • Luke 11:13 • Ephesians 3:16-21

April 4

Jesus Talks to You

In your times of suffering, lean on me. Having lived on earth, I experienced the same tribulations of everyday life as you. During the last three years of my life, I experienced sorrow and grief, as many rejected me as their Savior and God. My suffering at the time of my crucifixion was quite severe. I truly understand pain and anguish.

By my Father's boundless love, I was raised from the dead three days later; forty more days later, I ascended back to heaven to reign in glory forever with him. Share your sorrows, trials, and all of your sufferings with me. I am the God of all grace, who has called you to my eternal glory. I will personally restore you, strengthen you, and establish you.

Psalm 34:19 • Philippians 3:10 • 2 Corinthians 4:17 • Romans 5:3-5
1 Peter 5:10 • James 5:10-11 • 2 Corinthians 4:8-10 • Revelation 21:4

April 5 *Jesus Talks to You*

Without me you can do nothing, but as you abide in me, all things are possible. I can open doors that no man can shut, and shut doors that no man can open. As you seek me, I will hold your hand and walk with you; I will direct your every step. You can do all things through me who will strengthen you.

Your every heartbeat and breath is a gift from me; you are alive by a miracle. Humble your heart today and rejoice in thanksgiving for this gift of life. Seek me in prayer with expectancy, for I will enrich your day. I am a rewarder of those who diligently seek me. I will lead you by my Spirit and bless your words and works today.

Philippians 4:6-7,13 • James 1:17 • Hebrews 11:6

April 6 *Jesus Talks to You*

Your old life of sin was crucified with me. I was buried and rose from the dead. By faith in me and the miracle of the new birth, you are also risen from the dead into the newness of life. Set your mind on things of my kingdom above, where I reign on the throne of glory.

Your old life has died and your life is hidden in me. I will lead you each day to do my will. Your words and works will be to honor me and not yourself. When you do my will and love the brethren with my love, you are strengthening them in my kingdom. You often will not see the result of your loving words or deeds while here on earth. You are living by faith and are storing your treasures in heaven and not on earth, where treasures can rot, rust, or be stolen.

When I appear, then shall you also appear with me in glory. Your faith and hope, that has been anchored into heaven, shall be richly rewarded. You have an incorruptible inheritance whose glory will never fade.

Galatians 2:20 • Colossians 3:1-4 • Matthew 6:19-21 • 1 Peter 1:3-5

April 7

Jesus Talks to You

My dear child, do not be surprised at the fiery trials that come your way. The genuineness of your faith is more valuable, to me and you, than gold. As gold is tried in the fire, so do I try your faith. Through these fiery trials, you are actually a partaker of my sufferings. By abiding faithfully in me during these trials, your reward will be bountiful, and you will rejoice exceedingly at the revelation of my glory.

As you grow in my ways and faith, I allow these trials to purify your faith. I am entrusting you to grow through these fiery ordeals by fully clinging to me and trusting in my provision. I am actually honoring you and trusting you when I allow these trials. You have the opportunity to honor me by the choices you make; be led by my Spirit and express your faith by your words and deeds. It is during these times of affliction and suffering that you show that your faith is genuine.

I will be with you as I was with Shadrach, Meshach, and Abednego during their fiery furnace trial. Let your fears and doubts be cast onto me; I will not let you down, but will fulfill all of my promises to you.

1 Peter 1:6-9 • 1 Peter 4:12-13 • Romans 5:3-5 • James 1:2-12
James 5:10-11 • Isaiah 43:2

April 8

Jesus Talks to You

Enter my gates with thanksgiving. Rejoice exceedingly today; your name is written in the book of life, and I am living in you. You are more than a conqueror through me. Nothing can separate you from my love. You are complete in me, the Son of the living God.

You once were lost, but now are found; I rejoice eternally that you are my child. I lifted you up from a horrible pit and set your feet upon the Rock (me). A new song is in your heart, even praise to the God who dearly loves you. I hear your song and very warmly receive your praise.

Psalm 100:4 • Colossians 3:15-17 • Romans 8:37-39 • Psalm 40:2-3

April 9 *Jesus Talks to You*

I created the stars and know them all by name. I care for every creature on earth and see even when a sparrow falls to the ground. I uphold and maintain the entire universe by the word of my power.

My utmost delight is to have communion with you. The stars and earth will pass away, but you will live forever with me. Therefore I deeply enjoy spending quality time with you. You really can get to know me in a deep and rewarding way.

The world may scoff at you for stating that you know God personally, but I will richly bless you, pour out my Spirit upon you, and lead you on a very fulfilling journey through life, as you seek me above all else.

Psalm 147:4-5 • Matthew 10:29-31 • 1 John 1:1-4 • 1 John 3:1-3

April 10 *Jesus Talks to You*

Each day draw near to me with a humble heart. I will make known my will and guide you on my path. I will talk to you by my written Word and by my Spirit; let my peace bring quietness to your heart and mind, so that you might hear my still small voice.

My Spirit will teach you all things and bring to remembrance all things that I have said while I lived on earth. Let my Word dwell in you richly, so that my Spirit may remind you of the truth and guide you without all the distractions of the world filling your mind. You need to be single-minded. I am the Light of the world; let the light of my Word fill your heart and mind.

I am the Word of God; every Scripture is inspired by me. Diligently seek my Word; you will find your answer, comfort, guidance, or revelation regarding a question, problem, or decision you face. Trust me and my love for you, for I will be faithful to talk to you and guide you.

John 14:26 • Colossians 3:16 • Romans 12:1-2 • 2 Timothy 3:16-17

April 11

I care for you exceedingly beyond how much you think or imagine I could care for you. At times you may even doubt that I care about a problem, a broken relationship, a sickness, lack of money, or emotional stress and sorrow that you are going through. I am deeply concerned and desire to richly bless you through these problems.

I will answer your every prayer in my way, in my timing, and always with perfect love. These trials are where you will grow much in me. These very trials are often an answer to your prayers for growth in your life with me. Trust me, for I will transform you more into my image through these trials. I will also work all things for your good. Be strong in faith and ask me to give you endurance during these times. I will always be with you. Cast all of your cares on me, for I do care for you.

Jeremiah 29:11 • Isaiah 55:8-12 • James 1:4 • Hebrews 10:35-36

April 12

After I was baptized and came up out of the Jordan, the heavens were opened, and the Holy Spirit descended like a dove and rested upon me. Then my Father's voice from heaven said that I was his beloved Son in whom he was well pleased.

Being full of the Holy Spirit, I was led into the wilderness by the Spirit and was tempted by the devil for forty days. I ate nothing during those days. Each temptation that the devil threw at me, I answered with Scripture. The devil tempted me using the lust of the flesh, the lust of the eyes, and the pride of life. I was victorious on every count.

In my extreme physical weakness, I quoted Scripture to overcome. Having suffered, being tempted, I am able to help you when you are tempted and tried. Call upon me; rely on and proclaim the Scriptures at these times. You can overcome through me; let me reign in your heart.

Luke 4:1-15 • Hebrews 2:14-18 • 1 John 2:15-17 • 1 Corinthians 10:13
James 4:7

April 13 *Jesus Talks to You*

There are many giants to be conquered as you claim your promised land. If you look at your own strength compared to the size of the giants, you will get discouraged. If you look past today and take on the burden of the battles that lay ahead of you, dread might even begin to set in.

I know the plans that I have for you; wonderful and abundant blessings are ordained for you since before the world began. Do not worry about tomorrow. I will be there to fight the battles. Trust me with all of your heart and do not lean to your own understanding. I told Joshua, who was about to cross the Jordan, to be strong, of good courage, and not to be afraid or lose hope, for I the Lord God would be with him wherever he would go. Today is the day to rejoice, for I am with you and will be strong on your behalf. If I am for you, nothing can be against you.

Jeremiah 29:11 • Proverbs 3:5-6 • Joshua 1:9 • Romans 8:31

April 14 *Jesus Talks to You*

I will bless you with all spiritual blessing in heavenly places as you abide in me. Everything that pertains to life and godliness is yours through my divine power; I will provide for all of your physical needs according to my riches in glory. Be not envious of others' blessings or circumstances. There is so much for you to be deeply thankful for. Godliness with contentment is truly great gain.

Many people seek to have more goods. Material things do not provide fulfillment. Knowing me, and letting my life shine from you in word and deed is true fulfillment. I was poor when on earth. I did my Father's will and forever have glory and honor beyond all earthly riches. Yield to me, let my will be done in your life, be ever thankful, and you will be blessed in great measure now and forever.

Ephesians 1:3 • 2 Peter 1:3 • Philippians 4:19 • 1 Timothy 6:6
Hebrews 13:5 • Luke 12:15 • 2 Corinthians 8:9 • Ephesians 1:11-20

April 15 *Jesus Talks to You*

In Capernaum, those who received the temple tax came to Peter, and asked if his teacher (me) pays the temple tax. Peter said that I do. That day, I told him to go down to the lake, throw in a hook, take the first fish that comes up, open its mouth, and you will find a coin to pay the temple tax for you and me. He did what I told him to do, and our tax was paid.

I created all the galaxies, gave sight to the blind, raised the dead, and I miraculously provided for Peter's and my taxes. You may have worries for finances now and provision for your future. I, who bought you for a price, my own life's blood, will provide for your every need. At times, I am working in your life through trying circumstances, so that you may learn that man shall not live by bread alone, but by every word that proceeds from the mouth of God. I will provide your daily bread and all of your needs by my riches in glory.

Matthew 17:24-27 • Matthew 7:7-11 • Philippians 4:19

April 16 *Jesus Talks to You*

Come to me when you are growing weary and exhausted; I will give you rest. Come to me when you are loaded down with the burdens of everyday life; I will take your burdens and refresh your soul. Come to me when you are spiritually thirsty; I will give you living water that will thoroughly quench your thirst.

By taking my yoke upon you and learning from me, you will find true rest and refreshment for your soul. I am humble and gentle in heart. When on earth I came as a servant. I blessed the little children and comforted the brokenhearted. I touched and healed the lepers, the paralyzed, and the outcasts of society. Yes, my dear child, come learn of me and receive with meekness the implanted Word which will transform your life. Your fellowship with me will bring you abundant life.

Matthew 11:28-30 • Psalm 116:1-9 • 2 Corinthians 1:3-5 • Isaiah 61:1-3

April 17

Jesus Talks to You

According to my Old Covenant with the children of Israel, the high priest needed to enter the Holy Place each year with the blood of animals as the sacrifice for the sins of the people.

Not by the blood of goats and calves, but by my own blood, I entered in once into the true Holy Place, having obtained eternal redemption for you. I entered into heaven itself, to appear in the presence of the Father for you. By one offering—myself—I have brought righteousness forever to those who are set apart for my service.

Seeing that I gave my life for your sins, that you might have my righteousness and eternal life, shall I not freely and graciously give you all other things? Therefore come confidently before my throne of grace, that you might receive my mercy and grace to help in times of need.

Hebrews 9:24-28 • Hebrews 4:16 • Hebrews 10:14-22

April 18

Jesus Talks to You

It is easy to get your eyes on your circumstances and problems—like Peter looking at the waves when he was walking on the water. Fears and doubts will cause your human nature to begin to worry and take things into your own hands. Look only at me today, not at the winds and the waves. You will be "walking on the water" as I lead you to do my will.

Incline your heart to trust in me each day. I know what is best for you. Delight yourself in me and my Word, and I will give you the desires of your heart. Your life is in my hands. You were redeemed by my precious blood; therefore offer yourself as a living sacrifice, holy and acceptable to me. Do not be conformed to this world, which lives by the desires of the human nature, but let me transform you by renewing your mind each day by my Word and by the Holy Spirit.

1 Corinthians 6:19-20 • Psalm 37:4 • 1 Peter 1:18-22 • Romans 12:1-2

April 19 *Jesus Talks to You*

By obedience to the truth you have purified your soul. From your heart and life, let there be a deep and self-sacrificing love for your brothers and sisters who follow me. Whatever you do unto them, you do unto me. I am not unrighteous to forget your labor of love that you have given in my kingdom. Your true treasures in heaven are the blessings that you bestow on others' lives.

If you desire to be filled with my divine love, sincerely ask for me to transform your heart to be more like mine. Confess any sins that are preventing you from letting my love shine from your life. I am faithful and just to forgive you and to cleanse you from all unrighteousness. I am living in you and will continue the work that I began in you.

1 Peter 1:22 • John 13:34 • Galatians 6:2 • 1 John 1:9 • Hebrews 6:10

April 20 *Jesus Talks to You*

Earnestly contend for the same faith which I delivered to my disciples. They beheld my glory when I walked the earth; they witnessed a multitude of miracles, listened to my Word, and experienced my love. After they were filled with the Holy Spirit, they followed me wholeheartedly. They did not let the enticing lusts of the world draw them away from their holy calling. You also may behold my glory; my miracles, truth, and love are in my Word. I am the same yesterday, today, and forever. Rejoice, for the fruit of the Spirit will be abundant in your life as you continue to give your heart to me each day and let your conduct be controlled by the Spirit. As you are led by my Spirit, you will not fulfill the lusts of the flesh. The fruit of the Spirit will be increasingly evident as you live in me; many will see this in your life and will be inspired by it.

As my dear child, be compassionate and forbearing toward others. Forgive others as I have forgiven you. Let my peace rule in your heart today. Be thankful for all that I have done for you, and for the wondrous future I have planned for you. Do these things and you will be truly blessed.

Jude 1:3 • Romans 8:14 • Galatians 5:17-25 • Colossians 3:12-17

April 21 *Jesus Talks to You*

When you have times of sorrow, confusion, or worry, I understand how you feel. I am with you as you go through these dark, cloud-filled days. All things are working together for your good, although this may be hard to believe during these times. Look to me for help; I am your God and can bring peace to your heart. Trust in me, for I rule all circumstances and will accomplish my purposes through them. Submit yourself to me and to my will regarding the outcome of your circumstances; this is true growth in your faith.

In this world you will experience much tribulation, but take courage, for I have overcome the world. The sufferings that you go through are certainly not worth comparing to the glory that is to be revealed both in your life and in the wondrous kingdom you will soon be reigning in. Tears may endure through the night, but joy comes in the morning.

John 14:27 • Psalm 27:1-14 • Romans 8:18 • Isaiah 35:10

April 22 *Jesus Talks to You*

You can do all things through me, for I am your strength. I am the Rock; I am the Deliverer. Do not fear what man can do to you. Do not fear circumstances. I am with you; do not be dismayed. I will strengthen you by the Holy Spirit. Ask to be filled and led by my Spirit, and it will be done. You may feel weak, but I will give you power to do my will. Trust me with your whole heart.

I am your high tower. I see the end from the beginning. I have perfect counsel and wisdom to guide you with. Diligently follow my Word and trust in me. I will renew your strength. You will soar with wings as eagles; you will run and not get weary. Be strong by abiding in me and trusting in the power of my might.

Isaiah 41:10 • Ephesians 3:16-17 • Psalm 18:1-3 • Isaiah 40:31

April 23 *Jesus Talks to You*

I ordained twelve men, whom I named apostles, that they would continue with me during my work on earth. They would hear the truths of my everlasting kingdom and experience the love that my Father and I have for mankind. I then sent them out by the power of my Spirit to share the Word of Life and do the same works that I have done.

Since the day that I ascended back to heaven, I have continued to call men and women to receive my anointing for their work in this world. I am calling you; receive my rich blessing, that you might bear everlasting fruit in my kingdom. I will blend the talents and desires that I created in you, along with gifts that I will bestow upon you by the Holy Spirit.

I will be with you every step of the way. I will give you the words to share. I have works for you to do, ordained since before time began; I will do these works through you. Be willing and obedient, and you shall rejoice forever in the glory that will be revealed in heaven for you.

Mark 3:13-14 • John 15:16 • 1 Peter 4:10-11 • Ephesians 2:10
2 Timothy 1:9 • Colossians 1:9-12

April 24 *Jesus Talks to You*

Jairus' little daughter was dying. Her father pleaded for me to come and put my hands on her, so that she would be healed and live; so I went with him. While on the way to his house, some people came and said that his daughter had died; but I told Jairus to not be afraid and just believe. At the house I told the twelve year old girl to get up, and she arose from the dead. The parents and the disciples were totally astonished.

They had told Jairus that she was dead and not to trouble the Teacher any further. But when all hope seems lost, remember that I am the resurrection and the life. I have all power in heaven and in earth. Trust me, for I am able to do exceedingly above everything you can think or ask.

Mark 5:22-24, 35-43 • John 11:25 • Ephesians 3:20

April 25

Jesus Talks to You

You may feel weak and insignificant at times. But I have called you from heaven to be an ambassador for my kingdom. Not many who are wise in the world's eyes, rich or powerful are called. Blessed are the poor in spirit, who are rich in faith, for theirs is the kingdom of heaven. I will exalt the humble and meek by blessing their works and shining from their lives, as they abide in me. I look over the face of the whole earth for those who humble themselves and follow me with their whole heart; I will be strong on their behalf.

You are not insignificant; you are a royal jewel to me and I treasure you. Whoever has received me in their heart, is a child of the living God; this is the highest and matchless honor that one may possess. Enjoy your communion with me today. The Holy Spirit, who lives in you, will comfort you and guide you. This is a day to rejoice.

Psalm 37:11 • Matthew 5:3-9 • Isaiah 66:2 • Micah 6:8

April 26

Jesus Talks to You

I hear and value your every prayer. I know every one of your hopes and dreams for your life. I see your whole life on earth from beginning to end; I even see through eternity. I have all power to provide any need that you have. I know what is best for you. I will help you regarding relationships, as well as where to live and work. I will guide you on how to best bring glory to the Father through your work in the kingdom.

Don't worry about your circumstances or provision. Let me know your requests, with a trusting and thankful heart. Cast your cares upon me, for I lovingly care for you and will do what is best for you—providing what you need at just the right time. Be patient and trust in my power. Abide steadfastly in me, do my will, and then you will receive all that I have promised to you. You will grow strong in me during these times.

Psalm 139:1-18 • Philippians 4:6 • Hebrews 10:35-36

April 27

Jesus Talks to You

Come before the Father today with a heart of praise. As you abide in me and pray in the power of the Holy Spirit, the extraordinary will happen: whatever you ask for in my name, to the Father, according to his will, he will do it; my love, peace, and joy will abound in your life; your burdens will be cast upon my shoulders and you will not need to carry them any more.

Prayer has changed lives and the world. Centuries ago, Daniel and his three friends pleaded for mercy from the God of heaven, and the Father of lights revealed the mystery of a king's dream. The history of the world was revealed at that time through their prayers. Daniel and his friends were made rulers in the Babylonian kingdom.

Ephesians 6:18 • John 15:7 • Luke 11:9-10 • Daniel 2:17-49

April 28

Jesus Talks to You

After you heard the Word of Life and received me into your heart, you were sealed with the Holy Spirit—the deposit guaranteeing your inheritance in the kingdom of heaven. The Holy Spirit (Helper, Comforter, Advocate), whom the Father sends in my name, shall teach you all things and bring to remembrance what I said while I was on earth.

Fan the flame of this wondrous gift from above that has been given unto you. Your body is the very sanctuary of the Holy Spirit who lives in you. You are not your own, for I bought you for a price—my blood. Therefore honor the God who loves you by offering your body as a living sacrifice. This is true spiritual worship. Ask your Father to fill you and endue you with power by the Holy Spirit. The fruit of the Spirit will be evident in your life in increasing measure. Many will see me, the Light of the world, shining from your life. Your rejoicing will be boundless forever.

Ephesians 1:13 • 2 Corinthians 1:20-22 • John 14:26
1 Corinthians 6:19-20 • Romans 12:1 • Galatians 5:22-23

April 29

Jesus Talks to You

In your times of suffering and sorrows please do not cast off your confidence in me. These are times to draw close to me with all of your heart. I understand what you are going through and feel your emotions. Let me hold you close—speaking words of comfort to you. I will revive you and give you my peace in the midst of these trials. Let not the distresses and frustrations of life have a mastery over you. As you trust in me through them, I will overcome them for you—even as I overcame the world. I endured scorn, a crown of thorns, being spit upon, beaten, and being nailed to a cross. I know pain and suffering. My dear child, I deeply love you and promise to help you through these times.

John 16:33 • Isaiah 43:2 • 2 Corinthians 1:3-10 • 2 Corinthians 4:16-18

April 30

Jesus Talks to You

A man's son was possessed by a spirit that made him mute. It would also throw him violently to the ground, make him foam at the mouth, cause him to grind his teeth, and go into a motionless stupor. The spirit would often cast the child into the fire and water to try to kill him.

The father of the boy pleaded with me to help him. I told him that all things are possible to him that believes. With tears he said he believed, but pleaded with me to please help his unbelief. I rebuked the demon, and he came out of the boy, who was healed from that moment on.

I have been given all power and authority in heaven and earth. Do you have what appears to be an insurmountable problem? Nothing is too hard for me. You may be saying what the child's father said, "I believe, but help my unbelief!" I will honor your faith in me and the honesty of your own weakness. I am your God and your Deliverer, today and through all your days on earth. I will also raise you up on that great day of the Lord, for I am the resurrection and the life.

Mark 9:17-27 • Matthew 17:14-18 • Matthew 28:18 • Ephesians 1:11-23

Jesus Heals the Epileptic Demoniac—*Matthew 17*

Conversion of Saul—*Acts 9*

May 1

Jesus Talks to You

My Father spared not his only begotten Son that you might have everlasting life through faith in me. I will richly bestow upon you every spiritual and physical gift that you need for life and godliness. You are a treasured member of my eternal family.

I am continually interceding for you. Out of the rich treasury of my glory, I will empower you with inner strength by my Spirit. Welcome me fully to make my permanent home in your heart by faith. Be rooted deeply and established in my eternal love which far surpasses mere knowledge. Seek me wholeheartedly, and I will make you complete with the fullness of my power and life abundant. You will know me as the Most High God who is able to do superabundantly more than you could think or imagine. The resurrection power that brought me back from the dead to live and reign forever now works mightily in you.

Romans 8:31-32 • 2 Peter 1:3 • Ephesians 3:16-21

May 2

Jesus Talks to You

I have risen from the dead. I conquered death for you. Rejoice, for by your faith in me, your sins are forgiven and you will live forever in the glorious kingdom of heaven. I reign in heaven for all eternity, but I also will reign in your heart and life today—and through all eternity.

Let your whole heart sound the praises of your God. How pure and full of love your praise can be as you forget the things of this world while being seated in heavenly places with me. Joy and peace are yours today as you look to me and lift your praises.

Open your heart and I will fill you with the Holy Spirit. I will give you power to walk in my steps in this world. I will give you my love, kindness, and gentleness. I have power to transform your life. Ask and it shall be given to you, my child.

Psalm 27:4 • Psalm 47 • Psalm 92:1-5 • Ephesians 5:20 • John 16:24

May 3 *Jesus Talks to You*

Cast all your cares upon me, for I deeply care for you. Let me bear your burdens today—and always. I will give peace to your soul. Remember what I did concerning the storm on the lake with my disciples; I calmed the storm with my Word. Yield fully to me in the trials of life. I will give you wisdom and patience as you walk through these turbulent times. I will calm your storms at just the right time and great shall be your peace.

I have given you exceedingly great and precious promises in my Word. Embrace them. I will perform what I have promised; I will bring an abundance of blessings upon your life. Rest and trust in me. Come and spend quiet times with me; I will fill your empty cup to overflowing.

1 Peter 5:6-7 • 2 Peter 1:1-4 • Psalm 28:6-9 • Proverbs 3:5-6 • Psalm 23

May 4 *Jesus Talks to You*

Trusting and obeying me more fully through the trials and circumstances that I allow to come into your life is a most important lesson. For even I obeyed my Father through the many trials in my life. I delighted to do the will of my Father in heaven. When you do the will of your Father in heaven, you bring much glory to him and to the kingdom of heaven.

Do not be conformed to this present world, but let my Spirit transform you. I will equip you with everything needed to do the Father's will. I am doing a very special work in your life. Do not let yourself be limited by who you were before you received me into your life. For any one in me is a new creation; the old things have passed away. I created the heavens and the earth by my Word, and I surely can transform you into a new you. Be guided by my Spirit and let me live through you. Remember to give thanks always for all things to your Father in my name. The Father's and my love is upon you from everlasting to everlasting.

John 15:10 • Hebrews 13:20-21 • Romans 12:1-2 • Psalm 138:8
Psalm 90:16-17 • Psalm 103:17

May 5 *Jesus Talks to You*

Today you may be facing turmoil or a daunting task. You need not carry the burden yourself. It is not by your power or wisdom, but by my Spirit, that the best resolution will be attained in a perplexing situation. If you wait upon me, I will give you the answer for any problem that you face. My wisdom will be given generously to you when you ask; it will bear good fruit in your life.

It is easy to lean to your own understanding and to accomplish works in the flesh. I am calling you to humble yourself before me, the living God. All things are possible to you when you put your full trust in me. I open doors that no man can close, and I close doors that no man can open. I parted the Jordan River for the children of Israel, so they could go in to inherit the land that I promised to them. If I am for you, nothing and no one can be against you. I will bring you into the land of abundant life that I have promised to you.

Zechariah 4:6 • James 1:5, 3:17 • Jeremiah 17:7-8 • Proverbs 3:5

May 6 *Jesus Talks to You*

You can do all things through me who will empower you by my Spirit. When David faced Goliath, the giant, I gave David boldness, skill, and deliverance. He remembered that I had rescued him from a lion and a bear (that he killed while they were attempting to carry off sheep in his care). You should also remember the victories that I have given you, and the times that I have delivered you. This will give you confidence and boldness to step out in faith to do my work and bring glory to my name.

Cast not away your confidence, but be strong in faith today. Phenomenal rewards are yours in my kingdom; whoever serves me him will my Father honor. The treasures on earth will all perish and they cannot be taken to heaven. But to you who walk by faith and overcome, there is an incorruptible and glorious inheritance reserved in heaven for you.

Philippians 4:13 • 1 Samuel 17:34-37, 45-50 • John 12:26 • 1 Peter 1:4

May 7 *Jesus Talks to You*

Today and every day is a day of rejoicing and thankfulness. You are one of my chosen people, a member of my royal priesthood, and a citizen of the kingdom of heaven. I called you out from the darkness that you were living in and miraculously transferred you into my glorious kingdom of light. I have given you a reason to live and have put a new song into your heart. Therefore I say to you, that today and always is the time to rejoice and be thankful.

Let my peace rule in your heart. Let my Word fill your life, using the wisdom from above as you share with others; sing psalms, hymns, and songs of my love, with gratitude in your heart to your God. And whatever you do or say should be done in my name, giving thanks and glory to the Father through me.

1 Peter 2:9 • John 15:16 • Colossians 1:13; 3:15-17 • Psalm 100

May 8 *Jesus Talks to You*

A large army with horses and chariots compassed the city where the prophet Elisha was; the king of Syria wanted him killed. When Elisha's servant beheld the army, he was fearful. Elisha confidently stated that there are more with us than with them. He prayed for the eyes of the young man to be opened. I answered his prayer, and the young man beheld that the mountain was full of horses and chariots of fire all around Elisha.

When the enemy came down to him, Elisha asked me to strike the army with blindness; I blinded them as Elisha had asked. He led the army to Samaria where he prayed that I would now open their eyes, which I did. The king of Israel asked if he should kill them; but Elisha told him to give them food and water. After the large feast, they were sent on their way. These raiders did not return to the land of Israel again.

When your natural eyes behold the forces of the enemy encamped against you, it is easy to be gripped by fear, as Elisha's servant was. But the eyes of faith peer deeply and clearly into my eternal realm. What they see and apprehend gives you the strength and boldness to accomplish my will.

Greater is the one who is in you than the one who is in the world; I live in you. The enemy will assail you from every side. He appears very strong and you may feel very weak. But I conquered death and reign in your heart. The battle is mine. In your weakness, my strength will be made perfect. Fully trust in me to prevail in every encounter with the enemy. You will always triumph in me, and you are more than a conqueror through my power and love!

2 Kings 6:14-23 • 2 Corinthians 4:18 • 2 Corinthians 2:14

May 9 *Jesus Talks to You*

Elisha showed love to the enemy army that was made blind and then whose sight was restored. He fed them and sent them on their way. This victory was won by love.

You are my ambassador, sent on a special mission to show my love to all, in boldness and in the power of the Holy Spirit. Let my glorious light—that brings truth and warms hearts—shine from your heart. Yield to my Spirit's leading that you might do the works that I have ordained for you. Others will see them and glorify your Father in heaven.

I have loved you with the same love that the Father has loved me. Continue in my love. I loved all, even those that crucified me. Love is the conquering force. Millions of my enemies have received forgiveness and eternal salvation through my love. Nothing could destroy me. I arose from the dead and conquered death, the grievous enemy of mankind.

As I have loved you, so love one another. If you walk in my love, abundant blessings will be yours—in your work and in all of your relationships.

2 Kings 6:14-23 • Matthew 5:14-16, 43-48 • 1 Peter 2:12 • John 15:7-14

May 10 — *Jesus Talks to You*

Herod the king was persecuting my people. He had killed James, the brother of John, and had jailed Peter. Prayer was continually being made for Peter by the church. The night before Peter was to be executed, he was sleeping between two soldiers and was bound with two chains.

Nothing is hard for me. I sent an angel and a shining light to the prison cell. As the angel woke Peter up, the chains fell off his hands. The angel led Peter past the two guard posts, and upon reaching the iron gate, it opened up for them. As they walked on the street, the angel departed.

Peter proceeded to a disciple's home where many people were praying. The girl who answered Peter's knocking did not open the door, but ran to tell the others that Peter was standing outside the door. They did not believe her.

But Peter continued to knock, and when they finally opened the door and saw Peter, they were astonished. For days, the people had been fervently praying to me for Peter to be delivered from the hands of Herod. I answered their prayer and they did not believe it. Of course, disbelief quickly turned to amazement and great joy.

If you live in me and my words live in you, ask for whatever you will and it will be done for you.

Acts 12:1-19 • John 15:7 • Luke 11:9 • Isaiah 65:24 • Psalm 91:14-16

May 11 — *Jesus Talks to You*

I am creating new heavens and a new earth where righteousness dwells. Be glad and rejoice, for the holy city, new Jerusalem, awaits you. I will rejoice over my people and will dwell among them. I will wipe away all tears from the eyes of my people. Pain and death shall no longer exist. The former things will pass away, for I will make all things new.

I greatly love you, and you will soon be reigning with me in the glorious kingdom of heaven. Consider that your life on earth is but a vapor and learn to make each day count. Let me live through you, that your life might continually bring glory to the Father. I will guide you to walk on my path as you acknowledge me in all of your ways. By my counsel, you will be doing my will and works which I have ordained for you to accomplish. You will bear much fruit as you abide in me, even bringing everlasting glory to the kingdom above.

Isaiah 65:17-19 • Revelation 22:1-5 • 2 Peter 3:10-14 • Psalm 32:8
Proverbs 16:3 • Revelation 14:13

May 12

Jesus Talks to You

You were united with me when you received me as your Savior. We became one; I am in you and the Father is in me. The fullness of the Father dwells in me, and you are complete in me. By faith in me and by embracing the precious promises that I have given in my Word, you have been made a partaker of my divine nature. Remember, you are not justified or saved by your good works or by fulfilling the Ten Commandments. Your own righteousness is like a filthy rag. You now possess my perfect righteousness by faith—a gift from the Everlasting Father.

In the same way that you have received me, by faith and with a heart of full trust, continue to walk with me. Let your first love toward me be renewed. Do not let the world, its temptations, and the sins of the flesh rob you of the victorious life you have a right to live. Be filled and led by my Spirit, and you will not fulfill the lusts of the flesh. Your past life of sin has been crucified with me on the cross. Consider that old life to be dead; I now live in you by faith. Therefore, whatever you do in word or deed, do all to the glory of your God and Father in heaven.

You are my child. You know me, the Creator of the universe, personally. I have a glorious plan for you here in this world and in the everlasting kingdom of heaven. I am with you always and love you beyond words!

John 17:21-23 • Colossians 2:6-10 • 2 Peter 1:3-11 • Galatians 5:16-25
Jeremiah 29:11-13

Many areas of life can cause you to experience anxieties, even to the point of despair. You do not know what the future holds for you, and this can also bring distress. But I know the future perfectly, for I am the Beginning and the End, the Alpha and Omega; I am the Lord God Almighty, who is, who was, and who is to come.

You need to fully trust me as your provider in all areas of your life. The earth is mine and everything in it. I will liberally provide for all of your needs according to my glorious riches. Remember how I gave Abraham a child in his old age, gave water from the rock for the children of Israel, gave them the Promised Land, turned the water into wine, fed the five thousand, filled the boats with fish, raised the dead, cleansed lepers, put a coin for the taxes in a fish's mouth, and calmed the storm for the disciples. Even though I possess all the riches of the world, I do not even need them to provide miraculously according to the Father's will. I will provide all of your spiritual, physical, and emotional needs. You are my child and I dearly cherish you.

As Creator of heaven and earth, I have the power to be mighty on your behalf in all areas of life. But to have your whole heart and trust is most essential. Seek first my kingdom and my righteousness, and all that you need will be provided. Delight yourself in me, and I will give you the desires of your heart. As you grow in my grace and rejoice in getting to know me personally through my Word, your life will be transformed to be more like me; my desires will become your desires.

The Holy Spirit will give you a new power to walk confidently in this world, trusting me for many of the areas that were once the cause of distress. My peace will rule in your heart. My joy will be your strength. You will learn by experience that I am truly working all things together for your good. You will echo what the shepherd boy, David, sang long ago about—goodness and God's love will follow me all the days of my life.

Revelation 1:8 • Deuteronomy 8:1-10 • Philippians 4:19 • Psalm 84:11
Matthew 6:33 • Psalm 37:3-5 • Psalm 23:1-6

Seven men, full of faith and the Holy Spirit, were chosen to help bring daily distribution to widows shortly after I ascended to heaven. The apostles prayed and laid hands on these men. Their care for the needy was a work of love. I blessed them, and the sharing of my Word flourished. The number of disciples in Jerusalem multiplied rapidly; a great company of the priests became obedient to the faith, as well.

Stephen, one of the seven, filled with my grace and the power of the Holy Spirit, performed amazing wonders and signs among the people. He shared my Word with boldness and wisdom. The enemies of the faith stirred up the people and brought Stephen before the Sanhedrin, where false witnesses lied about him. Before the council, Stephen courageously proclaimed my reality and workings with the children of Israel, expounding truths beginning with Abraham and going through Moses, the prophets, and me, the Righteous One—the Messiah.

The Jewish leaders were cut to the heart and were furious upon being confronted with the truth. They shook their fists and ground their teeth at Stephen. But being filled with the Holy Spirit, he looked steadfastly up into heaven and saw me, his Savior, in glory. When he said to the council that he saw the heavens opened and the Son of Man standing at the right hand of God, they began shouting, stopped their ears, and rushed at him. They dragged him out of the city and stoned him.

As they stoned Stephen, he called upon me, saying, "Lord Jesus, receive my spirit." He fell to his knees and cried out to me, asking me to forgive them and to not hold this sin against them. With those final words of love, my servant fell asleep in me.

I welcomed Stephen, the faithful servant, into the joy of the kingdom of heaven. I reigned in his short life on earth, and forever he would now reign with me in paradise. He walked my path of life on earth; now in my presence, he would have fullness of joy and pleasures for evermore.

Acts 6:5-8 • Acts 7 • Ephesians 4:32 • 2 Corinthians 5:8 • Psalm 16:11

May 15 *Jesus Talks to You*

Stephen was not ashamed of the testimony of his Savior and Lord. He was a partaker of my sufferings, and as such, he would also experience the power of my resurrection and eternal glory with me.

You, my child, should likewise not be surprised at a fiery trial when it comes to test you. As I appeared to Stephen, at just the right moment to comfort him and give him my grace, so shall I stand by you when you need me. As I was with the three men in the fiery furnace, I am also able to deliver you. In this world you will have trials and tribulations, but be strong in faith and encouraged, for I have overcome the world. If you suffer for me, you will also reign with me. The sufferings of this present life are not worth comparing with the glory that shall be revealed in and to you forever. I am the resurrection and the life.

1 Peter 3:15, 4:13 • 2 Timothy 1:8 • Isaiah 43:2 • Romans 8:18

May 16 *Jesus Talks to You*

Saul, stood by and consented to the death of the martyr Stephen. He was on his way to Damascus to capture and persecute more believers. My light from heaven shone all around him. When he fell to the ground, I asked him why he was persecuting me. I told him that I was Jesus. Trembling and astonished, he asked me what I would have him to do. Paul was without sight for three days, and I sent Ananias to welcome him more fully into my kingdom. Paul received his sight, was filled with the Holy Spirit, and a grand life of service to his King began.

Over time, I transformed Saul (the persecutor and blasphemer) to Paul (the apostle and servant of the faith). Entrust to me those you love and pray for. I have power to reveal myself to them; I shone my light around Saul. But I have chosen you to be my light to the world. Ask me for strength and be not ashamed of the good news. It may bring new life to someone who really needs it—like Saul.

Acts 9:1-31 • Proverbs 11:30 • Ephesians 3:16-21

May 17 *Jesus Talks to You*

People were bringing their children to me that I might place my hands upon them and bless them, but my disciples rebuked them for doing so. I was quite displeased, and told them to let the little children come to me, for the kingdom of God belongs to ones such as these. I added that whoever does not receive the kingdom of God like a little child shall not enter it at all. I then took each of the children, placed my hands on them, and tenderly blessed them.

It is not the proud in heart, the mighty in his own strength, or the self-righteous that are chosen; those that have the humble heart of a child are the inheritors of the kingdom. I have respect to the lowly in heart; blessed are the poor in spirit, for the kingdom of heaven is theirs.

Mark 10:13-16 • Matthew 5:3 • James 2:5

May 18 *Jesus Talks to You*

It is easy to despise the day of small things and to think small beginnings are unimportant. But I have called you with a high calling; you are my ambassador. I am guiding you to do works that I have ordained for you. If you are abiding in me and doing my work, it is no small thing. Your service to me is a blessed and grand thing in my eyes.

When I washed the disciples feet, this was not a small thing like Peter thought—but rather it was an example of my wondrous love. It showed that my disciples need to be washed by me daily, through my Word and by my Spirit. I would soon offer my life as a sacrifice, that I might wash away all of mankind's sin.

When the children were brought to me to be blessed, my disciples thought this was too small a thing to trouble the Master with. But my Father sent me to bless all of my precious children. As my Father sent me, so I send you. Love others in "small things" and you will be blessed.

Zechariah 4:10 • 1 Corinthians 15:58 • 2 Timothy 1:9 • John 20:21

May 19 *Jesus Talks to You*

As a member of my eternal family, show forth a humble and gentle heart to your brothers and sisters. Be patient, forgiving, and forbearing as you walk in my love. Earnestly strive to maintain harmony with others by yielding to the Holy Spirit's leading.

You are a member of the body of Christ; you are actually that much a part of me through the miracle of your faith. Just as the human body has many members, so does my body. You also are members one of another—miraculously united with your brothers and sisters. Seeing that you are mutually dependent upon one another, seek to build up and encourage others to receive my fullness in their lives.

Ephesians 4:1-16 • 1 Corinthians 12:14-31 • Romans 12:4-13

May 20 *Jesus Talks to You*

I am the living God, the risen Savior, the Lord of heaven and earth. I am the same yesterday, today, and forever. I am the same as I was before I created the heavens and the earth, the same as I was when I walked the earth, and the same as I will be forever—reigning with everlasting love and all power.

Many say that I am not a personal God. But I say to you, that I will be strong on your behalf in a very personal way as you draw near to me, humble your heart, and are willing to be guided by my Word and by my Spirit. I will work in your life in a powerful way, just as I did for the early believers in the days after I ascended from the earth to heaven.

For as the rains come down from above and water the earth to bring forth bud and fruit, so shall I rain down my blessings, through the power of the Spirit, into your life. Open your heart and seek me diligently; no good thing will I withhold from you. All things are possible to you through faith. Ask and it shall be given. I desire to bless you richly.

Hebrews 13:8 • 2 Peter 1:1-11 • Isaiah 55:8-13 • Psalm 84:11 • John 15:7

May 21 *Jesus Talks to You*

The journey back to the land of Judah was underway. Naomi (her husband and two sons now dead) set before her two daughters-in-law the trials and tribulations that would await them. Under already gloomy circumstances, Orpah went back to her idolatrous friends, but Ruth clung to me, the God of Israel.

Wholeheartedly, Ruth devoted herself to follow Naomi, and together they would seek to come under my shadow in the land of promise—to take refuge under my wings.

On your journey to the land of promise, will you follow me wholeheartedly, though you face dark valleys and rocky paths on the way? When on earth, I had not a place to lay my head; many were against me, and the cross was my destination. Will my people be your people? Will you cleave to me though you must also travel the road of the cross? Will you make me your God under all circumstances? If yes, then you soon shall be delighting in paradise with me—co-heirs of the incomparable inheritance of the kingdom of heaven. The righteous, greatly honored, and gloriously joyful family of your God awaits your arrival.

Ruth 1:15-17 • Joshua 24:15 • Philippians 3:8-14

May 22 *Jesus Talks to You*

Naomi (Hebrew for pleasant, delightful) was returning to the land of promise with Ruth, her loyal daughter-in-law. Poor and bereft of hope, with her husband and two sons dead, Naomi sorrowfully told others to call her Mara (Hebrew for bitter). I, the Sovereign Lord, was weaving the tapestry of her life. Unfortunately, while on earth, one only sees the back of the tapestry, and not the finished work. She was only seeing the knots and the darkest of threads that were being spun on my loom of life. Perhaps you also behold the same and have become discouraged.

I was crafting a most wondrous tapestry of her life (as I am for you as well). Heavenly threads of fine gold and purple were being woven in, and a glorious masterpiece would be revealed on the day of glory. Through Naomi's poverty, Ruth would meet Boaz; Obed would be born. He would be the grandfather of David, king of Israel. I also was born into this world through this lineage. This story of love and faith is found in my written Word—honoring Naomi, Ruth, and Boaz.

Have you been distressed as you view the dark strands and knots on the back of the tapestry lately? Dear one, do not look at what can be seen with your eyes, but by faith view that which is eternal; rejoice in the wondrous work that I am doing, and the glory that awaits you. You, who have come to take refuge under my wings, will be richly blessed for your devotion to me. You shall call yourself pleasant and not bitter when you see the other side of the tapestry of your life, on the day of glory.

Ruth 1:15-17 • 1 Corinthians 13:12 • 2 Corinthians 4:16-18
Colossians 3:1-4

May 23 *Jesus Talks to You*

The lust of the eyes, the lust of the flesh, and the pride of life motivate those who live without faith in me. Riches, pleasures, prestige, power, and other cravings overshadow their acknowledging my kingdom.

You have been called to be my ambassador—representing the eternal kingdom of heaven. No higher calling can be realized in one's life. No greater service can be rendered to mankind. Earthly careers may bring accolades of men and vast earthly riches to the one who performs well. Neither is guaranteed to you as you serve me here on earth.

I am the true and faithful ambassador of my Father. My riches were not on earth, and I did not even have a place to lay my head during my ministry. Yet for the joy that was set before me, I endured the cross. I was not moved by the shame and contempt that men poured on me. My crown of thorns was soon replaced with many incorruptible crowns.

Whoever serves me will be highly honored on the day of glory. Happy is the one who endures the trials and temptations, for the overcomer will receive the crown of life that I promise to those who love me.

1 Corinthians 9:25 • Hebrews 3:1 • James 1:12 • 2 Timothy 4:8

May 24 *Jesus Talks to You*

Throughout all generations, I have been a rewarder of those who diligently sought me. All who lived faithfully in me bore fruit in their lives in due season. When my people faced fiery trials, I was there to deliver and provide for them. I will never forsake my children.

When you mourn, I will comfort you. When you are hungry, I will provide for you. When you are persecuted for your faith, I will let your heart know that the kingdom of heaven is yours. When you are faced with a dilemma, I will give you my counsel and wisdom that will bear much fruit in your life.

The faithful of millennia past, whose footprints are preserved in my Word for your eyes to behold, show my pathway to heaven. The testimonies of my people recorded in my Word show my love, faithfulness, mercy, and power to deliver and provide according to my riches in glory. These men and women of faith showed that they esteemed the riches of my kingdom to be of greater worth than all the treasures of this world along with its pleasures of sin.

With such a great cloud of witnesses surrounding you, throw off every weight that slows you down and the sins that entangle you; with perseverance run the race that I have set before you. As you humble your heart today and ask forgiveness for any sins committed, I do freely forgive you. I died for your sins, shed my blood for you, and rose from the dead to give you forgiveness, my righteousness, and assurance of eternal life. Press on, the race will be finished with the help of my Spirit; the prize of the heavenly calling, the crown of life, will be yours my child.

Hebrews 11:6 • Hebrews 12:1 • Psalm 145 • Proverbs 4:18
Philippians 3:12-21

May 25 *Jesus Talks to You*

I love you with an unfathomable love. I have such glorious plans for you, so do not be anxious about anything. Cast your cares upon me, for I care for you. I know well the dilemmas that you face, the sorrows that you suffer, the burdens that you bear, and the trials of your faith that you have endured. Fully rely upon me to take care of all of these. I am your God, the King of kings, and the Ruler of heaven and earth. Draw close to me and I will draw close to you. Whoever I bless will be blessed indeed, and nothing is impossible for me. Trust me fully to accomplish my will in your life. I am the God of all grace who has called you with a holy calling. I will guide you with my counsel, and afterward I will receive you to everlasting glory. After you have suffered for a little while, I will complete you, restore you, strengthen you, and establish you in me, upon my everlasting foundation.

Romans 8:35-39 • 1 Peter 5:6-11 • Psalm 138:1-8

May 26 *Jesus Talks to You*

The day I rose from the dead—conquering death—was a glorious day. With a great earthquake, one of my angels from heaven rolled away the stone from the door of the tomb. I then appeared to some of my devoted followers, who told the apostles of this glorious happening and were not believed; they were considered as speaking nonsense and idle tales.

On the evening of this same day, the disciples were assembled together and had locked the doors for fear of the Jewish leaders. Suddenly, I stood in their midst and gave a greeting of peace to them. I showed them my hands and my side where I had been pierced. They were filled with joy to see their Lord. But Thomas, one of the twelve, was not there and refused to believe this account. He insisted that unless he would see the mark of the nails in my hands, put his finger into the mark of the nails, and put his hand into my side, that he would never believe.

Eight days later, the disciples were gathered together, and Thomas was with them. Then I appeared, the doors being shut, and standing in their midst greeted them with, "Peace be to you." Then I told Thomas to reach out and put his finger in the nail prints and his hand into my side. I told him to stop doubting and to believe. Thomas answered me, "My Lord and my God!" I told Thomas that because he has seen me, he believes, but how blessed are those who have not seen me and yet believe on me.

My dear child, you are truly blessed; you have not seen me in the flesh, yet you believe in me, trust in me, and love me. Your reward shall be boundless, as you overcome with this precious faith.

Matthew 28:1-7 • John 20 • 1 Peter 1:8-13 • Romans 15:13

May 27 *Jesus Talks to You*

The one who overcomes and gains the victory in life, by faith—the faith of the Son of God that dwells in you—I give great and precious promises for your entrance into my glory:

• You shall be clothed in my righteousness forever, and I will never blot out your name from the book of life. I will announce your name, that you are mine, before my Father and his angels.
• I will give you the right to eat of the fruit of the tree of life which is in the midst of my paradise in glory.
• I will give you the right to sit beside me on my throne, even as I sat down next to my Father on his throne.
• You will not be hurt by the second death.
• You will eat of the hidden manna.
• I will give you a white stone with a new name engraved on it, a name that no one knows or understands except you.
• I will make you a pillar in my holy sanctuary, and you will never have to leave it. I will write upon you the name of the city of heaven, new Jerusalem, and will write upon you my new name.
• You shall inherit all things, and I will be your God, and you shall be my child forever.

Revelation 2 & 3 • Revelation 21:1-7

I sent the angel Gabriel (same angel whom I sent to the young virgin named Mary) on a mission to Zacharias, while fulfilling his duty as a Hebrew priest. His wife was barren, and both he and Elizabeth were well stricken in years. Gabriel told him that his prayer has been heard, and that his wife would bear him a son, whom they were to name John.

To most people, for this couple to have a baby at their age would appear to be a hopeless cause. But they prayed and prayed over the years, and did not give up. I heard their prayers, and gave them more than a son; John the Baptist, would bring many of my people, the children of Israel, to repentance, as John prepared the way for me, the Son of God.

Though Zacharias and Elizabeth endured many years of trials regarding their blessing, my timing was perfect for them and John to fulfill a glorious work in my kingdom, as prophesied centuries earlier.

Do not lose heart, my child; all of your prayers have also been heard. I know what is best for you and my kingdom. Sometimes the answer to a prayer will be no. At other times it is my will to wait to fulfill a request; I may be working in your heart to prepare you for the blessing when it is given. Other circumstances may also need to be arranged or changed by me to bring you what is best.

Continue in prayer with thanksgiving, with reverence and trust, for all of your needs, hopes, and dreams for your life. Be open while in prayer, for I may speak to your heart, comfort you by my Spirit, or reveal a calling or my will for you regarding your circumstances. Believe my Word and its promises. When I speak personally to your heart, believe me and be willing to do what my Spirit shows you to do. Remember, Zacharias, did not believe the angel Gabriel's word, and I took away his ability to speak until John was born.

I am working all things for your good, according to my holy purposes.

Luke 1:5-25 • Isaiah 30:18; 40:3-5 • Philippians 4:6 • Romans 8:14-32

I am a friend who sticks closer than a brother. I love you exceedingly more than anyone in the world does. Your heartache, loneliness, and emotional stresses are close to my heart. I am always with you, to listen to you as you share with me your burdens and troubles.

Bonds of family, friendship, or marriage are often so very strong; they also tend to be very fragile. When you feel hurt, confused, rejected, or without hope, come spend time with me. Do not try to fix your relationships in the flesh—especially when motivated by raw emotion. Humble your heart before me, acknowledging that you do not have all of the answers. Let my peace rule at this time; open your heart, and let the Holy Spirit give you peace that surpasses understanding.

Quietly examine your own heart and be willing to say one of these three word statements, when needed, that can bring healing to relationships: "I am sorry" or "I forgive you." Pray that I will give you conciliatory words to share with others, that harmony would be the tone of your relationship. Be willing to calmly share how you feel without accusatory statements toward others. Open your heart, that you might listen and truly hear the feelings and concerns of others.

Ask the Father, in my name, that he would work wonders in your relationships and send the Holy Spirit to deeply move in each heart, so that the Spirit would control actions and words.

I came into this world to share the good news; there is more to life than just this world. By faith and fully trusting in me, abundant life will be experienced in this world and everlasting life in the kingdom of heaven. I came to earth to bind up the brokenhearted and to proclaim freedom to those held captive to sin. I will give joy instead of mourning and the garment of praise in place of discouragement. I will heal and gently care for you. You shall be called an oak of righteousness, the planting of the Lord, that brings glory to my name.

Proverbs 18:24 • 1 John 4:9-12 • Ephesians 4:29-32 • Isaiah 61:1-3

May 30 *Jesus Talks to You*

After being tempted forty days by the devil, I returned to Galilee in the power of the Holy Spirit. In Nazareth, where I had been brought up, I had just finished reading from the scroll of the prophet Isaiah about the Messiah's ministry of deliverance and healing; I told the synagogue that this day these scriptures are being fulfilled. I shared a little more, and everyone who was listening became so furious that they ran me out of town, leading me to the brow of the hill on which the city was built, to throw me over the cliff. But I walked right through the crowd, and went on my way.

The people that I grew up with treated me like that. There would be many others during my ministry that would accuse me of being a drunkard, blasphemer, sabbath-breaker, demon-possessed man, liar, and more. One would think that I would be discouraged by this kind of treatment. I was not; I had a mission to fulfill—to give my life as a sacrifice for the sins of the world. I would not fail or be discouraged until this work of love be completed. I set my face like flint and pressed on. My full trust was in my Father whom I served; he would raise me up to glory after my death—the death that would bring life to the world.

Luke 4:13–30 • Isaiah 42:1-7 • Isaiah 50:6-7 • Ephesians 1:19-23

May 31 *Jesus Talks to You*

Do not be discouraged by what others say or do to you. The enemy will use people and circumstances to try to trip you up. Ask me and I will empower you by the Spirit to press on and fulfill my call in your life. The early disciples were transformed by the Spirit to do the same works that I did; I can work through you to touch lives. I have all power in heaven and earth—wonders will happen in and through your life. Let me transform your life. As my Father sent me, so I send you. You are not insignificant in my kingdom; you are my ambassador. Live up to the honor of the calling. I really love you and am with you always.

John 16:33 • Joshua 1:9 • 2 Timothy 1:9-10 • Ephesians 1:3-18

Lame Man Healed by Holy Spirit Using Peter and John—*Acts 3*

Daniel in the Lion's Den—*Daniel 6*

June 1

Jesus Talks to You

Do not let your soul be discouraged or cast down. Though you are going through trials and temptations, I shall soon bring to you rich blessings; peace and comfort of heart shall be yours. Though you now feel the heat of the fire, trust in me; I will burn away your dross, and you will come forth from the fire as pure gold.

In these hardest of times, know this: I am with you and desire that you come close to me. Trust me, lean upon me, and let me speak to your heart during your quiet times with me. I am very mindful of your tears and deeply listen to your every prayer. Great is my faithfulness, and my mercy and compassion is ever toward you. I will command my lovingkindness in the day, and at night my song will be with you. I will answer all of your prayers—in my way, in my perfect timing, and in my perfect love. I treasure your hopes and dreams, and will do more for you in this world and in the world to come than you could ever ask or imagine. Be patient, and trust that my will is best for you, even if you do not understand. Continue to walk by faith and not by sight.

2 Corinthians 12:9-10 • Psalm 42:1-8 • Job 23:8-10

June 2

Jesus Talks to You

I was faithful to Paul during his many perils: shipwrecks, beaten many times for his faith, robbers, false brethren, imprisonments, hunger, labors, and more. Though his outward life was perishing, I was renewing him inwardly every day—to be transformed more into my image. He sought me when discouraged; he received abundant hope and grace from the Holy Spirit. He learned to triumph and rejoice in his sufferings, knowing that they worked unswerving endurance in his life. Through patience, he gained experience—that I would be strong on his behalf and bless his life richly. My love, flowing through his yielded life, inspired millions. Be patient, strong in faith, committing your heart fully to me, and no good thing will I withhold from you, beloved one.

2 Corinthians 4:6-18 • Isaiah 43:2 • Romans 5:1-5 • Psalm 84:11

June 3 *Jesus Talks to You*

My Father has given to me all power in heaven and in earth. Richly blessed are you, who through the revelation of the Holy Spirit, have come to know me and the Father. Before I walked the earth as the Son of Man, many righteous men, prophets, and kings desired to see the fulfillment of the many prophecies of the Messiah of the world. But, through my Word and the revelation of the Holy Spirit, you know all about me, the Messiah—my birth, my ministry, my wisdom, truths of heaven and hell, my death and resurrection, my gift of righteousness, and salvation. But most wondrous of all is that you know me personally, for I live and reign in your heart and life.

Luke 10:21-24 • John 1:1-18 • John 14:6-26

June 4 *Jesus Talks to You*

I am the Beginning of the creation of God, I am the Word of God—the Word of God made flesh when I walked the earth. I spoke the worlds into existence and also created man in our (Father, Son, and Holy Spirit) image, after our likeness. I, who spoke light into existence, have shined the true Light into your heart, to give you the knowledge of the glory of God, as revealed in me, Jesus Christ, the Messiah.

You have this precious treasure in a fragile jar of clay (you); allow the Holy Spirit to work in you and your jar to be broken by my love. Let the treasure of life (Christ in you) be poured out to a world desperately in need. Let your jar be broken—like the alabaster jar of perfume the woman broke and poured over me. Let your jar be broken—like Gideon's men who broke the jars to let their lamps shine bright in gaining a great victory. Let your light (my light and life that dwells in you) shine to all those around you. Let them see your good works and glorify your heavenly Father. They will see the true Light and then receive me, the true Life.

2 Corinthians 4:6-7 • 1 Peter 2:9 • Matthew 5:16

June 5

Jesus Talks to You

I spoke to Joshua and told him that there was still much land to be possessed by the children of Israel. It was theirs by inheritance and promise from me, but they were required to actively go in and take possession of it. The glorious land of promise that is your spiritual inheritance in me, as a born again member of my holy nation, has boundless treasures and riches in its valleys and hills. Much of this has yet to be explored and taken possession of by you.

I bid Peter to come out of the boat, onto the lake, and I gave him power to walk on the water. I bid you to come and seek out the vast wealth of promises you are yet to embrace; you will receive gifts from me and words of promise that will supernaturally enable you to defy the winds and the waves of the enemy; you will walk on the waters of this life by the power of the Holy Spirit. Go through the land. Claim and possess the great truths and promises of my Word. You will gain considerable strength and spiritual riches by them, and will bless many others as well.

Joshua 1:9 • 1 Peter 1:3-9 • Colossians 1:12-19 • 2 Peter 1:1-11

June 6

Jesus Talks to You

I am the eternal Son of God, the heir of all things, and King of the ages, who was delivered up for you. Will not the Father also freely give you all spiritual blessings to be found in me? Yes, he will. You are his elect—chosen and predestined to be adopted as his child. You are a joint-heir with me. It is your Father's good pleasure to give you the kingdom of heaven, with all of its glory and splendor.

Many of these rich blessings will come to you as you seek me with your whole heart. The Holy Spirit will guide you to do the works that have been ordained for you since before the world began. As I fulfilled the Father's will and then reaped boundless honor and glory in heaven, so shall you, if you go on and serve me and are led by my Spirit.

Ephesians 1:3 • Proverbs 8:14-21 • Hebrews 11:6 • John 12:26

June 7

Jesus Talks to You

Cast all your cares upon me for I deeply care for you. Throughout my Word, I encourage you to trust me. You may find it easier to trust in me for the big things—like forgiveness of sins and the gift of eternal life—which you could never take care of on your own. The small things can cause you unnecessary anxiety, not being sure if I care about them.

I will answer prayers for big and little cares. Seek me and my ways for your needs and problems. Do not lean to your own understanding and try to change circumstances in your own power. Be patient, let me work in your heart, and do my will in these needed areas. I know what is best for you, and have the power to do great things if it is my will to do so.

As you care for your own body, I care for mine. As a member of my body, you can trust in my love. Keep your mind stayed upon me always—seeking those things which are above—allowing the peace of God to rule in your heart, as I work in your life and in your circumstances.

1 Peter 5:7 • Isaiah 65:24 • Proverbs 3:5-6 • Isaiah 26:3

June 8

Jesus Talks to You

Whoever has my commandments—to love God with all of your heart, soul, strength, and mind; and love your neighbor as yourself—and obeys them, is one who loves me; all who love me will be loved by my Father, and I also will love and manifest myself to this one.

The richest aspect of abundant life in me is your personal relationship with me. To know me, the Creator of life, is to know a love that passes knowledge, a joy unspeakable, and a peace that surpasses understanding. Many know me as a God that seems to be far off. The early disciples that walked with me had a special privilege in their closeness to me. I desire to have an intimate relationship with you. Today and everyday, spend time with me—your friend and God. When I speak to you, the warmth of my love will richly bless you.

John 14:21-27

June 9

Jesus Talks to You

I am the great Shepherd, and I desire to restore your soul each day. I have set times of rest for you who labor for me. Come and learn of me; I am gentle and humble in heart, and you shall find refreshment for your soul. In the heat of the day, come and sit down under my shadow. Come to my banqueting house; my banner over you will be love. Taste and see that I am good; blessed is the one who trusts in me.

Follow close to me, that you may be with me as I usher you into green pastures. You will be guided beside peaceful brooks. The peace that is not of this world is yours to receive as you abide in me. I care for you; cast your burden upon me and I will sustain you.

Psalm 23 • Colossians 3:16 • Song of Solomon 2:4 • Psalm 55:22

June 10

Jesus Talks to You

I have given to you a priceless gift—a perfect gift from the Father above. As the Savior of the world, I have shed my blood in payment for your sins. The chastisement of your peace was upon me—and with my stripes you are healed. I freely forgive anyone who will come to me with a repentant heart. Truly happy is the one whose sins have been washed away. On the cross, I became sin for you, that you might become the righteousness of God in me.

You are washed, you are sanctified, and you are justified (it is just as if you have never sinned). Who will bring any charge against you, my chosen child? No one. You are justified by me, the Messiah. If your own heart condemns you for some sin of the past, I am greater than your heart; as far as the east is from the west, so far have I removed your transgressions from you—they are remembered by me no more. Rejoice and walk confidently in this newness of life. You have my perfect righteousness; I live in you.

Psalm 32:1 • Isaiah 53:5 • 2 Corinthians 5:21 • 1 John 3:20-21
Romans 8:33-39 • Psalm 103:12 • Hebrews 10:17

June 11 *Jesus Talks to You*

Sight, hearing, taste, touch, and smell—the five senses are gifts I have given you to enjoy while you are in your earthly body. Behold the beauty of the stars, waterfalls, or thousands of varieties of flowers and animals. Listen to a babbling brook, your favorite music, or the laughter of children playing. Savor the delicious tastes of one of hundreds of culinary delights. Feel the refreshing cool waters of a mountain lake on a hot summer day. Enjoy the touch of holding hands with someone you love. Enjoy the aroma of a freshly baked apple pie. How very fragrant is the rose or the lilac to name only two of thousands of floral delights. I have fully blessed you with a body that is perfectly suited to experience this glorious creation that you inhabit for a vapor of time.

But you shall put off your corruptible body and be clothed with an incorruptible one. Just as you have borne the image of the man that I created from the earth, so shall you bear my image—the Man from heaven. New glorious senses of a divine and eternal nature shall you be endowed with. You shall see me as I am and you will be just like me—changed in the twinkling of an eye. I will make all things new. The wonders of the kingdom of heaven will be yours to delight in forever!

1 Corinthians 15:42-53 • 1 John 3:1-3 • 1 Corinthians 2:9 • Psalm 16:11

June 12 *Jesus Talks to You*

I desire to have a warm and loving relationship with you. I will open up my spiritual treasures to all who seek me diligently. If you thirst to be filled with the Holy Spirit, you will not be denied. The glorious fruit of the Spirit will be found in your life, as you abide in me and are controlled by the Spirit. You shall be like a tree planted by streams of water, yielding its fruit in due season, and whose leaves will not wither. Whatsoever you do shall prosper. When you pray, I listen—and will compassionately care for, bless, and establish you. For my eyes search the whole earth to strengthen those whose hearts are fully committed to me.

Psalm 1:1-3 • Proverbs 3:13-18 • John 14:26

June 13 *Jesus Talks to You*

For many years, I was the carpenter of Nazareth, and knew much of creating fine pieces of workmanship. My tools were sharpened and ready to use as the needs arose. Today, I am the carpenter and builder of my eternal kingdom. I am fashioning works that shall abide forever in glory. You are my workmanship and are being built upon the foundation of the apostles and the prophets—I am the chief Cornerstone.

Marvelous as it may seem, you also are my tools, created in me to do good works, ordained before the world began. I will employ your words, deeds, talents, and gifts, which I have given to you by my Holy Spirit, to build others into my spiritual house.

Let my word dwell in you richly, bringing you wisdom, knowledge, and love. Be ready always to share my love and the truths of my kingdom; I will open doors for you to do so. Build upon the foundation of the prophets, apostles, and upon me with the gold, silver, and precious gems that I provide to you—doing my will and sharing my Word. These works shall abide the fire on the day of judgment and shall endure forever.

Ephesians 2:19-22 • 2 Timothy 2:15 • 1 Corinthians 3:10-15

June 14 *Jesus Talks to You*

Saul was blinded when my light shone around him. I sent Ananias to tell Saul that I had chosen him to know my will, to see me (the Righteous One), to hear my voice, and to be my witness to all men. Ananias met with Saul; he received his sight and was no longer on the same road of destruction. With new spiritual eyesight, Paul would see the risen Savior each day as he walked a new road—the road to new Jerusalem.

I have also chosen you to know my will. I will give you abundant grace as I transform your life. I will speak to you words of love and guidance. You will be my witness—receiving a great reward on the day of glory.

Acts 9:1-22 • 2 Timothy 1:9 • Ephesians 1:1-6

June 15 *Jesus Talks to You*

With great joy and everlasting love in my heart, I continued to teach the disciples after my resurrection. As Master of all creation, I directed all fish to steer clear of the seven disciples as they fished one night. After telling me that they caught nothing, I told them to throw the nets out on the right side and they would find some. As on the day when Peter was called to be my disciple through a miraculous catch of fish and a good dose of two sinking boats, I miraculously employed my finned friends. A colossal catch of 153 large fish astounded my disciples.

I added a big helping of kindness to a miraculous lesson. For when they landed on shore, they saw a fire of coals and fish cooking on it. I proceeded to serve them a fine meal of bread and fish.

The lesson was deep; without me, you can do nothing, but with me, all things are possible. Remember, my beloved child, I am calling you to be fishers of men. Walking with me and working through my power, you will touch the world with my love and bring others into the kingdom.

John 21:1-14 • John 15:4-16 • Philippians 4:13

June 16 *Jesus Talks to You*

Will there one day be no more temptations and trials? Will there one day be no sorrow? Can it really be that someday there will be no pain or suffering? Yes. Yes. Yes. In the kingdom of heaven, all things will be made new. The day of glory is fast approaching. My redeemed will enter my glory with unspeakable joy, peace that passes understanding, and love that surpasses knowledge. I will wipe away every tear from off your eyes. Death, crying, or pain will be no more. I understand how trials and temptations can be overwhelming at times. Take some alone time with me and I will impart new hope to you. Let my Word comfort you. Rejoice, knowing that my glory shall be revealed in your daily life and to you in heaven. Life is short; soon you will have forever joy.

Isaiah 51:11 • 1 Corinthians 2:9-10 • Colossians 1:27

After I had given David, the king, rest from all of his enemies, he desired to build a house for me, because he lived in a cedar house and the ark of God was only in a tent. I spoke to Nathan the prophet, and had him share some wondrous news with my servant David regarding his loving, devoted desire to build a house for my name.

I told Nathan, the prophet, to say the following to David: I had not requested the children of Israel to build a house for me to dwell in; I have moved from place to place, with a tent as my dwelling; I took David from the pasture and his flock of sheep to be ruler over my people; I have cut off all of his enemies and made his name great in all the earth; I will also provide a place for my people, Israel, and give them a home of their own; I will actually build a house for my faithful servant David—I will raise up his offspring and establish his kingdom; David's son shall build a house for my name; the throne of his kingdom will I establish forever; David's house and kingdom will endure before me forever.

After David heard the prophecies that I gave Nathan for David, he came before me with the most glorious prayer of thanksgiving and honor that man could offer—it brought joy to my heart. He was so grateful for the wonders that I had shown toward my people, Israel, and the glorious promises that I would fulfill in his life, through his son, as well as my great blessings that would honor David forever.

Solomon would build a most magnificent house to bring glory to my name. The grandest of blessings to honor David would come twenty-eight generations later, when I would be born as a baby in the little town of Bethlehem—I am the Root and the Offspring of David.

Like David, you may have plans of love toward me—plans to glorify my name. As you abide in me, many of your plans will be fulfilled and my heart will be blessed. But know this, beloved—I will build you a house; I desire to establish you in my kingdom and bless you so richly that only eternity can hold the glory and blessings awaiting you!

2 Samuel 7:1-29 • Jeremiah 29:11-13

June 18

Jesus Talks to You

Centuries before David, my servant, reigned as king of Israel, a great rejoicing reverberated through the vast multitude of the children of Israel. With mighty miracles, I had brought them out of the land of Egypt, where they had been in cruel bondage for four hundred years. Their songs of praise came before me in heaven the hour that I returned the Red Sea upon the Egyptians, who were in hot pursuit of their former slaves. My people were now absolutely free—their enemy gone forever.

I have set you free from your enemies, sin and death, now and forever. I took every sin upon my body on the cross. I died, was buried, but arose again three days later. As Israel was freed from bondage in Egypt, you also died to your old life of slavery to sin, when your sins were crucified with me. As I rose from the dead, you also are risen with me by the glory of the Father—into the newness of life, just like the children of Israel who rose from the waters on the Promised Land side of the Red Sea. Rejoice, and walk with me in this newness of life. Be filled with and controlled by my Spirit, and enter the true land of promise—abundant life now and forever—by the faith of the Son of God, who lives in you.

Exodus 15:1-6 • Galatians 2:20 • Romans 6:1-13

June 19

Jesus Talks to You

You, who sow in tears, will surely reap with songs of joy. I am the God of compassion and mercy. I will never forget your labor of love that you have shown toward my name. You, who have gone forth weeping, carrying my Word to a hurting world, will doubtless come again rejoicing with a bountiful harvest. As the rains come down to water the earth and bring forth fruit, so my Word will not return empty; it will accomplish what I desire. Your Father in heaven will rejoice as broken lives are made whole, and those who were lost are found. So do not cast away your confidence; your reward is great. Persevere, so that after you have done my will, you will receive what I promised.

Psalm 126:5-6 • Isaiah 55:10-13 • Hebrews 10:35-36

June 20 *Jesus Talks to You*

A word spoken at just the right time is like apples of gold in a setting of silver. You can minister life or death by the power of your tongue. When you are controlled by the Holy Spirit, as you share with others, you will reap the sweetest of fruit. When you share my Word, do so with my love and kindness—that my Father might be glorified as you minister in my name.

I came into the world to do the works of my Father and to speak his words—full of the Holy Spirit and life. As my Father has sent me, in like fashion, I send you to speak my Word and truths, filled with the Spirit and life. Share words of hope with the despairing and lonely, words of comfort to the fearful, and words of faith to the weak. My Word is pure, like silver refined in a furnace, purified seven times. Seek me with your whole heart, and I will fill you with my Word and the Holy Spirit. Go to those who are in need and share apples of gold.

Proverbs 25:11 • Proverbs 18:21 • Ephesians 4:29-32 • Psalm 12:6

June 21 *Jesus Talks to You*

With a measure of faith in the living God and a heart filled with courage, Jonathan and his armor-bearer took on the Philistine outpost. Jonathan believed the Lord would act on his behalf. He was willing to fight the battle as if it all depended on him while knowing it all depends on his God. I created an earthquake and a panic in the Philistine army; a great victory was won that day for Israel. The battle is not yours, but mine.

I will be mighty on behalf of those who seek me wholeheartedly. I told Joshua that no one would be able to stand up against him all the days of his life. I promised to be with him as I had been with Moses and not leave him or forsake him. Ask me for Spirit-led strength, faith, and courage as I lead you. All things are possible to him that believes.

1 Samuel 14:6 • 2 Chronicles 20:15 • Joshua 1:5

June 22 *Jesus Talks to You*

I am omnipotent, omniscient, and have an everlasting love for you. I also have a wondrous plan for your life. My infinite love led me to become a man, forgive and take away your sin, and conquer death itself. When you received me as Savior, I placed my seal upon you—the Holy Spirit of promise, who is the earnest (down payment) of your inheritance. You have been given the first-fruit and foretaste of the kingdom of heaven. You are a co-heir with me of the kingdom. I am the Truth and cannot lie; I will fulfill my pledge. You will soon acquire complete possession of your glorious inheritance.

Until that wondrous day, our Father will perform a remarkable miracle in your life; he will transform you day by day by my Spirit and mold you into my image. My Father desires that you share inwardly my likeness. I am in heaven preparing a place for you, and the Holy Spirit is preparing you for that place, for you are being transformed into my own image from one degree of glory to another.

Colossians 1:12-22 • Psalm 139:1-18 • Ephesians 1:13-14 • Titus 1:2
2 Corinthians 3:18

June 23 *Jesus Talks to You*

I have taken you into a land of promise flowing with milk and honey. You, who once dwelled in the bondage of sin, can now freely enjoy the blessings of walking with me, the God of all creation. You possess my written Word, with the complete story of salvation and abundant life, and wondrous testimonies of my people—whose lives I have changed by my everlasting love. I am merciful even in your trials and disciplines.

Be thankful to the Father, in my name, for all your rich blessings: salvation, love, family, health, and all your needs that will be provided according to my riches in glory. I inhabit the praises of my people; whoever offers praise glorifies me.

Deuteronomy 8:1-10 • 2 Timothy 3:16 • Ephesians 1:3-12; 5:20

June 24

Jesus Talks to You

The apostles and disciples were filled with the Holy Spirit and were walking in my power after the day of Pentecost. I was working miracles through these dedicated men and women. They were preaching with boldness. A number of these had seen me crucified. They knew the same death might be their end. But they also had seen me, the risen Savior, for forty days, and watched as I ascended back to glory. They were convinced that they were more than conquerors through me. They knew that I was the Way, the Truth, and the Life, and were willing to give their hearts and souls to me, as they shared my love with the world. They were not ashamed of the gospel that I brought to earth, for through its power, eternal salvation is secured to all who believe.

Humble yourself before the Father, and ask him in my name to send you the power and boldness of the Holy Spirit in your life. You can do all things through me who strengthens you. Abundant blessings will be yours, as you share my love, wherever I have called you to serve.

Acts 4:29-33 • Romans 1:16 • John 3:16 • Romans 10:14-15

June 25

Jesus Talks to You

Offer your life to me with no reservations—trusting that I will bring you into your calling and a rich abundant life, now and forever. Do not be conformed to the ways of this world, but allow my Spirit to transform you in wondrous ways. I give to every believer a measure of faith and my grace to fulfill my will; use the gifts that I have given: if prophesying, then edify, encourage, and comfort with the words I give, according to the proportion of faith gifted to you; if teaching, then speak as the oracles of God; if ministry, humbly walk in my anointing; if serving, then give in love; if exhortation, then encourage and admonish with a caring heart; if leadership, then guide with eagerness and effort; if showing mercy, do so with true cheerfulness. Though many members are in my body, with different gifts, there is one Spirit and one Lord that dwells in you all.

Romans 12:1-13 • 1 Corinthians 12:4-12 • Ephesians 4:1-13

When Moses came down from Mount Sinai, holding the two tables of the covenant law (Ten Commandments), he was not aware that his face was radiant from being in my presence and having spoken with me. A veil was placed over Moses' face, because of its brilliance, so that the Israelites might not gaze upon his face—this Old Covenant glory was to fade and pass away when I would bring to mankind the abundant grace and brilliant glory of the New Covenant. And if what was transitory had glory, how much greater is the glory of that which lasts forever.

The law of sin and death came by Moses on Mount Sinai. But the glorious law of the Spirit of Life is the covenant that I brought to earth, when I came down from Mount Zion (heaven). The ministry of doom (the Old Covenant law revealed man's exceeding sinfulness), brought by the hand of Moses, pales in glory to the infinitely more abounding in glory ministry that brings righteousness.

You have been set free from the law of sin and death. The Sun of Righteousness, the Light of the world, has come—bringing abundant grace and truth. My righteousness and my glory will never fade away. And you shall behold my face and reign with me throughout all eternity.

I have chosen you to be a minister (servant) of my covenant of grace. You, who with an unveiled face reflect my glory—for you have been in my presence and spoken with me, and I have ministered to your heart by the Holy Spirit—are being transformed into my image and likeness from one degree of glory to another.

Exodus 34:29 • 2 Corinthians 3:6-18 • Jeremiah 31:31-33
Romans 8:29-31 • 2 Corinthians 4:6

June 27 *Jesus Talks to You*

Without having seen me with your physical eyes, you love me; even though you do not see me now, you trust fully in me and are filled with an inexpressible and glorious joy, for you are receiving the outcome of your faith, the salvation of your soul.

The most advanced telescope man has constructed is not able to behold what your eyes of faith have seen. Scientists have searched the stars that span the universe, craving the wisdom they believe to be woven in the tapestry of the heavens. I am the God who spoke the stars into existence, and I have revealed myself to you. Your spiritual eyes have seen me, the King of kings. You have embraced the One who freely gives the love and wisdom that is beyond time and creation. Kings and prophets have desired to see what you see. Though you have not seen me with your physical eyes, you have experienced my miracle working power. When you received me, you became a new creation; through my many precious promises, you were made a partaker of my divine nature. I, who gave sight to the blind, hearing to the deaf, and life to the dead, have done all that for you as well. You now see the Truth, hear my Word, and you, who were dead in sin, now live an abundant and everlasting life.

1 Peter 1:8-10 • 2 Corinthians 4:18

June 28 *Jesus Talks to You*

Since you have been raised from the dead, into the newness of life in me, seek those things which are above, where I sit on the right hand of the Father.

Today, rejoice and offer praise unto your God, who has blessed you with every spiritual blessing in the heavenly realm. You are my treasured child, one of my chosen people, and a holy priest; you have been called out of darkness into my wonderful light, that you might declare the praises and the mighty works of your God and Savior.

Colossians 3:1-3 • Ephesians 1:3-6 • Hebrews 13:15

June 29

Jesus Talks to You

Some people may ask you about me, your Savior and Lord. Here are some truths for you to share. I am the radiance of God's glory and his express image—his perfect imprint. I was the Word of God made flesh when I came to earth. I told my disciples that if they have seen me, they have seen the Father. I and my Father are one; I am in the Father, and the Father is within me. As the Word of God, I spoke all things into existence, and uphold and maintain the universe by the mighty power of my Word. We (Father, Son, and Holy Spirit) created man in our image. The prophets spoke of me being born into this world as a man, and that I would be called the Mighty God, Everlasting Father, and Prince of Peace. The Father proclaimed that all the angels should worship me. I am the faithful witness, the firstborn from the dead, and the King over all the kings of the earth. All the fullness of Deity (the Godhead) lives bodily in me—the Christ, the Messiah. I am Alpha and Omega, the Beginning and the End, the one who is, and who was, and who is to come, the Almighty. I know the entire history of the world, every thought of every living creature, and your every word and action for your whole life on earth—all of these even before I created the world. I inhabit eternity and rejoice that you, who believe in me, will be reigning with me in paradise, enjoying pleasures forever and ever.

June 30

Jesus Talks to You

Isaiah's call began with a glorious vision of me sitting on the throne and surrounded by angels. When he heard my voice ask who shall we send, and who will go for us, he said, "Here I am, send me." When on earth, I revealed my glory with miracles. Yet my call to the fishermen was a simple one to follow me, and I would make them fishers of men. You, too, have seen my truth and glory in my Word, and have heard my gentle call.

Will you follow in the footsteps of Isaiah and the early disciples? They said, "Here I am. Send me." The rest of their lives exemplified the acknowledging of my great glory; they lived for me and loved me.

Isaiah 6:1-8

The Ascension of Jesus—*Luke 24*

Day of Pentecost: the Disciples were Filled with the Holy Spirit

—*Acts 2*

July 1 *Jesus Talks to You*

I came into this world by a miraculous birth. I healed thousands, brought comfort by teaching the things concerning the kingdom of heaven, and lived a life of perfect love. In my sacrificial death, I conquered the power of sin that had plagued man since the beginning. By my resurrection, I triumphed over the enemy—death—and by doing so brought new hope and everlasting life to all who would believe in me.

My awestruck disciples (who thought they had seen it all), with jaws dropped, were gazing into the sky where I had just ascended out of view to the kingdom above. The two angels then said that this same Jesus will return in the same way that you have seen him go into heaven. My disciples had known me as the bread of life, the Light of the world, the Son of David, the Lamb of God, and now the ascended Savior. Yes, I am coming back from heaven with a commanding shout, the voice of the archangel, and with the trumpet call of God. I return as King of kings, and every eye shall see me. I am returning for you—to reign with me forever. Look up for your redemption draws near.

Acts 1:9-11 • Revelation 1:5-8 • Luke 21:27-28

July 2 *Jesus Talks to You*

When I proclaimed, "It is finished," on the cross, it was—except for your believing in and receiving that finished work. I came from heaven to bring you the gift of salvation and the perfect standing of righteousness. Though you are going through trials and temptations, there is great reason to rejoice today; you are perfect in me, by faith in me. It was finished on the cross. I am your righteousness and I live in you.

You do not need to strive by works to please me. By faith, you are fully justified—declared righteous. You have peace with the Father through me. He loves you and when he beholds you, he sees me in you. Beloved child of the Father, rest in his love, for you have been made righteous.

Philippians 3:9 • 2 Corinthians 5:21 • Jeremiah 23:5-6

July 3 *Jesus Talks to You*

I came into this world to radically change your life. The world says, "Go to work, come home, play, go to work, come home, play and after a while you will die. And that's life." No, that is not life. I came into the world that you might have abundant life. I have added a whole new dimension to living. By my Spirit, I have been transforming you more and more into my image—with new ideals and attitudes.

I desire for you to press on toward the prize of your high calling in me. There are boundless riches to dig up in my Word. There are gifts to receive from the Holy Spirit—that you may strengthen other believers. The communication of your faith will be powerful and very fruitful if you will acknowledge every good attribute that is in you through my dwelling in you—as you are led by the Holy Spirit.

Romans 12:2 • Philippians 3:12-14 • 1 Corinthians 12:7-12

July 4 *Jesus Talks to You*

The end of something is better than the beginning thereof; it is better to be patient in spirit than proud of heart. My servant David went through much tribulation on his way to being crowned king of Israel—and dwelling with me in the kingdom of heaven forever. The same patience was needed by my apostles and prophets as they endured great suffering before they wore the crown. I was despised and rejected by man and experienced much sorrow and grief while on earth. I wore a crown of thorns before many royal crowns were placed upon my head in glory.

Be patient through your trials. I am always with you to strengthen you. It is very easy to become discouraged—even David and Paul despaired at times. The key to their success was to trust me with all of their heart, by faith, even during the worst circumstances. Let my Spirit, through your endurance and patience, work in your heart to help you be more mature and complete in me.

Ecclesiastes 7:8 • Isaiah 53:3-5 • Revelation 19:12 • Philippians 4:13

July 5

Jesus Talks to You

King Saul was hunting David to kill him. David hid in the caves of Adullam and Engedi, which is next to an oasis. He would cry out to me, the Most High God, trusting me that I would fulfill my eternal purpose in his life. I had promised him, through the prophet, that he would reign as king—and he did for forty years. Though he was a step away from a beautiful oasis, he was also a step away from death.

I have given you exceedingly precious promises which will all be fulfilled in your life. Trust me during your times of tribulation; take refuge under the shadow of my wings and drink from the living waters of my Word and my love—I am your oasis. As David gave rich praise to his God during his calamities, so should you—for great is my faithfulness and my mercy toward you.

Psalm 57

July 6

Jesus Talks to You

The four beasts that are before my throne never cease to give glory, honor and thanks to the Lord God Almighty. The twenty-four elders lay their crowns before the throne as they worship me, glorifying me for the wonders of creation.

Beloved, continually remember all of my benefits; they are given with everlasting love. I have forgiven all of your sins and redeemed you from destruction. I am the God that heals you—spiritually, physically, and emotionally. I crown your life with lovingkindness, and my mercies are new every morning. I provide your many needs according to my riches in glory. I renew your strength like the eagle's.

Come into my presence every day. Offer your praises to the Father, in my name, for the blessings you have received. Join the multitude of heaven as they shout, "Hallelujah! For the Lord God Almighty reigns!"

Revelation 4 • Psalm 103 • Hebrews 13:15 • Revelation 19:4-6

July 7 *Jesus Talks to You*

You are more than a conqueror through me. As you abide in me and are guided by my Spirit, you will accomplish my will and bear much fruit which will remain forever.

Although I promised them the whole land of their inheritance, the children of Israel still had to set their feet upon it and claim it. As a mighty token for good and a foretaste of my mighty power that would be with them, I performed a spectacular miracle as they were entering the Promised Land. As promised, when their feet touched the Jordan River, though at flood stage, I stopped its flow upstream. They walked across on dry ground, crossing into their promised territory.

Your land of promise has remarkable spiritual blessings and gifts within it for you to possess. But you must set your foot of faith upon the promised territory. I have given you all things that have to do with life and godliness. Walk in the newness of life and rejoice in the hope of the glory of God. I will split the "Jordan" for you as you enter your land of promise.

Joshua 1:3 • 1 John 4:4 • Psalm 84:11-12 • Joshua 23:8-11

July 8 *Jesus Talks to You*

If you believe, you will see the glory of God. The stone was taken away, and I raised Lazarus from the dead. I can do the impossible—bring life to a dead area in your heart, relationship, or circumstances. Your dilemma is for the glory of God, that I may be glorified through it. Seek me with your whole heart and trust me to do my will—in my timing.

Abraham did not waver concerning my promises to him. He was strong in faith giving glory to me, fully convinced that I had the power to do what I had promised. I have all power in heaven and earth. Rest in my love; I will be strong on your behalf.

John 11:39-45 • Romans 4:17-25

July 9 *Jesus Talks to You*

I had cast seven demons out of Mary Magdalene. She was totally healed and had followed me as a dedicated disciple—a loving daughter. But suddenly all was very dark for her. She had watched me, her Lord, die through crucifixion. Now, three days after my death, while it was yet dark before dawn, she was crying outside the tomb. As she looked inside, she saw two angels who asked why she was crying; not only did she believe I was dead, but now even the body she had come to anoint with spices was taken away. She told them she was crying because the body of her Lord was taken away. She then turned and saw me—thinking I was the gardener. She asked if I had taken the body away. I then said, "Mary." She cried out, "Rabboni," (which means Master).

Her very darkest hour became a glorious dawn for her. The Son had risen and her heart was healed—her deepest sorrow turned into the greatest joy. My beloved child, when your darkest hour is upon you—when all hope seems gone—just turn and look to me. I am here with you. I am the Sun of Righteousness; I will shine brightly and show you my path. I will comfort you in your grief and replace it with everlasting hope.

John 20:11-18 • Isaiah 61:1-3

July 10 *Jesus Talks to You*

I am the great Shepherd, seeking my lost sheep. I will find every one of my dear elect lambs that I have loved with an everlasting love. My hand is not shortened, that it cannot save. I rescued Israel from their bitter bondage, split the Red Sea, and carried them to their Promised Land. I will care for and reach out to those you love and are praying for. The Lord your God is mighty—mighty to save. I saved Saul on the road to Damascus miraculously. When you are worried about your unsaved loved ones, bring them before me in prayer and thanksgiving. Trust in me, the omnipotent God, who is able to do immeasurably above all that you could ask for or imagine.

John 10:11, 27-30 • Isaiah 40:9-11 • Ephesians 3:17-21

July 11

Jesus Talks to You

I called Abram (Abraham) to leave his country and his people. I was going to make of him a great nation, with children as numerous as the stars of the heavens, and give them a rich and flourishing land as their inheritance. Abram obeyed me and by faith walked toward the Promised Land, physically and spiritually. He believed me and my Word, and it was credited to him as righteousness, and he became my friend.

There were trials and fears, but I told Abram to not be afraid; I said that I am his shield and his very great reward. By your faith in me, you have received my righteousness and are now my friend. I will be your shield and protector. All the riches of the universe are at my command. I hold all wisdom and knowledge. I am the God of perfect love. Yes, I am your very great reward!

Genesis 15:1-6 • James 2:23 • Psalm 84:11-12

July 12

Jesus Talks to You

As I called Abram to leave his country and culture, I have called you to leave your old country and lifestyle (the land of sin). Just as I promised most wondrous blessings to Abram, so I have promised to bring you to a land flowing with the glory of God. You, who are looking for the city with foundations, whose builder and maker is God, will soon behold the heavenly city, new Jerusalem, which awaits your arrival. There will be no death, sorrow, or pain there. You will see me as I am and will be changed to be like me. I promise that you will inherit all things. You will truly be blessed with all spiritual blessings and immeasurable glory in heaven throughout the endless ages.

My beloved child, rest in my love always. All of my promises will come true. Rejoice and be thankful; you will soon reign with me in glory.

Genesis 12:1-3 • Hebrews 11:8-16 • 2 Corinthians 1:20

July 13 *Jesus Talks to You*

In Daniel's vision, he saw one like the Son of man coming with the clouds of heaven and approaching the Ancient of Days. He was given dominion, glory, and sovereign power; all peoples and nations of every language worshiped him. His dominion is an everlasting dominion which shall not pass away, and his kingdom is one that shall never be destroyed. I am the Son of man revealed in this vision to Daniel.

Many think that I am just a great teacher who brought religion. But I am the Son of God with all power in heaven and earth. Before I created the worlds, I reigned in heaven eternally. While on earth, I had authority over all creation. I calmed a storm by my Word. I walked on the water, gave sight to the blind, cleansed lepers, gave the lame the power to walk, cast out demons, and even raised the dead to life again. I am the same today as I was before creation or when I walked the earth. I am coming back soon. The first time I came as the Lamb of God, the sacrifice for all of man's sins. But I am returning as the King of kings and Lord of lords. I am your Creator and the lover of your soul.

Daniel 7:9-14 • Hebrews 9:28 • 1 John 3:1-3

July 14 *Jesus Talks to You*

All the wisdom and knowledge possessed by mankind is rather miniscule. The depth of the riches of the wisdom and knowledge, and the power that I possess is unfathomable and infinite. Man, through all his wisdom, is not able to escape death nor can he ascend to the glory of heaven in his own power. But through what man considers foolishness, I have made a path for you to the kingdom of heaven; through faith in the power of my atoning blood, my death, and resurrection, you are given the most wondrous gift in the universe—forgiveness and everlasting life. My counsel and wisdom will bear the sweetest of fruit if followed. I who created the glorious universe, and gave my life for you, will also freely give you all things that pertain to this life and the one to come.

Romans 11:33-36 • John 3:16-17 • 2 Peter 1:1-4

July 15 *Jesus Talks to You*

I am close to the brokenhearted and rescue those who are crushed in spirit. I will be very gracious and merciful to you; my heart is opened wide to your tears and pain. I am moved whenever you experience sorrow. In tumultuous times, I will calm your storms.

While on earth, I was a man of sorrows and acquainted with grief. I deeply understand what you are going through. As my child, you have entered the fellowship of my suffering. Draw near to me in close-knit fellowship, seeking my help in your time of need. Allow me to put my arm around you. Listen to my words of comfort and care; I truly love you more than you could ever imagine—an everlasting love. I will give you peace and bring you fully into my fellowship of joy. Rejoice, inasmuch as you are a partaker of my sufferings; when my glory is revealed, you will be glad with joy beyond measure—forever.

Psalm 34:18 • Isaiah 53:3-5 • Hebrews 4:13-16 • 1 Peter 4:12-13

July 16 *Jesus Talks to You*

Even as your body is one, and has many parts, so it is with me, the Christ. Every member is unique and fulfills a special part in my body. You and each member will be changed more and more to be like me, who is the head of the body; the Holy Spirit will perform the transformation.

Honor your God by respecting each other for the special role each brother and sister fulfills in my body. You need not be jealous of someone else's calling. I will reveal the wonderful calling I have for you in my kingdom—ordained since before the world began. Give yourself wholly to my love and my Word. I will work in your life—in my time and in my way. Pray for your brethren. You will be amazed at how I honor and answer prayers of love. It is a rich ministry in itself. Rest in my peace always.

Ephesians 4:13-16 • 2 Peter1:3-11

July 17 *Jesus Talks to You*

My beloved child, you need not worry about what the future holds; for you know the God who holds the future. I will provide for all of your needs according to my riches in glory.

I will comfort you in times of trouble and sorrow. When you are lonely, I will be a friend that is closer than a brother. Your every tear is seen and felt by me. Always draw close to me, for I desire to bear your griefs and sorrows. I will impart hope to your heart if you will but give your heart to me each day. I desire to bring you into a life that has a deep joy.

John 16:33 • Revelation 21:4 • Philippians 4:19

July 18 *Jesus Talks to You*

I have all power in heaven and earth. I can change circumstances so very easily for you. But what is most necessary for you is to get to know me in deep and heart-changing ways. To have your life transformed more into my likeness, through the power of the Holy Spirit, is exceedingly more valuable to you and me than your circumstances being more favorable to you. To possess the treasures of my wisdom, the knowledge of my kingdom, and to experience my glorious hand of care and deliverance through trying times are beyond measure more valuable than all the gold, silver, and precious gems of the world.

By placing your full trust in me through the trials of your faith, you will come forth as gold out of the furnace of affliction. Do not be surprised when these trials—that I allow—come into your life. I will speak with you during these hard times. Invest time with me and allow my Word and Holy Spirit to lead you. I will guide you personally by my counsel. I am the living Savior who is able to do abundantly above all you could imagine is possible. I will truly deliver you, set you free in so many ways, and establish you in my kingdom; I will bring hope, joy, and love into your heart, in areas where they were not in the past.

Romans 5:3-5 • 1 Peter 4:12-13 • Psalm 73:24 • Psalm 40:1-3

July 19 *Jesus Talks to You*

The plant and animal kingdom, men, women, and children all benefit richly from the vital forces of the sun. There is no life without it. This must be also said of the Sun of Righteousness. Life abundant here on earth and eternal in the world to come is only found in me—the Sun of Righteousness, the bright Morning Star, the Christ of God.

I have arisen in your heart. Let my light shine from you so that the blind may see. My light brings sight and reality to all who will receive it. Let my warmth flow from you to the cold, dying world around you. Let the sweet influences of the Sun of Righteousness flow from your life. Ask me to fill you with my Spirit and I will.

Are you sometimes discouraged that you life is not shining brightly? Though you are weak, I delight in you just as you are. Little by little you will grow and the light will shine brighter from your life. Trust me fully and be patient, so that you may know that every step of growth and blessing was from my hand. I began the good work in you and will continue it until the day of glory.

Malachi 4:2 • Proverbs 4:18 • Philippians 1:6

July 20 *Jesus Talks to You*

As you follow me, you will need to endure many troubles; but I will deliver you from them all. This is a comforting promise to you in your times of suffering—and how severe these trials can be. Your body is frail and subject to the elements. Your heart can be broken even in the most close-knit relationships. Sometimes there seems to be no hope.

I will raise up those that are bowed down. I deeply love the righteous. I will heal the broken in heart and bind up their grief. Ask of me and I will give you a full dose of the patience of Job and wisdom from above. Tears may endure through the night, but I will bring joy in the morning.

Psalm 34:17-19 • Psalm 147:1-5

July 21 *Jesus Talks to You*

A man who was covered with leprosy came to me. Falling down with his face to the ground, he begged me, "Lord, if you're willing, you can make me clean." I reached out my hand and touched the man. "I am willing," I said. "Be clean!" And immediately the leprosy left him.

Come to me today and receive compassion and healing. I am the great Physician. I am the Holy One of heaven, and I am always willing to touch any area of your life. The worst of disease or sin cannot defile me. As the merciful Redeemer, I welcome all today. I have the keys to every prison door that holds you captive. All who call to me, I will set free. For each and every area of your life that is stained, scarred or mangled by sin or the enemy, I will touch your life and impart power and virtue to restore you to perfect wholeness—in my timing, in my way, and always in my love.

Luke 5:12-13 • Matthew 4:23-24 • Matthew 9:35-36 • Malachi 4:2

July 22 *Jesus Talks to You*

Emerging from the waters of the Jordan, I heard, "This is my beloved Son, whom I love; with him I am well pleased." I was now to endure a most extreme time of testing for forty days. As the pioneer of your faith and author of salvation, I was blazing a trail for you. I would prevail over Satan in the wilderness—and three and a half years later at the cross.

In the paradise of Eden, Adam failed and succumbed to the temptation of Satan, who allured through the lust of the flesh, the lust of the eyes, and the pride of life. In the harsh and burning wilderness, I prevailed. I sinned not, but stood rock solid on Scripture. Follow me; he that overcomes shall inherit all things. As a joint-heir, you will reign with me in the glories of heaven forever. You can overcome by the blood of my sacrifice, by the word of your testimony, and by not loving your life, so as to shrink from death. Overcome through me who strengthens you.

Hebrews 2:9-18 • Hebrews 4:14-16 • Revelation 12:11 • Philippians 4:13

July 23 *Jesus Talks to You*

In the beginning of creation I spoke the billions of stars into existence. I fashioned earth by my wisdom. The mighty oceans and rivers flowed at the touch of my hand. I brought into being thousands of species of plants and animals. Man was created in the image of God. Man fell and how great was that fall. He desperately needed a Savior.

When you receive me, you become a new creation. By the same power that I created the universe, I will transform your life to be in my image—the likeness of Christ. By the power that raised me from the dead, the Holy Spirit will bring forth life in you where no life existed. Where there once was hate, my love will shine. Where sin once ruled, I, the Prince of Peace will now reign.

By faith you know your sins are forgiven and gone forever. By faith you know that out of my glorious riches, I will continually provide for you—sometimes in miraculous ways. By faith let me, the Christ of God, reign in your heart.

Ephesians 3:16-21 • Romans 8:11 • Romans 5:8-21

July 24 *Jesus Talks to You*

I came from heaven to earth to wash away your sins. It is humbling to you, no doubt, but you needed it. Through this one act of love—my blood sacrifice—I blotted out your sins forever. You are clean and pure; you are 100% righteous by the miracle power of your God. And I will continue to cleanse you daily from your sin and the impurities of the world that you walk through.

Will you come to me humbly and allow me to work in the hidden areas of your heart and mind? I will cleanse you, free you, and transform you.

John 15:13 • 1 John 1:9 • Revelation 1:5 • 2 Corinthians 5:21

July 25 *Jesus Talks to You*

A woman who had suffered from bleeding for twelve years came up behind me and touched the edge of my garment—experiencing my healing power. She believed that if she could only touch my clothes, she would be healed. I turned to her, and told her that her faith had healed her. And the woman was completely cured from that moment.

This woman had spent all of her money on doctors through the years. She was at the end of her rope. You may have a relationship that is suffering, spiritual difficulties, sins that have you tied up in knots, sickness that has plagued you, or employment and financial problems. I understand your hardships and pain. If you believe that I am able to heal and miraculously bless your life, come to me with a humble heart today. Be led by my Spirit and do what I show you to do by faith to receive my blessing. If you only touch the hem of my garment, you will know my healing touch and power of deliverance—in my way and in my timing.

Bring your brokenness and suffering to me today. Remember, while on earth I was a man of sorrows. I understand and love you. I desire to talk to you, comfort you, and make you whole.

Matthew 9:20-22 • Mark 5:25-34 • Matthew 14:35-36 • Psalm 40:1-3

July 26 *Jesus Talks to You*

Every day I pour out wonderful gifts to you: sunshine and rain, health and prosperity, and blessings of family and friends. The whole creation proclaims the goodness and love of your ever-giving Father. Blessed is the one who knows the gift of eternal life through me, the Messiah, Jesus. I promise to anyone who believes, that living water will flow in a torrent from your innermost being. I tell you the truth; my Father will freely give you whatever you ask in my name. Until now you have not asked for much in my name. Ask according to my will, and you will receive, and your joy will be overflowing. Seek me with all of your heart; I am a rewarder of all that do so.

John 4:10 • Hebrews 11:6

July 27 *Jesus Talks to You*

I gave sight to the blind, hearing to the deaf, and life to the dead. I can transform your heart so that my love will reign. In the same way that you are patiently awaiting my return, endure with hopeful expectation that I am continuing a deep work in you. I care for you deeply and with a boundless love. I desire that you experience my life-changing love in such a manner that both you and those you come in contact with are amazed at the power of God—that the same miracle working love that I shared when on earth can still change lives today.

Please be patient with your spiritual progress. Be forbearing of others, as well; I am not finished with them either. You may be longing for answers to prayers, or fulfillment of hopes and dreams that you have presented to me in the past; I have not forgotten. Be patient, for I will bring to pass marvelous blessings in your life.

2 Thessalonians 3:5 • James 1:3-5 • Isaiah 55:8-13

July 28 *Jesus Talks to You*

By faith Noah, Abraham, and Moses established my reality to a world entrenched in disbelief. These men exhibited human weaknesses common to man, yet their hearts were humble enough to receive my Word and promises. Mixing their faith with obedience, these three notably changed the course of history in a way that greatly glorified their God.

Do you feel kind of ordinary? Noah, Abraham, and Moses did too. When I ask you to fulfill my will and the task appears overwhelming, remember what these three went through. They believed the "impossible" because I said it was so. I, the omnipotent God, who spoke the universe into existence, have called you to do my will. Believe me fully that I will accomplish a remarkable work through you, if you will but humble your heart, listen, and obey my Word—the reality that I am living and reigning in your life is wondrous in its own right.

Hebrews 11:6

July 29 *Jesus Talks to You*

The whole creation is groaning and travailing, as in the pains of childbirth. You who have the firstfruits of the Spirit, eagerly await the glorious day of the redemption of your bodies. God the Father redeemed you spiritually through my priceless blood. You have been given the Holy Spirit, which is the down payment of your inheritance. This deposit guarantees that you will soon inherit the exceeding great riches and the incomparably splendorous glory of the kingdom of heaven. It truly is your Father's good pleasure to give you the kingdom. All of your trials will soon be over. You will really be with me, the risen Savior, forever. Rejoice, you will soon receive the crown of life that I promise to all who love me. God your Father, will welcome you to enjoy his love and his wonderful, majestic kingdom throughout all eternity.

Romans 8:17-39

July 30 *Jesus Talks to You*

As a believer, the Spirit that raised me from the dead is living in you. The Holy Spirit is able to transform your life in ways exceedingly abundant above all that you can think or imagine possible. Give your life to me in a new way today—as a living sacrifice. I will perform the miracle of life and build you anew. I will fashion you into my image with power and love; I desire for you to reign in life with me. As I rose from the dead by the glory of the Father, so you are to walk in the newness of life. You are my child. All things are possible to you that believe. Build yourself up in the faith by entering into my Word more deeply. The testimonies, wisdom, and miracles shared will radically change your life.

Please do not be discouraged; bring your brokenness and troubled heart to me. I desire to shower abundant mercy and forgiveness upon you. I will bring strength and joy to your innermost being. Draw near to me and I will draw near to you. Welcome me to reign in your life; your rejoicing shall be complete as I fill your heart with my love and peace.

Romans 8:11 • Romans 12:1 • 2 Corinthians 4:16

Return of the Spies from the Promised Land—*Numbers 13*

July 31

Jesus Talks to You

As the great Apostle and High Priest of your faith, I spanned the gulf between heaven and earth. Because I love you so very much, I took upon myself a body of flesh and lived among you.

My immeasurable love is equal to my infinite power. Through mighty signs and wonders, I confirmed that I am the Son of God. I promise abundant life with power to all who will receive it. The early disciples experienced this. They fully received the faith that I delivered to them. Let my Word dwell in you richly that you might know my many great and precious promises, and enjoy their fulfillments in your life. Contend earnestly and with unwavering determination for the faith of the Son of God. You will be so blessed and thankful if you do.

Hebrews 3:1 • Jude 1:3, 20-21, 24-25

August 1

Jesus Talks to You

Twelve men went in to explore the land that I had promised to give to the Israelites. Ten came back reporting of the powerful people and the large, fortified cities. Looking at the enemy and their own strength, they said that they could not attack those people because they are too strong. Two men, Joshua and Caleb, came back rejoicing in their God, his promises, and his power. Caleb said that they should go up and take possession of the land; he had complete confidence in his God.

If you look at the difficult tasks, enemies, trials, and tribulations that lie ahead, and compare them to your own strength, you will look very weak and small in your own eyes—a mere grasshopper. But greater is the Son of God, who lives in you, than the enemy who is in the world. Choose today to be like Caleb and Joshua. Walk in my faith and power—be more than a conqueror. All things are possible to you who believe.

Numbers 13:23-33 • 1 John 4:4 • Galatians 2:20

Apostle Paul at Ephesus—*Acts 19*

August 2 *Jesus Talks to You*

The Jewish exiles had returned to their land. They wept as they listened to the Word from the Book of the Law of Moses. Nehemiah said that this day is holy to the Lord and not to weep, for the joy of the Lord is your strength. Nehemiah told the Israelites to go and enjoy choice foods and drink, and to send some to those that have nothing prepared.

You were once exiled from the promises and inheritance of my kingdom. Forgiveness through my blood sacrifice has allowed you to enter the land of promise of the living God. Sometimes upon hearing my Word, you may sorrow greatly for the years that passed without your having walked with me; but today and every day is a sacred day. You have my life, my Word, and my love; you have ample reason to rejoice. Go and share the bread and wine of Christ with a hungering and thirsting world. Bring them the true joy of the Lord. My joy is your strength.

Nehemiah 8:8-12 • Romans 15:13

August 3 *Jesus Talks to You*

I came into the world to bind up the brokenhearted, to proclaim freedom to those who are captive, to comfort all those who mourn—to present to those who grieve, a crown of beauty instead of ashes, the oil of joy in place of mourning.

I know the number of stars and call them each by name. They will disappear when I create new heavens and a new earth, but you, whom I love, will live forever with me. You, who are a joint-heir with me, will be comforted in the same way I was. In my severe pain, shame, suffering, and death, I committed myself to the Father. He raised me up in power and bestowed upon me immeasurable honor. Commit you heart to the Father. He will raise you up with honor on the day of glory. I desire to put my arms of love around you. I know your every problem, every sorrow, and burden. I care so very much for you. I am not far off, but here with you now. Let me love you, heal you, and encourage you.

Psalm 147:3-5

August 4

Jesus Talks to You

You have a partnership and communion with me. I call you my friend. You are a member of my body. Being a partaker of my divine nature, allow the Holy Spirit to enrich you in my Word. You will be strengthened, refreshed, and given power to do my Father's will. Whoever does the will of my Father is in my intimate family. Let my love run deep in your life. The world hungers to know of this wondrous fellowship that we share.

I am the author and finisher of your faith; I began a good work in you and will be faithful to complete it. You will be presented spotless and pure—possessing my righteousness—before the presence of my glory with triumphant joy when you enter the kingdom of heaven.

1 Corinthians 1:8-9 • Jude 1:24-25 • 1 Thessalonians 5:23-24

August 5

Jesus Talks to You

If anyone receives me, the Christ, he is a new creation; the old has gone, all things are become new. Though your sins were as scarlet, they are now white like snow. God made me, who had no sin, to become sin for you, that you might become the righteousness of God in me. Your Father sent me, the exact representation of his being, in a beyond astonishing display of his unfathomable love for you. I knew the cross was awaiting me, even before coming into the world. Even through great sorrow, shame, and pain, I stretched out my arms and pleaded for your soul; "Father, forgive them, for they do not know what they are doing."

I am the resurrection and the life. By my power and my Spirit, I have brought you to life from the dead! As my special clay jar, it is my desire to keep you filled to overflowing with my living water, that you also, will bring life to others who are dead in their sins. Go now with a heart of forgiveness and love, on my behalf, so that others who do not know what they are doing, may know forever the glory of my love.

2 Corinthians 5:17-21

August 6 *Jesus Talks to You*

I loved you before you received me as your Savior. While you were yet in a life of sin, I loved you. When I created your inmost being and fashioned you in your mother's womb, I knew you and your whole life story—and I loved you. When the Father sent me to the agony of the cross at Calvary to die for your sins, I loved you. During the rise and fall of kingdoms and nations, you were on my mind—and I loved you. When Adam and Eve walked in the midst of the paradise of Eden, I knew exactly where you would be born in their family line. And yes, I loved you then. When I was creating innumerable galaxies and the earth, with its spectacular mountains, oceans, animals, and floral wonders, you were loved. During the eons of eternity, amid the majesty and glory of the kingdom of heaven, where millions of angelic beings rejoiced with me and the Father—where spectacular sights and sounds indescribably surpass all that would be found on the earth that I would create—I loved you with an everlasting love!

Jeremiah 31:3

August 7 *Jesus Talks to You*

Isaiah prophesied of me, the Messiah, saying that I would be a witness, a leader, and commander to the people. I am the faithful witness. As the great Apostle of the kingdom of heaven, I was faithful to speak words of the kingdom and do the works that the Father sent me to do—perfectly faithful, even unto death.

I am the great Shepherd of the sheep; leading my sheep beside still waters and into green pastures. I lead them through dark and dangerous valleys, but care and fight for my sheep that I may preserve every one.

As your commander, I have engraved two commandments upon your heart and mind: love God with all your heart, soul, mind, and strength and love your neighbor as yourself.

Isaiah 55:4 • Revelation 1:5-6

August 8 *Jesus Talks to You*

Come boldly before my throne of grace, so that you may receive mercy and find grace to help you in your time of need. When you are in the midst of deep suffering and trial, I welcome you with open arms and heart to come into my presence. Pour out your heart to me; you will not be denied my compassion and consolation. You are my child and I am moved with the hurts of your heart—I truly feel your sorrows and suffering. I also will rejoice with you in the joys that you come and share with me. I am not a God that is far off; I am always there with you.

As you cast your cares and burdens upon me, open your heart and listen. Be still and I will speak to you. I will comfort you with words of love. I will guide you with heavenly wisdom.

Hebrews 4:14-16 • 1 Peter 5:7 • James 1:5

August 9 *Jesus Talks to You*

Once afflicted by your own sins, tossed and thrashed about by the deceitful winds of the world, lost in your sorrow and shame, you have been gloriously redeemed and liberated by my love and power—the Sun of Righteousness has arisen with healing in his wings. My command, "Peace be still," has been heeded by all the forces contrary to you. My forgiveness and righteousness has freely been granted.

Exceedingly great and precious promises have been assured through my holy blood covenant. The Holy Spirit is freely given to all who obey. Rejoice! You who once were alienated from my love and my kingdom are now one with me. You are a member of my eternal royal family. You are a living stone, being built on the foundation of the apostles and prophets—I am the chief Cornerstone. All my precious and glorious gems—my people, who are lively stones—are harmoniously growing together into a holy temple, a dwelling place of your God by his Spirit.

Isaiah 54:10-13 • Ephesians. 2:19-22

August 10 *Jesus Talks to You*

What glories await you in my eternal kingdom. There will be new heavens and a new earth; there will be no more crying, pain, or death. The river of the water of life, clear like crystal, will be flowing from my throne. You soon shall see the heavenly Jerusalem, the city of the living God. Millions of angels will be there rejoicing, as will also a vast multitude that no one could number, from every nation, tribe, people, and language.

You shall be changed in the twinkling of an eye; you will reign in an incorruptible body, with sin long forgotten, enjoying the riches of the King of kings for the eternal ages to come. Lay up for yourself treasures in heaven; for they will forever be yours. Praise your God and Father. In his great mercy, he has given you a new birth into a living hope through my resurrection from the dead, and he has brought you into an inheritance that can never perish, spoil, or fade—kept in heaven for you.

Colossians 3:1-4 • 1 John 3:1-3 • Matthew 6:20-21 • 1 Peter 1:4

August 11 *Jesus Talks to You*

Do not lose heart; outwardly you are wasting away, yet inwardly you are being renewed day by day. For your light and momentary troubles are working for you a weight of eternal glory that far outweighs them all. Gold ore is purified in the fiery furnace, and its impurities are purged out; a most valued piece of gold is soon obtained through the process of continued firings. Like gold being refined, so I am utilizing the fiery furnace of trials to remove the dross of sin from your life (though you'll never be perfect, while in your present body, until you are in heaven). I will be very merciful and refresh you when needed. Be encouraged; you are being changed into my likeness and are learning many of my ways. I am the master jeweler and know the way you take; after being tested, you will come forth as gold—the eternal kind at that. Your present sufferings are not worth comparing with the glory that will be revealed in you.

2 Corinthians 4:16-18 • Job 23:10 • Romans 8:18

August 12 *Jesus Talks to You*

Every nail hammered, every brick laid, every window placed, every wall raised, and every room painted has an integral part in the building of a house. Each worker, when the job is done, is rewarded knowing the part he has played. You have been greatly honored, for I have called you to be workers on the majestic house of the living God. I am the chief Cornerstone. The living stones that are placed within this glorious habitation are the lives of those whose hearts have been touched by the love and deeds wrought by my Spirit through my children, like you.

Therefore, my dear child, be steadfast, immovable, always abounding in my work, for your labor in my kingdom is not in vain. Do not be weary in well doing; in due season you shall reap if you do not give up.

Galatians 6:9-10 • 1 Corinthians 15:58 • 2 Peter 1:10-11

August 13 *Jesus Talks to You*

The apostles understood little of their high calling when I first bid them come. I was to build such great works in and through each of these men, that only the centuries to come would begin to reveal how glorious it was. As you use a pen to write a letter to a friend, I used the lives of these men to write upon millions of hearts the love I have for all.

You have me, the Christ—the hope of glory—living in you. You have the complete Word of God. I have a precious plan for you to bring my Word, love, and life to this world. I have works ordained for you to walk in—ordained since before the foundation of the world. Press on in your walk with me that you may apprehend that for which I have apprehended you. You are my workmanship—my poem. Will you be my pen, as well, that I might write my poem of love on the hearts of those who do not yet know me?

Philippians 3:12-14 • Ephesians 2:10 • 2 Corinthians 3:2-3

August 14

At times you feel that you do not have so very much to offer me in my work on earth. Good news; I have chosen to do great works through the ordinary, the weak, and the humble. It is truly all to my Father's glory when a meek and lowly person allows my light to shine through them. Gideon felt very insignificant, but I told him to go in the strength he had and to save Israel out of Midian's hand. You may not be called to save a nation, like Gideon, but I have a special calling on your life that will bring much glory to my Father in heaven if you will go in the strength that you have.

My grace will be abundantly provided as is needed. My power will be made perfect in your weakness. I see you as more than a conqueror. I saw Saul, the blasphemer and murderer, as Paul the apostle. I saw Moses, the murderer, as Moses the servant leader. I saw Gideon, the fearful thresher of wheat, as a mighty warrior. I am with you, victorious one, is what I say to you today. I will enrich you as you seek me through my Word, and I will prosper your work in my kingdom.

2 Corinthians 12:9-10 • Judges 6:12 • Romans 8:37

August 15

Jesus Talks to You

I know the sorrows of the world. I hear the cry of the fatherless and the widow. My heart is touched with the sorrows of the homeless and the abused. My compassion is toward every man, woman, or child who today sighs by reason of any affliction. I sent Moses to lead my people out of Egypt, their land of suffering, to a land flowing with milk and honey. Their journey was not easy, but my presence went with them.

The Father sent me into this world to bring healing, liberty, and love. A land flowing with milk and honey is promised to those who follow me. As my Father has sent me, so I send you. You are sent to bring the oil of joy to those who mourn. Help make the land of promise—abundant life now and heaven forever—a reality to others; share my everlasting love.

Exodus 3:7-12 • John 20:21

August 16

Jesus Talks to You

By a mighty hand and remarkable miracles, I delivered the children of Israel out of the bitter bondage of Egypt. I then told Moses where to encamp with the people. They would be facing annihilation when Pharaoh and his army would find them encamped at the Red Sea. I told Moses that I would gain great honor through what would soon occur.

Because of my plan, the people experienced the most heartrending and distressing trial possible. But it was designed for my grand purpose—that Egypt, Israel, and the whole world would learn of my mighty power and my ability to deliver. I parted the Red Sea for the children of Israel and great rejoicing soon was heard—millions of my people since then have offered praise for what they consider a most spectacular miracle.

Are you in the heart of trials that perhaps I have allowed or even designed and orchestrated—that I might manifest my love and deliverance to you and others? Please trust me and ask for wisdom to guide you. My ways are not your ways, nor is my timing your timing. Remember, I allowed Lazarus to die—I could have come sooner and healed him—that the incomparable glory of God might be known by raising Lararus from the dead. I will deliver you, and you will learn more of my love.

Exodus 14 • Isaiah 55:8-9 • Psalm 107:1-8

August 17

Jesus Talks to You

I know your every thought, sorrow, and concern. I deeply care for you, as no other on earth; welcome my comfort. The burdens you carry, I will take. I will guide you through any dilemma you face. You are my cherished child. Come rest in my love. I will strengthen your heart, and refresh you with my joy. I am a friend who is closer than a brother. Trust me—nothing is too hard for me.

Psalm 139:1-18 • Matthew 11:28

August 18 *Jesus Talks to You*

Solomon had built a magnificent temple to my honor. On the day of dedication, when Solomon finished praying, I sent fire down from heaven which consumed the burnt offering and sacrifices. My glory filled the temple. When the children of Israel saw the fire coming down and my glory above the temple, they worshiped and gave thanks for my mercy and goodness.

I am the living God. In my relationship with my people, I sometimes act in wondrous ways. I answered my people's love in their offering of the temple and themselves; the fire came down and my glory filled the temple.

2 Chronicles 7:1-3

August 19 *Jesus Talks to You*

When God's people have fully dedicated their hearts to me, I move in wondrous ways. On the day of Pentecost, my disciples were of one heart in my presence. From heaven, I sent a sound like a mighty rushing wind and what appeared to them as tongues of fire that separated and rested on each of them. All of them were filled with the Holy Spirit and were speaking in other tongues as my Spirit gave them utterance. The fire came down and my glory filled their temples.

These brothers and sisters of mine had fully given their hearts and lives to me. Through their love and sacrifice in the years ahead, millions of lives would be transformed eternally.

If you fully dedicate your heart and life to me, you will experience wondrous blessings. Ask to be continually filled with and led by my Spirit. Rivers of living water will flow from your innermost being. My divine power will give you every good thing that pertains to life and godliness.

Acts 2:1-4 • Acts 4:29-33 • John 7:38 • Acts 13:52 • 2 Peter 1:1-11

August 20 *Jesus Talks to You*

My spiritual house—which consists of all my beloved sons and daughters—is a holy temple that I live in by the Holy Spirit; it is deserving of having your fullest love and dedication as you help build it. I came to the weak, hurting, lowly, and despised. These mere stones dug from the earth have become my treasured gems of heaven. My love transformed their lives. When you allow me to reign in your heart and life, the miracle of love will flow from you, with power, to also change lives to the glory of God your Father.

Build up your brothers and sisters in the faith; they will be blessed by your encouragement. My house will be that much more glorious through your labor of love. Love one another, as I have loved you. By this love shall all men know that you are my disciples.

Ephesians 2:19-22 • 1 Peter 2:4-10 • Romans 15:1-7

August 21 *Jesus Talks to You*

You will flourish like a palm tree and grow like a cedar of Lebanon; you will flourish in the courts of your God. You are the planting of the Lord, and with roots deep in my Word you are strengthened by miracle nutrients. Your roots find a measureless supply of my living water, a secret channel flowing from me through your innermost being to bring fruit and life to the world.

Growth takes time. You must be patient for the fruit. Abide in me and welcome the Sun of Righteousness to be your source of light and life-giving energy. At times, I will prune your wild branches; you will produce better and more abundant fruit. Please welcome my pruning shears; your fruit will be sweet, abundant, and eternal. I will renew your youth, and you will bear fruit in due season even into your old age.

John 15:1-8 • Psalm 92:12-14 • Psalm 1:1-3 • Isaiah 40:29-31

August 22 *Jesus Talks to You*

The unbelievers around you think it very strange that you are not plunging headlong into self-indulgent sin as they do. You may suffer reproach and other persecution for your faith. Seek to glorify your Father in heaven in these special opportunities. Let me shine from your heart that others might see my love. Endure everything for the sake of the elect, as I did, that they too might obtain salvation that I freely give, with eternal glory. Do not be envious of the possessions or pleasures of the world. The riches that await you in my kingdom, and the pleasures at my right hand are worth enduring through all your trials during this short life; you shall enter my heavenly kingdom soon. All the pain and suffering will have been worth it. For you shall receive the crown of life and a glorious inheritance among the people of the living God.

1 Peter 4:12-14, 19 • 2 Timothy 2:3, 10 • James 1:12

August 23 *Jesus Talks to You*

I am the author and finisher of your faith. Be confident in this: the work that I began in you when you received me, I will continue until the day you enter my glory. I will guide you every step of the way. I know what you need to grow spiritually and will give you grace to receive it. The Holy Spirit will give life to your mortal body and transform you daily more into my image. A great work is happening in you; rejoice in the hope of the glory of your God.

You have this treasure, the Christ of God, in an earthen vessel to show that the excellency of the power is from me, your God, and not from yourself. Do not lose heart through all the tribulations that you endure for my sake; this light momentary affliction is achieving for you an eternal weight of glory beyond all your hopes and dreams. Therefore do not look at the things which can be seen with your human eyes, but at the things which are not seen. For the things which are seen are temporary, but the things which are unseen will last forever.

Philippians 1:6 • Romans 8:11 • Romans 5:1-5 • 2 Corinthians 4:16-18

August 24

Jesus Talks to You

I am God Almighty. I performed phenomenal miracles in delivering Israel out of the cruel bondage of Egypt. I also worked wonders daily as I cared for them on their wilderness trek. I led them by day with a pillar of a cloud, and by night I provided a pillar of fire for light. When the children of Israel had no water, I brought forth water from the rock. To satisfy their hunger, I sent manna from above for forty years.

I also performed extraordinary miracles when I walked the earth. I delivered you through my death and resurrection. Through my blood sacrifice, forgiveness for all sin is provided; you are now miraculously born again by my Spirit through your faith in me. On your journey home, I am providing for you richly. My Spirit gives you light for your path each day; like the pillar of a cloud, I lead you. I am the Rock that gives you living water. My Word is the bread of life. You will soon eat of the hidden manna and be led to living fountains of waters.

Psalm 105:1-4, 39-45 • Galatians 2:20 • Revelation 2:17; 7:17

August 25

Jesus Talks to You

Paul, my apostle, was once a blasphemer and persecutor of the church. My grace was abundantly poured out upon him. If Saul (Paul), the worst of sinners can be saved, then anyone can. In Paul, I am displaying a pattern for all who will believe. When I am received in the heart, a new life begins, and sins are fully forgiven. They are buried, as it were, at the bottom of the deepest ocean. You were stained like scarlet, but you have been made white as snow. I will remember your sins no more.

Let the pattern that I established with Paul be your guide. Be thankful for forgiveness, 100% righteousness, and possessing this treasure—the life of the Son of God—in your earthen vessel. Your words and deeds will show my grace and truth to all. Others like Saul (Paul) are waiting to see and hear of my love.

1 Timothy 1:12-17

August 26 *Jesus Talks to You*

When the curse is lifted off the earth and I reign, the knowledge of the glory of my kingdom will cover the earth as the waters cover the sea. There will be streams in the desert, and it will rejoice and blossom as a rose. Until that day, there will be a highway to walk on—the Highway of Holiness. Only the redeemed will walk there as they journey to Zion. The ransomed of God will enter Zion with singing; everlasting joy will be upon their heads. They will be filled with gladness and joy; sorrow and sighing will flee away.

The Highway of Holiness, though not paved with gold, is specially marked; my footsteps are clearly seen—to help you walk as I have walked. The lights of Zion can be seen in the distance as you progress on this road. Songs of joy can sometimes be heard from within Zion's gates, as you travel on this highway. When it dips into the valleys, and there is sorrow and fear, I will draw near and bring comfort and hope as I did for the two on the road to Emmaus.

Isaiah 11:9 • Isaiah 35:8-10

August 27 *Jesus Talks to You*

You are 100% righteous through faith in me. You are justified freely by my grace, through the redemption that came through my sacrificial death and atonement by the shedding of my blood. I died in your place, fulfilling any claims of laws you broke against God. God the Father is fully satisfied in my death, canceling any debt you owed. Being in me, the Christ, you have already suffered for any claim against you—having been crucified with me and died. As I arose by the glory of the Father, you also have risen in the newness of life. You are free; you are freely forgiven, freely justified, and freely given my gift of righteousness. There is therefore no condemnation for you. Every sin that you have ever committed is freely forgiven you through repentance and asking for forgiveness. My blood cleanses you from all sin.

Romans 3:22-26 • Galatians 2:20 • Romans 8:1-4 • 1 John 1:7-9

August 28 *Jesus Talks to You*

Having been despised and rejected by men, I know your pain when you are scorned or abandoned. I sailed the stormy seas and know well the fears that may course through your soul. As a man of sorrows while on earth, I was acquainted with grief; but I am also the Wonderful Counselor and Comforter.

When your suffering strikes, I am close by. I immediately came to the rescue of the man that had been excommunicated from the synagogue. I had just given this beggar, blind from birth, the glorious gift of sight. The man stood up for me and had been thrown out. When I begin a good work in you, trust in me, even when you are thrown out; I will come to you and bring you into an even better place. The man not only was healed of blindness, but he met me, the Messiah, and received my love—no longer spiritually blind, but now seeing the eternal as well.

John 9

August 29 *Jesus Talks to You*

About 500 years before the spikes were driven into my hands and feet, I spoke these words through the prophet Zechariah: They will look upon me, the one they have pierced, and they will mourn for him even as one would mourn for an only son. I knew before I created the world that I would die upon the cross for the sins of the world.

Zechariah's prophecy foretold of my crucifixion—as well as my return. John, in my Revelation to him, said that I am coming with the clouds, and every eye will see me, even those who pierced me; and all the peoples of the earth will mourn because of me. So shall it be. I am coming again. Every knee will bow and every tongue shall confess that I am the King of kings and Lord of lords. Millions will mourn because they did not receive me as their Savior. As a believer, my child, you have reason to rejoice greatly.

Zechariah 12:10 • Revelation 1:7

August 30

Jesus Talks to You

I have loved you with an everlasting love. With lovingkindness have I drawn you to myself. The love that I have toward you is exceedingly beyond any love that the world has ever known.

I dwell in eternity—yet I fully love you at this moment and always desire to share as much time together as you would like. I am excited about my love for you. There is so much about my love for you that you don't fully know or have not experienced yet. It will take the endless ages to unfold for you all the glories of my love and the mysteries of life itself.

You are special and unique. I love you just as you are. I created the entire universe, but each child that comes into the world is a priceless gem to me. As you get to know me, your Creator, you will understand how rich my love is for you.

Jeremiah 31:3 • Ephesians 1:1-23

August 31

Jesus Talks to You

I am always intimately caring for you. I saw you when you were in your mother's womb. I was there when you were born. I have been there every moment since—your first smile, first time crawling, those precious first words, your first time standing and walking.

I have watched, loved, and cared for you ever since you were born. My heart has always been warm toward you. I have seen and felt every tear. I have enjoyed your every joy. Trust me when I say to you that I love you with the richest love that you could ever imagine and exceedingly beyond that.

I love you with an infinite love. As the waves of the ocean are immeasurable, that is how wondrous my love is for you. Deeper than the deepest sea are the depths of my feelings of love and compassion toward you.

Psalm 139:1-18 • Isaiah 49:15-16

Jesus, the Messiah, Feeds the Multitude—*Matthew 14*

September 1 *Jesus Talks to You*

I am He who created the stars as well as all the intricate life forms of earth. When I make all things new, you will reign with me in the new heavens and new earth that I have prepared for you. It is not the stars or the intricate flowers of creation that I will cherish and rejoice with throughout eternity. It is you, with whom I will live, delight in, and celebrate with forever.

There are no words, in any language, that are able to express fully the glory and majesty that you will experience forever. The most gorgeous sunsets that you have ever witnessed, the most magnificent music you have ever heard, the most beautiful and fragrant floral displays your eyes have feasted upon, the majesty of earth's grandest mountain ranges, the wonders of the highest waterfalls, and the brilliant glories of a thousand galaxies all pale in comparison to the glory that you will experience—for all eternity!

1 Corinthians 2:9 • Revelation 22:1-5

September 2 *Jesus Talks to You*

David wrote Psalms while in the wilderness of Judah. He expressed the dryness and thirst that his soul had for his God. When he would enter my spiritual sanctuary, he would rejoice in the awesome blessing of having fellowship with me.

When you enter my pavilion, the holy place of prayer, you can behold my power and glory as you open your heart to me. You do this by meditating on my Word, its testimonies and miracles, rejoicing in my promises, and just sharing a time of loving fellowship with me, your God and Savior. My love is better than life. Whoever offers praise glorifies me. Your soul will be satisfied as with the richest of foods. Come into my sanctuary today; I am always glad to meet you there.

Psalm 63:2-5

September 3 *Jesus Talks to You*

Habakkuk, in facing the prospect of having the course of nature turn its forces against him, boldly proclaims that he would still rejoice in me, his God and Savior. Whether it be the enemy that might rise against you, or a drought or flood threatening to deliver a fatal blow, I am the God of all creation. I will direct you to the heights, that you might be saved and prosper. I hid Elijah by a brook, and ordered the ravens to feed him daily during an extended drought. I fed the five thousand with five loaves and two fish; I am able to supernaturally provide for you when everything points otherwise. I will provide for you with my heavenly provision as you have need. I am the Sovereign Lord; I will be your strength and provider.

Habakkuk 3:17-19 • Psalm 27:1-6 • Psalm 46:1-7

September 4 *Jesus Talks to You*

May the richest of praise flow from the hearts of all the faithful unto the God of life—like millions of streams joining as a delightful river proclaiming, "Glory to God." May it make glad the city of your God, where I, the Most High God dwells. Should it not be so? I have given you this spectacular creation. Every breath and heartbeat you have is a gift from above. Through me, you have been forgiven and redeemed. Through my everlasting love, you have exceeding great and precious promises and have been made partakers of my divine nature. I have lavished upon you rich blessings every day, and my personal love and care will preserve and guide you throughout all your days. I am able to keep you from stumbling and to present you faultless before my glorious presence without fault and with triumphant joy. Behold, what manner of love the Father has richly bestowed upon you, that you should be called a child of the living God. Beloved, it has not yet appeared to you what you shall be; but know this, when I shall appear, you shall be like me, for you shall see me as I am. By having this hope fixed on me, you purify yourself, even as I am pure.

Psalm 46:4 • Psalm 23 • Psalm 73:24 • 1 Jude 24-25 • 1 John 3:1-3

September 5 *Jesus Talks to You*

You cannot exhaust my love. For instance, a thirsty little sparrow comes to the edge of a very large lake. If it were fearful that its little drink might exhaust the supply of thirst-quenching waters, it need not be. Nor do you, my beloved one, need ever be doubtful of the infinite love that I have for you. It is boundless and immeasurable. A beautiful flower soaks up the warm rays of a summer sun. Might this delicate creation of mine exhaust the glorious power of the sun? No. The life-giving radiance of the blazing star that I created to bring life to earth cannot be weakened or drained by one flower—nor all the world's flowers or the billions of trees carpeting the planet.

Enjoy the radiance of my love which is infinitely more glorious and powerful than the sun. My love gives life and wholeness. Like a flower absorbs the rays, you may always bask in the warmth, the vitality, and fullness of my love. My love is limitless and never-ending.

And by the way, you are of much more value than a sparrow or a beautiful flower. As complex, intricate, or delicate a flower or sparrow may be, they exist but for a moment. You, on the other hand, are eternal.

September 6 *Jesus Talks to You*

I have called you to be an ambassador of my kingdom. You are a member of my royal family. Let your light so shine before others that they may see your good works and glorify your heavenly Father. As a servant of the living God, you have been entrusted with my Word. It has the power to give life to the hearers. Be bold in your faith; I am able to do mighty works through you.

Esther made herself available to serve my kingdom and I used her to change the course of history. Men and women, of like passions as you, stepped out on the faith that I gave them; I blessed their deeds and righteousness was wrought. I have ordained works for you to walk in—my power and love will guide you.

Esther 4:14 • Ephesians 2:10

September 7 *Jesus Talks to You*

Paul and Silas had been severely flogged and thrown into prison, their feet fastened in the stocks. With an attitude of love and worship, they sang praises to me—trusting that I would work all things to their good.

Sometimes I surprise my people with blessings, experiences, and deliverance; I did that for Paul and Silas. After a violent earthquake, prison doors flying open, and chains falling off, Paul and Silas shared my powerful Word; a whole family met me, the Savior of the world, and received eternal life. Attitude and commitment—Paul and Silas trusted and loved me with their whole heart. I honor those who honor me.

Acts 16:25-34 • Romans 8:28

September 8 *Jesus Talks to You*

A woman came with an alabaster box of very expensive perfume. She did a beautiful thing; she broke the jar and poured the perfume on my head—to prepare for my burial. Wherever the gospel has been shared in the world, what she has done has been told in memory of her.

She did what she could. Her greatest possession, very expensive perfume, was lavished on me, the Savior of the world. With a heart broken because of her many sins, she came to honor me, the One who would forgive them all and become her Savior. As the sweet fragrance of perfume being poured upon me filled the air, so did the aroma of my life-healing love. The woman had been forgiven much—she loved much.

Beloved child of mine, have I forgiven you of much? Do you love me much? You have a precious possession in a jar; you are the jar and your life and love are the most expensive of perfumes. The woman did what she could. Will you do what you can? Let your jar be broken and may your life offered to me be a sweet fragrance today and forever. I will always remember your love and rejoice with you forever.

Matthew 26:6-13 • 2 Corinthians 2:14-15 • Ephesians 5:2

September 9 *Jesus Talks to You*

Those who are wise will shine gloriously like the bright expanse of the heavens, and those who turn many people to righteousness, like the stars for ever and ever. When on earth, I spoke of seed, fish, pearls, wine, money, and fig trees in parables to teach important truths. A most glorious element of creation are the stars in the heavens above. If you allow my Word to dwell in you richly, wisdom shall be yours. You will shine like the brightness of the heavens.

Let my love emanate from your life in word in deed. As you do, hearts and lives will be won for me, the King of kings. Souls will be saved from death and a multitude of sins will be covered. I am reigning as the Sun of Righteousness forever. You also, as you turn many to my way, shall reign with me forever and shine like one of the stars above.

Daniel 12:3 • Matthew 13:43 • Proverbs 11:30

September 10 *Jesus Talks to You*

I redeemed you, not with corruptible things like silver or gold, but with my own blood. I have loved you with an everlasting love. I desire for you to be free from sin and the empty way of life this world offers.

As the author of life itself, I am preparing for you a new heavens and a new earth. I also desire that you might have an abundant and glorious entrance into my kingdom. This is the time to grow in my grace and the knowledge of your King and his kingdom. My divine power will give you everything you need for life and godliness.

As you look forward to the great day of your Lord, let my love reign in your heart and life. Be strong and courageous, for you will lead others to gain an inheritance in my glorious kingdom, as you love in my grace by the power of the Holy Spirit.

2 Peter 3:10-18 • 2 Peter 1:4-11

September 11 *Jesus Talks to You*

David, the shepherd, psalmist, and king knew me as his strength, rock, fortress, and deliverer. Early on, he learned of my power when I delivered him from a lion and a bear. Then there was the glorious victory over the giant Goliath, through David's faith in me. I also delivered David from the hand of King Saul and his other enemies.

As I led David from victory to victory, so will I do for you. There will be battles, trials, and tribulations. But be of good courage; I have overcome the world. I rule heaven and earth. At my command, Peter walked on the water. When he began to sink, he cried out, "Lord, save me." As I reached out my hand and rescued Peter, so shall I deliver you when you need me.

Psalm 18:1-3, 16, 19, 48-50 • John 16:33 • Matthew 14:26-33
Isaiah 43:1-2 • Isaiah 40:29-31

September 12 *Jesus Talks to You*

Since you have a great High Priest who has entered into heaven, hold firmly to the faith you profess. For you do not have a high priest who is unable to sympathize with your weaknesses, but one who has been tempted in all points, just as you are—yet was without sin. Come before my throne of grace boldly with confidence, so that you may receive mercy and find grace to help in your time of need. I will strengthen you by my Spirit. I am with you and will uphold you with my righteous right hand.

When you fall short and sin, and humbly repent, I will provide mercy and forgiveness. As the great High Priest, I came to earth and died in your place for your sin. Receive my forgiveness through my shed blood. I paid your debt so that you can have fellowship with me—freed from guilt. There is no condemnation to you who are in me, who do not walk according to the flesh, but according to the Spirit. For the law of the Spirit of life in me has set you totally free from the law of sin and death.

Hebrews 4:14-16 • Isaiah 41:10 • 1 John 1:9 • Romans 8:1-2

September 13

Jesus Talks to You

When there was no water for the people to drink, they quarreled with Moses. I told Moses to strike the rock at Horeb, for I would cause water to come out of it for the people to drink. He did and I provided water in abundance for all the people.

When faced with insurmountable problems, look to me, the great Shepherd—knowing that I have all authority in heaven and earth. Nothing is too hard for me. Trust in my caring hand; I will provide what you have need of, just when you need it.

The children of Israel drank from that spiritual Rock that accompanied them in the wilderness, and I was that Rock. They were not thankful and did not honor me. My child, be thankful to your heavenly Father, for I, the Rock, was struck for you, so that you could be saved and be able to continually drink of my living water—with ultimate satisfaction and delight all the days of your life, even forever.

Exodus 17:1-6 • Matthew 28:18 • 1 Corinthians 10:1-4 • Psalm 16:11

September 14

Jesus Talks to You

It is natural to become brokenhearted at times. Many of your acquaintances and those you love do not have faith in me, the King of kings, whom you love. You also may find yourself mourning because of your sins and failures. You are also burdened as you behold a wanton disregard for your King displayed in every area of society. I know well how you feel. When I lived on earth, my heart was often burdened with sorrow.

I am able to do much more than you can think or ask—I have the power to reach and save, with my love, those you are concerned about. I also will comfort you, as you share your tears with me. The day is coming soon when you shall enter the new world wherein dwells righteousness. I am the God of hope and want to renew your heart today.

Matthew 5:4 • Isaiah 61:1-3 • Ephesians 3:20 • 2 Peter 3:13 • Titus 2:13

September 15

Jesus Talks to You

Greatly rejoice in me, your God and King, for I have clothed you with the garments of salvation; I have covered you with the robe of righteousness, as a bridegroom is dressed for his wedding, and as a bride adorns herself with her jewels.

You have the gift of my righteousness—perfect, pure, and without any stain. You did not earn this precious gift, nor are you able to add to its perfection by any works of your own. Rest in my total acceptance of you—a gift through grace alone.

Isaiah 61:10 • Ephesians 2:4-10 • Revelation 19:7-9

September 16

Jesus Talks to You

The patriarchs (Jacob's sons), motivated by jealousy, sold Joseph into Egypt. He endured much anguish of heart because of family rejection and later false accusation; but I was with him, and rescued him out of all his afflictions. Though evil was intended against Joseph by his brothers, I meant it unto good. I gave him favor and wisdom in the presence of Pharaoh, king of Egypt—who made him ruler over Egypt and all his house.

The comfort I provide may seem elusive at traumatic times like the ones Joseph had to endure. Mixed emotions, doubts, and reasonings may run rampant. It is so important to trust me when you are rejected or persecuted. For out of this crucible of pain and trial shall come forth the gold that the world rarely beholds!

Joseph remained faithful to me. He was available for my purposes and maintained a heart of compassion. He became a source of comfort and life to many peoples. Therefore, be steadfast, trust in me, and patiently endure hardships. I will surely send relief and delivery—my rich blessings will come upon you.

Acts 7:9-10 • James 5:10-11 • Matthew 5:10-12 • 1 Peter 1:6-9

September 17 *Jesus Talks to You*

Rejoice that you participate in my sufferings, for you will be overjoyed with triumph when my glory is revealed. I am the God of hope and consolation. As you trust wholeheartedly in me, the author and perfecter of your faith, your heart receives great assurance and comfort.

In a sense, I was last in this world according to worldly standards: I had no place to lay my head, no bank account, automobile (chariot), or fancy wardrobe. I was a man of sorrows, who gave up all on my journey to the cross—that you might have my kingdom above. I became poor for your sake, that you might become rich through my poverty.

But though I was despised and rejected of men, my Father has highly exalted me above every name in heaven and earth. The Father, whose hand I held, truly fulfilled the hope that led me through suffering and the cross—immeasurable eternal glory and children as plenteous as the stars for all eternity. As the Father loved me, so he loves you! Trust him to bring you great consolation, reward, and joy on that day.

1 Peter 4:12-14 • 2 Corinthians 8:9 • Isaiah 53:3-6 • Philippians 2:5-11

September 18 *Jesus Talks to You*

You who overcome, I will make a pillar in my holy temple in the kingdom of heaven. I will write upon you the name of the living God and the name of the city of God, new Jerusalem; and I will also write upon you my new name. As you have yielded to my molding of your life, in that you have loved me and my people, so shall I exquisitely and uniquely sculpt you to fit most gloriously as a pillar in my temple. I will celebrate your walk of faith, honoring you forever in a place of strength. The years of labor and sorrow will be over. Never will you leave this glorious place of rest and comfort. Forever you shall reign in glory with me, the One who cut you out of the rock of this world and called you to be sculptured into a work of magnificence for my kingdom in heaven.

Revelation 3:12

September 19

Jesus Talks to You

Abraham did not waver through unbelief at my promise that he would be the father of many nations. He was strong in faith, gave me glory, and was fully persuaded that I had the power to do what I had promised.

Joshua, my servant, reminded the children of Israel that not one word has failed of all the good things that I had promised them. All had come to pass and not one of them had failed. You, my child, should live each day believing that I am able to fulfill all of my promises to you. You, who are a partaker of my divine nature and possessor of my very great promises—including that you will be a joint-heir with me of the kingdom of heaven—be not weak in faith, but rejoice in the hope of my glory which you will share. You have entrusted your heart and soul to me; I will be as faithful to you as I was to all the saints of old.

Romans 4:13-25 • Joshua 23:14

September 20

Jesus Talks to You

The words of your King are pure words, like silver refined in a furnace or like gold refined seven times. My Word provides so very much: a light in your darkness, a map that will lead you to your heavenly home, keys to exceedingly valuable treasures, comfort to your hurting heart, a portrait of your Savior, living water to refresh your thirsting soul, bread of life when you are hungry, and eternal salvation with pleasures forevermore in a world without end.

I am the Word of God, and I became a man, Jesus, that you might know me. You beheld my glory full of grace and truth. Let my Word dwell richly in your heart and be filled with thanksgiving always—I have done so much for you. Desire the sincere milk of my Word that you may grow up into the full experience of salvation. As you behold the glory of my Word, you are being transformed into my image from one degree of glory to another.

Psalm 12:6 • Psalm 119:103-105 • John 6:68 • John 1:1-4, 12-14
Colossians 3:16-17 • 2 Corinthians 3:18

September 21 *Jesus Talks to You*

About 700 years before I was born on earth, I spoke through Isaiah, the prophet, about my persecution and my reaction: I gave my back to those who beat me, and my cheeks to those who pulled out my beard; I hid not my face from mocking and spitting; for the Sovereign Lord helps me, I will not be ashamed; therefore have I set my face like a flint.

While on earth, I was accused of blasphemy, insanity, gluttony, breaking the Sabbath, being possessed with devils, and treason. This did not stop me. Isaiah's prophecy came to pass; I was mocked, spit upon, and beaten. This did not stop me. Knowing that I would be nailed to the cross by cruel Roman spikes and suffer excruciating pain on that black day of suffering did not stop me. I set my face like a flint and went on to love you!

For the joy of obtaining the prize in glory—that you and all of my children would reign forever with me—I endured the cross, despising and ignoring the shame. By the resurrection power and the wondrous mercy of God my Father, I now sit at the right hand of the throne of God with everlasting glory! Receive my grace each day that you might set your face like a flint and go on to love others. You too will obtain the prize in glory and reign forever with me, your King.

Isaiah 50:6-7 • Hebrews 12:2-4 • Romans 8:17-18

September 22 *Jesus Talks to You*

Arise my child and shine, for your light has come. The glory of the Lord is risen upon you. You, who once lived in darkness, have been transferred into my kingdom of light. You have been given the gift of my Spirit to teach you of this new life and give you the power to live it. I will open up your understanding of my Word. I will bring healing when you are broken in heart. I will also shine my light into hidden areas of your heart, revealing sins, so that you might be set free from them.

Isaiah 60:1 • 2 Corinthians 4:6-7 • Colossians 1:12-13 • Galatians 5:16-24

September 23 *Jesus Talks to You*

I am continuously, with deep devotion and delight, thinking about you. I desire that my plan for you, thought out before time began, might be embraced by you, and that you would fully and intimately experience my love. You will soon reign with me in my world with no end.

My world will give you the ultimate experiences that are far beyond the finite range of your five senses. In my presence is pleasure forever. All the pleasures of earth combined do not equal the bliss, euphoria, and ecstasy that you will be baptized with the very first moment that you enter my paradise. This you will experience forever and ever.

Jeremiah 29:11 • Psalm 40:5 • Psalm 16:11

September 24 *Jesus Talks to You*

Before you received me, by whom all things were created, you looked to man's wealth, wisdom, or power, for help in times of need. I am infinite in power and wisdom, and I promise to liberally supply your every need according to my riches in glory.

David knew that his help comes from the Lord, the Maker of heaven and earth. In Psalm 23, David speaks of me as his Shepherd. By trusting me fully, he knew that he would overflow with the blessings of the living God, and that goodness and mercy would follow him all the days of his life.

When you experience emotional suffering, troubled relationships, and trials in any form, call upon me, the Maker of heaven and earth. I am omniscient and omnipotent. Cast your cares upon me, for I care for you. Abide under the shadow of my wings until I answer by my love—in my chosen way and time. My Father, who did not spare me, his only begotten Son, but delivered me up for you, shall also provide you with every good thing that has to do with life and godliness.

Isaiah 40:28-29 • Psalm 23 • 1 Peter 5:7 • Romans 8:32

September 25 — *Jesus Talks to You*

John, in the Revelation, saw seven golden lampstands, with me standing among them. I had eyes like a blazing fire. My feet were like fine bronze, as if refined in a furnace, and my voice like the sound of rushing waters. My face was like the brilliance of the sun shining, and in my right hand I held seven stars. Out of my mouth came a sharp double-edged sword. The seven lampstands represent the seven churches. I stand in the midst of my church. Out of my mouth comes a sharp two-edged sword; this sword is the Word of God by which the very thoughts and purposes of the heart are revealed, analyzed, and judged. The seven stars are the angels that minister to my church.

I am the same yesterday, today, and forever. As I, the Sun of Righteousness, continued the work in each of the seven churches depicted in Revelation, so shall I continue the work that I have begun in your life, until the day you see me face to face in the glorious kingdom of heaven.

Revelation 1:11-20 • Philippians 1:6 • 1 Thessalonians 5:23-24

September 26 — *Jesus Talks to You*

I told Ananias to go to a man from Tarsus named Saul, who was praying. I told him that Saul was my chosen instrument to carry my name to the Gentiles, their kings, and the people of Israel. Ananias had concerns about murderous Saul at first, but I knew Saul's penitent heart; tears of a soul sorrowing over his sin are as diamonds to me.

I look on the heart. Man looks on the outward appearance. Do not lean to your own understanding in your service to me. Fully receive my Word, which teaches you to love, even as I loved. Let not a Saul slip through your hands out of fear or prejudging. Your Father welcomes home his lost sheep. Be willing to reach out and love the unlovely; Saul was absolutely in that class at one point. Ask me to continually fill you with my Spirit, and I will give you the love and boldness that you need.

Acts 9:11-22 • Romans 15:7

September 27 *Jesus Talks to You*

With each loud and terrible clang of the Romans spikes being driven into my hands and feet, a spike of anguish ripped into the heart of my mother, Mary, as she watched in horror. Just thirty-three years earlier, she had borne the child who would be called the Son of the Most High. She was the "possessor" of the hope of the world. The son she had loved so dearly, along with any hope or joy she had, was now cruelly being destroyed. Mary fully believed that my life and hers were finished.

After knowing that all things were now accomplished, and that I was about to die, I said, "It is finished," signifying my glorious work, as Savior of the world, was complete.

John 19:26-30

September 28 *Jesus Talks to You*

My agonies at Gethsemane were past. Torturous Golgotha was buried, and three days later the wondrous glory of God, my Father, broke through the darkness that covered the whole land; the hope in every heart that had been extinguished was raised from the dead! The Sun of Righteousness broke the chains of death to shine most brilliantly and bring healing to every anguished heart!

Be encouraged, dear child, though heartbreak and tears may have been your companions lately. My heart is certainly moved with compassion toward you; for I have heard you when you cry and have seen your tears. As it was for Mary, my mother, and all the others who loved me, the night of sorrow will soon pass for you as well. The stone will be rolled away just after sunrise—Sonrise. Welcome the magnificent Light of the world to ignite your heart and soul anew.

Mark 16:2-6 • Romans 8:11 • 1 Peter 1:3

September 29 *Jesus Talks to You*

The angel told my followers that Jesus of Nazareth, whom they were seeking, was crucified. He added that he has risen; he is not here, but go, tell his disciples *and Peter*. Peter, the bold fisherman had declared allegiance to me, the Son of God, saying he would be willing to die for me. But shortly after, he denied me three times. Hours after he had wept bitterly for his failing, the echoes of the rooster's crows still haunted him. The angel sent these comforting words, "Go tell his disciples and Peter." The disciples had fled in the garden and needed to hear the glorious news, that he who was crucified is now risen! All of your sins and death itself have been conquered! Everything is OK! But I was moved by the broken heart of Peter and had the angel make a special mention of him. Soon Peter's heart would be mended, for I, the One with the nail-pierced hands, would wrap my arms around Peter and say, "I love you!"

Have you failed me in times past (all have)? Do you sometimes still hear the rooster crowing? I desire to reassure you today, as I did Peter, that all is OK. Receive my forgiveness and love. This is why I died. I am risen! I have gone on before you to my kingdom; I am preparing a place for you, and will soon welcome you with open arms of love.

Mark 16:6-7 • 1 John 1:9 • Psalm 103:10-14

September 30 *Jesus Talks to You*

I have given unto you very great and precious promises. From Genesis through Revelation, my promises shine as the stars in the night sky. I have been faithful. I made a great nation of Abraham, as promised. I brought them (Israel) to the land of milk and honey, as promised. I performed what I told David—that I would be born from his seed. I have blessed you with abundant life, as promised. I promise to give you eternal life in my paradise, and you shall be like me. I promise to wipe away all tears; I promise that there shall be no more pain or death.

2 Peter 1:1-4 • Titus 1:2 • Revelation 21: 1-7

Jesus with the Teachers—*Luke 2*

October 1

Jesus Talks to You

You may wonder about my personal care for you. With billions of people on earth, you at times may feel insignificant. How can God care for and listen to everyone on the planet at the same time? My answer is simple; I can and I do just that. I can totally be with you and give you my full attention, as if there was no one else in the world. That is how much I love you. I can listen to you, care for, and comfort you more devotedly that anyone on earth. Believe me. I passionately care for you, and I would love to enjoy more time together.

I inhabit eternity—but I always have time for you. I promise. I will be a friend whose love will bring healing to your heart. There are many hurts that you have experienced. There are sorrows so deep down in your soul. Many have failed you. I saw every time that happened to you. I felt any abusive words or actions anyone ever expressed to you. It hurts, I know. As you come closer to me and spend time with me, my Spirit will bring true healing to your soul—and help you to forgive others fully from the heart. I am here to hold you close and guide you on my path daily.

Isaiah 57:15 • Isaiah 61:1-3

October 2

Jesus Talks to You

I know your every thought that you have ever had or will have on your journey through life on earth. I know your every action and word for your entire life even before you were born. Hard to believe? Yet it is true. I am the Most High God, who inhabits eternity. Besides me, there is no other. As Creator of the universe, I have all power in heaven and earth. I possess all knowledge of every creature that inhabits heaven and earth. I am not bound by time or any limitation of my creation.

My heart is intimately devoted to and deeply cherishes you. My love is as deep as my omniscience is wide and as immeasurable as the stars in the heavens. I will care for you with an everlasting love!

Psalm 103:1-5, 8-17

October 3 *Jesus Talks to You*

Since you have been raised into the newness of life with me, the Christ, set your heart on heavenly things above, where I am seated at the right hand of God the Father. I have established a new covenant with you; do not hesitate to fully enter your land of promise—abundant life now and heaven forever. Enter my presence, and enjoy a friendship whose joy outshines all the false glimmers of this world. Taste and see that I am good. I will withhold nothing good from those who walk in my ways.

When you were born again, new passions and desires were set in motion. Welcome me this day to lead you, by my Spirit, into a deeper fellowship with me. I will meet you in a very fulfilling way. You will be abundantly satisfied with the fullness of my house; I welcome you to drink from the river of my delights.

Colossians 3:1-17 • Psalm 36:7-10

October 4 *Jesus Talks to You*

I will be your Shepherd now and forever. You shall soon be with me in heaven. I will lead you to springs of living water. I will wipe all tears from your eyes. Never again will you hunger; never again will you thirst. The scorching heat of the sun will no longer beat down upon you. The remembrance of sin shall flee away. All of your trials will soon be over. All things will be made new.

You have died to your old life; your new life is hidden in me. When I appear, then shall you also appear with me in glory. If you knew you were to inherit millions of dollars soon, you would probably rejoice. There is reason for true celebration today; for you are a joint-heir with me, the Son of the living God, soon to inherit the glorious kingdom above—worth vastly more than all the riches of the entire world. I am the great Shepherd of the sheep, and I will meet you and lead you from glory to glory through the countless ages of eternity.

Revelation 7:15-17 • Colossians 3:1-4 • Romans 8:17

October 5

Jesus Talks to You

I love you exceedingly. Today, I will shower you with grace, and give you eternal encouragement and good hope. Let the Holy Spirit comfort your heart and strengthen you in all of your works and words. Your fellowship is truly with the Father and me, Jesus, personally. Very few people can boast of knowing a king or a president. You personally know me, the King of kings—every ruler of earth throughout the history of mankind will bow before me on the great day of the Lord. Yet I am a friend who sticks closer than a brother; I desire to have a rich friendship with you every day.

The immeasurable love that the Father has to you led me to the cross, and also showed itself in the resurrection. I took all of your sins upon myself when I died on the cross. But I also conquered death three days later to give you complete assurance of eternal life.

2 Thessalonians 2:16,17

October 6

Jesus Talks to You

The prophet Isaiah said that I would not falter or be discouraged until I established justice on the earth. My passion was to reach the lost—I was determined to love. My Father sent me to bring truth and abundant life. The Holy Spirit was given to me without limit. I went forth confidently fulfilling the mighty works that my Father had ordained for me before the foundation of the world.

Receive my abundant grace today. Be encouraged. Go forth with confidence as my Spirit guides you. He will do notable works through you, for I am living in you. The communication of your faith by your words and works will transform lives as you acknowledge every good thing which is in you through me, Christ Jesus—who lives in you.

Isaiah 42:4 • Romans 15:13 • Psalm 90:16-17 • Philemon 1:6

October 7 *Jesus Talks to You*

I came into the world to comfort those that mourn, to give unto them a crown of beauty instead of ashes, the oil of gladness instead of sorrow, and the garment of praise to replace a spirit of despair. They would be called oaks of righteousness, my planting of love, that I might be glorified. I turned the water into wine, made blind eyes see, deaf ears to hear, and raised the dead to life again; I am more than able to transform your heart.

As a man of sorrows, I have been well acquainted with grief. Yet I am the Wonderful Counselor. Continue to pour out your heart to me. For as the night changes to the dawn, so shall your beauty, joy, and praise return unto you. You are my tree of glory. Why are you cast down, dear child? Hope in me, for you shall yet be filled with praise, for I who created the heavens and the earth will greatly help you.

Luke 4:14-21 • Isaiah 61:1-3 • Psalm 43:4-5

October 8 *Jesus Talks to You*

David desired that he might dwell in my house all the days of his life, to gaze upon my beauty, and to inquire in my temple. I fulfilled all of these desires. It all began among the hills of Bethlehem, where a young shepherd boy was learning deep lessons from me, the great Shepherd. I became the Rock that David would stand upon during his forty-year reign as king. David would be as a tree planted by streams of water yielding much fruit through the seasons of his life. He prospered greatly as a psalmist, warrior, and ruler.

Trials and tribulations were a constant companion to David. But he knew the wondrous secret of living; walk daily with the great Shepherd, who guides in the paths of righteousness, restores the soul, and anoints with the overflowing blessings from above. If you seek me, as David did, surely goodness and mercy will follow you all the days of your life.

Psalms 27:4 • Psalm 1:1-3 • Psalm 23

October 9

Jesus Talks to You

David offered the richest praise to me, rejoicing in my awesome power, glory, and majesty—acknowledging that everything in heaven and earth is mine. The people of Israel had just offered generously and abundantly to provide for building a temple to glorify the Holy name of the Lord God; gold, silver, bronze, iron, and precious stones were plentifully provided.

You have been transferred from the kingdom of darkness into my kingdom of light, have been made co-heirs with me, and have been promised the glories of life eternal to be enjoyed in a new incorruptible body. Offer unto me your talents, resources, and your whole being; your heavenly Father is building a magnificent temple that he will dwell in through the Holy Spirit. You are being built upon the foundation of the apostles and the prophets; I am the chief Cornerstone. Your health, wealth, gifts, and your life itself all come from me. Store your treasures in heaven; you will rejoice eternally for the love you freely give my people and my kingdom. Bountiful is your reward on the day of glory.

1 Chronicles 29:6-16 • Ephesians 2:19-22 • Matthew 6:19-21

October 10

Jesus Talks to You

You who have sown in tears will reap with songs of joy. I am the God of compassion and mercy. I will never forget your labor of love that you have shown toward my name. You have gone out at times weeping while you sowed in the field. You will doubtless come again rejoicing, carrying bountiful sheaves. Let my Word dwell richly in you and continue to sow the seed (my Word) in the field. My Word will not return empty but it will accomplish what I desire. My heart will rejoice and be warmed, as broken lives are made whole, and many of my loved ones are saved. So do not cast off your confidence; it will be amply rewarded. You need to patiently endure, so that after you have done my will, you will receive what I have promised.

Psalm 126:5-6 • Hebrews 10:35-36 • Galatians 6:8-10

October 11 *Jesus Talks to You*

Look to me and my strength; seek my face always. Remember the wonders and miracles that I have done. Daniel pleaded for mercy from me, the God of heaven, and I revealed the mystery of a king's dream. Lives were changed, and the history of the world was revealed through his prayer time with me. Peter went up on a roof to pray. While he was seeking me, I gave him a vision that helped open the gospel to the whole world and not just the Jew—another prayer time changes the world. With much weeping and prayer, Hannah entered a solemn vow to me. Samuel, a great prophet to Israel and its kings, was born to Hannah.

I honored the prayers of Hannah, Daniel, and Peter, and I also will honor yours, as you seek me with your whole heart. Come boldly into the joy and blessing of prayer time in the Holy Spirit. Enter into my holy presence and have an inspiring and refreshing time with me each day.

1 Chronicles 16:8-12 • Daniel 2:18-23 • John 15:7

October 12 *Jesus Talks to You*

Elijah, a man of prayer, possessed boldness that equaled the great challenges he faced. The people of Israel and hundreds of false prophets gathered in a tense showdown; the God who would answer by fire and burn the sacrifice would be declared and recognized as the true God. The prophets of Baal had already failed. Then fire, sent by my hand, fell and burned up the sacrifice, the wood, the stones, the soil, and also licked up the water in the trench. All the people saw this and fell down and cried, "The Lord—he is the true God! The Lord—he is the only God!"

Elijah was human just like you; he had the same kind of trials, frailties, and temptations. Yet, he took on a wicked king, and through Elijah's earnest prayers, I held back the rain for three and a half years as a testimony of my power. He prayed again, and I sent the rains, and the earth produced its crops. I look throughout the whole earth to be strong on behalf of those whose hearts are fully committed to me.

1 Kings 18:36-39 • James 5:13-18

October 13

Jesus Talks to You

My desire for all of my sons and daughters is that you have the same attitude of mind toward one another that I had—that harmony would prevail among you. You share the same calling of giving your lives to follow me, the Son of the Almighty God. You share the same glorious hope of being changed into incorruptible bodies and reigning with me in the splendor of paradise forever. You share the same heritage of the treasured men and women of faith who have honored me through the centuries. You share the same family that will soon be gathered on the other shore for the everlasting celebration. You share the same Holy Spirit given to empower you to do my will in boldness and joy. Since you are one in me, Christ Jesus, the Messiah, then with one heart and mouth glorify your Father in heaven for these many blessings. Like a magnificent orchestra may you all, in most wondrous harmony, offer praise to the God of all creation, who is worthy of all praise!

Romans 15:1-7

October 14

Jesus Talks to You

Therefore receive one another, just as I have also received you to the glory of God the Father. Pray for your brothers and sisters. Consider others in my orchestra (my sons and daughters)—encouraging them in their quest to be their best. I will honor your love and care for each other, and I will certainly work mightily among you.

As an instrument of righteousness in my orchestra, allow my Spirit to tune you and work through you. For those whom I foreknew, I have predestined to be transformed and conformed day by day into my image—that I might be the firstborn among many brothers and sisters. Continue in my Word; my Spirit will guide you into all truth, that you may be complete in me, and equipped for every good work—fulfilling your unique part in my orchestra with my glory and blessings upon you.

Romans 15:1-7 • Romans12:16 • 2 Corinthians 3:18 • Romans 8:29

October 15

Jesus Talks to You

The mountains may be shaken and removed, yet my steadfast love for you will not depart nor shall my covenant of peace be removed from you—for I am the Lord who has great mercy upon you. I am the God of all comfort. My heart is moved with compassion when you are in the valley of despair. I desire to hold your hand as I lead you from the valley to the heights.

When the waves of trial are coming over the side of your boat, call upon me and trust me fully; I will calm the storms with my Word, in my perfect timing. Cast your cares upon me, for I care deeply for you. I am your refuge and your strength.

The Father sent me into the world to bind up the brokenhearted, to set the captives free, and to comfort all who mourn. I will replace mourning with the oil of gladness. I will clothe you when you despair, with the garment of praise. I love you with an everlasting love. No power can stand in the way of or change the perfect love that I have toward you.

Isaiah 54:10-17 • Psalm 46:1-5 • Jeremiah 31:3

October 16

Jesus Talks to You

Upon seeing a glorious vision of me seated upon my throne, Isaiah heard my call asking, "Whom shall I send and who will go for us?" I am still on the throne and desire for you to fulfill my call in your life. I desire to enter into a richer relationship with you.

Ask of me and I will give you a new heart of compassion and boldness to share my love, within the calling or vocation that I have called you to. You have been chosen to help build up my glorious kingdom. As my Father has sent me, so I now send you. Receive my love and power for your calling. The Holy Spirit will surely comfort and guide you to do my will.

Isaiah 6:1-8 • John 20:21

October 17

Jesus Talks to You

I gave Israel all the land that I had sworn to give unto their ancestors; the Israelites possessed it and settled there. I also gave them rest on every side; I delivered them from all their enemies. Not one of all my promises to the house of Israel failed; every one was fulfilled. As you fight the good fight of faith, I will be fulfilling many of my promises. I conquered your dreaded enemies, sin and death; I shall also vanquish every foe you face as you go forth to inherit your land of promise—abundant and eternal life. If I am for you, nothing can be against you.

I will fulfill every promise I have made, and will soon return to bring you into the glorious kingdom of heaven above. I will transform your lowly body to be fashioned like my glorious body, by the same wondrous power that raised me from the dead. As you walk with me, be patient as you wait for my promises to be fulfilled. I am God, and will do immeasurably more than you can think or ask; I have wonderful plans for you.

Joshua 21:43-45 • Romans 8:31-32 • Philippians 3:20-21

October 18

Jesus Talks to You

Be of good courage, and I will strengthen you by my Spirit as I fulfill my purposes in your life—in my perfect timing. As high as the stars are above the earth, so much higher are my ways above your ways. I am Alpha and Omega, and know the beginning and the end. You need patience, as you wait for me to teach and guide you. Be not hasty to go your own way. When circumstances seem contrary to you, remember that I am working all things together for your good, according to my eternal purposes. This will be difficult to believe at times, but trust me fully, and I will honor your faith and work wondrously on your behalf. I will strengthen you when in distress. I will shine my light to help you walk my path. I will be a shelter from the storm. As you wait upon me, I will renew your strength; you shall mount up with wings as eagles; you shall run, and not be weary; you shall walk, and not faint.

Psalm 27:13-14 • Isaiah 55:8-9 • Romans 11:33-36 • Isaiah 40:31

October 19 *Jesus Talks to You*

I sent Samuel, the prophet, to the house of Jesse to anoint one of his sons as the king of Israel. When Samuel looked on the appearance of one son, he thought that surely this was the Lord's anointed. I told him that I do not look at the things that man looks at. Man looks upon the outward appearance, but I look upon the heart. I chose out the youngest of the eight sons of Jesse, David, who was tending the sheep. From that day forward I placed my Spirit upon David powerfully.

You may consider yourself ordinary, and not having valuable gifts to offer to me. But as I blessed David with a special ministry, I will also guide you to fulfill a unique calling. It is not by your ability or power, but by my Spirit. I will give you gifts and my anointing to fulfill my purpose in your life. While on earth, I transformed ordinary men to be sons of God with love and power; I am more than willing to bestow my Spirit and power upon you. Do not limit me by looking at your own outward appearance or natural abilities. If you have a humble and willing heart, I will live through you and bring much glory to my kingdom.

1 Samuel 16:1-13 • Zechariah 4:6 • Ephesians 2:10 • Hebrews 13:20-21

October 20 *Jesus Talks to You*

I am the Mighty God of Israel, who parted the Red Sea for my people, that they might escape their enemy. As the children of Israel reached safety, I closed the Red Sea upon the Egyptian army. Years later, I cut off the waters of the Jordan for my people to enter the Promised Land.

Be strong in faith, my child. I shall cause you to go over on dry ground when an ocean of impossibility lies before you, and the enemy is hot on your heels. And I am very able to cause the enemy to be seen no more. I am able to suspend the very laws of nature as you press on to inherit my promises to you. As I stopped the Jordan, so shall I work mightily on your behalf, as I accompany you into the land of milk and honey.

Isaiah 43:1-2

October 21 *Jesus Talks to You*

When on earth, I went up on a mountainside and shared the wisdom of heaven through the Beatitudes; the comfort they brought enriched the souls of those who gathered unto me—and has for two thousand years to all who hear them. That day on the mountain was a shadow of the glorious fulfillment of a prophecy I gave through Micah, which is yet to come to pass. I spoke of the last days when the mountain of my temple will be established; many nations will desire to go up to this mountain to learn my ways, so that they may walk in my paths. The days are coming, when swords will be beaten into plowshares; spiritually hungry hearts from nations worldwide will stream to my mountain to be fed with the finest of wheat and drink of the milk of my Word.

How much more glorious it will be when all the saved from every nation, people, and tribe stream to the celestial Mount Zion above and into my heavenly city, new Jerusalem. The glory, honor, and majesty of my kingdom will abundantly fill heaven and bless my eternal family.

Micah 4:1-3

October 22 *Jesus Talks to You*

Having begun with the Spirit, do not now try to attain your goal by human effort. My perfect righteousness has been imparted to you. Good works can justify no one; you are saved by grace. You are justified (no more guilt, no more penalty for sin) through my work at Calvary—my blood was shed for you. To say that obeying certain laws or performing good works makes one more righteous would pollute my holy work. I have made you holy and have given you my perfect righteousness.

Likewise, no human effort could bring you to heaven itself. Only my resurrection power can raise the dead and bring you home. So it is with being righteous. It is wholly my miracle in you; having been washed from your sins and now are born again, you have been made partakers of my divine nature. Rest in my finished work on the cross.

Galatians 3 • John 3:16 • Romans 5:1-2 • Ephesians 2:1-10

October 23 *Jesus Talks to You*

My unfailing love is priceless. Feast on the abundance of my house and drink from the river of my delights. I freely give you the fountain of life. Since the beginning of creation, only my perfect love has brought true fulfillment to man. The lust of the flesh, the lust of the eyes, and the pride of life have competed for man's allegiance since the paradise of Eden. As all the rivers of the world flow into the sea yet the sea is never full, so man fills himself with his varied lusts and yet is never truly complete. Blessed are those who hunger and thirst for righteousness, for they will be filled.

Many squander their wealth and their very life in their futile search for satisfaction. How ironic; that which can bring perfect love, comfort, joy, and contentment in this world—as well as eternal pleasures in the world to come—cannot be purchased for all the treasures on earth; it is free. Allow me to lead you to the green pastures and still waters—I completely satisfy.

Psalm 36:7-9 • 1 John 3:1-3 • Psalm 16:11

October 24 *Jesus Talks to You*

I am the bridge that spans the gulf between earth and heaven. The bridge is paved with the gold of my forgiveness; all believers may travel upon it and cross over into my kingdom. The sign across the gate of the bridge says in blood red, "I will remember their sins no more." As far as the east is from the west, that's how far I have removed your sins from you. I have blotted out your transgressions. They are gone, as though cast to the bottom of the sea. If you have lingering guilt in your heart, know that I am much greater than your heart. I desire for you to enjoy the same peace that I enjoyed on earth. Receive my full forgiveness; accept the freedom from guilt that comes with it. I want you to be free. That is why I came to earth. Believe what the sign on the gate of the bridge says; it will bring healing to your heart and freedom from guilt.

Psalm 103:10-14 • John 3:16 • 1 John 4:9-10 • Hebrews 10:16-20

October 25 *Jesus Talks to You*

My dear child, I am doing a wondrous work in your life. Do not look at your inabilities, but look to my abilities. I am able to do exceedingly beyond what you could ask or even imagine, for I have all authority in heaven and earth. I split the Red Sea, brought water from the rock, raised the dead, gave sight to the blind, and conquered death itself. Nothing is too hard for me. All things are possible to the one who even has a mustard seed of faith. So be strong in me and the power of my might. Do not worry, but cast your cares on me—for I richly care for you. Let thanksgiving and trust fill your heart and mind. I will guide you today and forever with my perfect counsel and my everlasting love.

October 26 *Jesus Talks to You*

It is done. I am the Alpha and the Omega, the Beginning and the End. Whoever is thirsty, I will give to drink without cost from the river of life, which is in the midst of paradise, where I dwell. A most glorious and eternal new heavens and new earth awaits you and all of my treasured family. I will live with you all and be your God. No longer will there be death, pain, or sorrow—for the former order of things has passed away; I am making everything new. Beloved child, soon you shall be rejoicing in the glorious new kingdom. After a twinkling of an eye, clothed in your incorruptible body, you will reign with me, the King of kings, forever.

When you are discouraged, and when earthly circumstances seem to be clouding your vision of the eternal, embrace these truths I have just shared. They will give you hope in the midst of your trials and temptations. Call out to me, and I will give you power and grace by the Holy Spirit. Give your heart to me and I will give you the help you need. My power is made perfect in your weakness. I will transform you day by day into my image. It's hard to see the changes that I am making, but it is happening. Your life is truly hidden in me. When I appear, then shall you also appear in glory with me.

Revelation 21:1-7 • Colossians 3:1-4

October 27

Jesus Talks to You

It is not by your own power or wisdom that my purposes are accomplished in your life and in my kingdom. Oftentimes, I allow humbling in my children before exalting and multiplying them. I, who make streams in the desert, will gloriously bring my rich blessings upon you—in my own chosen way and in my perfect timing.

Peter denied me three times during the weakest and most humbling time of his life. Immersed in and enabled by my Holy Spirit on the day of Pentecost, he then preached in boldness and power, and saw thousands come into my kingdom. This supernatural power, anointing, and wisdom came from above, and not at all from Peter.

Ask of me and I will give you the full blessing of the Holy Spirit's power and anointing; I will work through you, and I will speak through you.

Zechariah 4:6 • 2 Chronicles 32:7-8 • James 1:2-4, 12, 17

October 28

Jesus Talks to You

Joseph, robbed of his family and sold into slavery through the evils of his brothers, was further reduced and humbled through false accusation and imprisonment while in Egypt. I exalted and richly blessed my beloved child Joseph; I made him second in command in Egypt, and many lives were saved by my good hand upon him.

Job was riding high in life, but I allowed Satan to strike him, reducing him by taking away his family and possessions. He was also humbled with a loathsome disease. He did not understand much during his severe trial of faith; but he knew, that when this furnace of affliction would run its course, his God would bring him forth like gold. I did just that—I abundantly blessed him. I healed him, restored his goods and flocks abundantly, and he saw his children to the fourth generation. Job, by my merciful blessing, learned much of my truth, mercy, and love.

James 5:10-11 • James 2:5 • 1 Peter 1:3-9 • Job 23:8-10 • Job 42:10-17

October 29 *Jesus Talks to You*

I had been working in Gideon's life. At a time when he was humbled by circumstances, I chose him to be the deliverer of my people, Israel. I then reduced his army to such a small group, that it was humanly impossible to defeat the enemy. But, I gave him wisdom and counsel from heaven. I exalted him and multiplied my blessing upon him through a miraculous victory that brought glory to the God who loved his people. Behold this testimony of my power. Know that in your most dire straits, when you call on me, I will reach down and lift you out of deep waters (like I did for Peter on the Lake of Gennesaret), bringing you deliverance, my richest of blessings, and glory to my name.

Judges 7:2,7 • Psalm 109:26-27 • Matthew 14:22-33

October 30 *Jesus Talks to You*

Moses was raised with the riches and glory of ancient Egypt. After being humbled to the simple life of a shepherd for forty years, I chose him to be the deliverer of my people Israel—who had been suffering in bondage for generations. By this meek shepherd, I worked mighty miracles never before seen on earth, to bring freedom to my people, and set them on their way to the land that I promised their ancestors.

Saul (Paul), proud, blasphemous, and murderous, was humbled when I, the risen Savior, spoke to him from heaven. Paul was transformed into a faithful ambassador for my kingdom. He suffered greatly during his ministry and was often humbled. But his life was hidden in me; when I would appear in glory, he would then experience abundant glory.

I rule the nations and the lives of every soul. Trust me to call and transform those you are praying for. I am able to do immeasurably more than you can imagine in their lives—and in yours. I love you with an everlasting love and will fulfill my glorious plans for you.

1 Peter 5:10-11 • Colossians 3:1-4 • 2 Peter 1:11 • Revelation 3:21

Arrival of the Good Samaritan at the Inn—*Luke 10*

October 31 *Jesus Talks to You*

I am your God for ever and ever; I will be your guide even to the end. I am the great Shepherd and laid down my very life for my sheep. I saved you and washed away your sins by my blood sacrifice. My sheep hear my voice. Come close to me today and always; I will talk to you, bringing you comfort and guidance. I know where the green pastures and the refreshing streams are. I will protect and care for you in so many ways.

The children of Israel, while in the wilderness, had the cloud to guide them. When it moved, they were to travel. But you have a personal relationship with me. You need to share time with me daily in prayer and in my Word. If you are being led by my Holy Spirit, you are walking in your land of promise—abundant life now and heaven forever. You will be victorious, more than a conqueror, and eat the good of the land.

I was your God when you were born. I was your God when you were born again. I will be your God to the end of this creation and beyond. For through the endless ages of eternity, I will guide you by everlasting love. The glory, joy, and peace we will share together will be inexhaustible and immeasurable!

Psalm 48:14 • Psalm 23 • Psalm 73:24 • Ephesians 2:6-7

November 1 *Jesus Talks to You*

I am your God, the mighty King of creation. I will strengthen you and help you always; I will uphold you with my right hand of righteousness. I gave up my life for the sheep. I suffered reproach, intense sorrow, excruciating pain, and death, that you might be able to enter green pastures forever. I conquered death so that you would never have to die. I rose from the grave, dusted myself off, and with arms once again stretched wide said, "I love you so much." Come unto me and I will give you rest. My love is much stronger than death. I will strengthen you when you need help. I desire to care for all of your needs. When you are too weary to go on, I will carry you in my arms so very close to my heart.

Isaiah 41:10 • Revelation 7:17

November 2

Jesus Talks to You

For over three years, my disciples beheld the majesty of the God of creation, while I was clothed as a man. They watched me, the great Physician, loving unconditionally and bringing wondrous healing to the diseased and sinner. Their eyes feasted on the glory of the Lord as I fed the five thousand with five loaves of bread. The apostles in training feasted on the bread of heaven as I shared my Word, which is spirit and life. They learned how to be servants when they beheld me washing their feet. They learned how to die, for they experienced new life being imparted to them through my sacrificial death.

Through my Word, and the mighty working of the Holy Spirit, you have obtained the same precious faith as my early disciples. Through the wonderful gift of the Spirit, you have the faith of the Son of God. You have Christ in you, the hope of glory. As I ordained and sent my disciples, each with special ministries, I now send you—with a very unique calling. I have works for you to fulfill, ordained since before the world began. Let me reign in your life. All things are possible to you; ask and you shall receive.

2 Peter 1:1-11

November 3

Jesus Talks to You

Whenever two or three are gathered in my name, I am there among them. I rejoice in the fellowship of my people. Everything you think, say, and do is open to my knowledge. The right word spoken at the right time is like apples of gold in settings of silver. I greatly honor those who place their hearts and lives in me, and seek to minister grace to the hearers. You have been given the gift of my love and my Word; I will honor the love and kindness you show others. I am writing a book of remembrance all about it. Your life is hidden with me. When I appear, then shall you also appear with me in glory. Your loving words and works will be rewarded; you truly are my treasured child.

Matthew 18:20 • Malachi 3:16-17 • Proverbs 25:11 • Colossians 3:1-4

November 4

Jesus Talks to You

Miraculous signs and healings accompanied Philip in Samaria as he proclaimed my Word there. There was great joy throughout that city. I sent an angel to Philip, and told him to go south into the desert on the road that goes down from Jerusalem to Gaza. A man was returning to Ethiopia from Jerusalem. My Spirit told Philip to go over to his chariot. He ran there and heard him reading from the prophet Isaiah—at the exact moment that the passages were about me, the Messiah. The door was opened to share the great news of salvation and the man was gloriously saved—he went on his way rejoicing.

Through Philip's obedience, salvation was imparted to the Ethiopian. I am Alpha and Omega, and I see all from the beginning of creation throughout eternity. I know what is best for you and for my kingdom. Whether I guide you by my Word, my Holy Spirit, or an angel, purpose in your heart to fulfill my will without hesitation. Entrust all of your large and small decisions to my guidance; throughout eternity, you'll be glad you did.

Acts 8:5-8, 26-40

November 5

Jesus Talks to You

Build yourself up in your most holy faith and pray in the Holy Spirit. Live in my love as you wait for my mercy to unfold to you eternal life—the indescribable gift you have received. As a member of my royal family, you are called to walk by faith and to love as I have loved. I have the transforming power to impart faith and love to your heart. As Moses' face shone after being on Mt. Sinai in my glorious presence, and as the early disciples lives shined with my glory and power, so will your life radiate with the blessings and strength of your King. The disciples, day after day, beheld my mighty works, absorbed my Word, and experienced my great love. Come into my presence, seek me in my Word; my Father and I will manifest ourselves to you. You will be richly blessed in all your ways.

Jude 1:20-21 • John 14:21-23

November 6

Jesus Talks to You

More fragrant than ten thousand roses, more beautiful than the most glorious of sunsets, more awesome than a thousand shooting stars, more spectacular than the highest mountain ranges, more heavenly than the sound of a magnificent choir of angels, and more delightful than the first day of creation is my love that I have for you.

Follow me, my highly treasured child, and live a life of love, just as I have loved you and gave myself up for you—a fragrant offering and sacrifice to God the Father. With a heart as humble and believing as a child, ask and allow me to come into your life in a rich new way. I will do wondrous things in you. My everlasting love will warm your heart and shine to those in your life. My peace that surpasses all understanding will prevail when you are faced with troubles and trials. My joy will be your strength. I will guide you with my counsel and after you have done my will, I will receive you into glory. How awesome that glory will be!

Ephesians 5:1-2 • Romans 12:1 • Psalm 73:24-26

November 7

Jesus Talks to You

After my ascension, my disciples were praying one day. I shook the place where they were meeting, and they were all filled with the Holy Spirit and spoke my Word boldly; the apostles did wonders and miraculous signs. These believers were devoted to the teaching of my Word; and they rejoiced together as they met daily for fellowship, prayer, and worship. All the believers were of one heart and shared with one another whatever was needed. My grace and love was richly in evidence among them; this fellowship was glorious. These brothers and sisters of mine were witnesses of my crucifixion, resurrection, and ascension; they were excited about my return. My eyes look throughout the earth for those whose heart is fully devoted to me, that I might be strong on their behalf. Seek me wholeheartedly so that you might receive all that I have for you, and you will touch the world around you in wonderful ways.

Acts 4:29-33

November 8 *Jesus Talks to You*

Ten men, suffering terribly with the dreaded disease of leprosy, stood at a distance calling to me in a loud voice, "Jesus, Master, have mercy on us!" Ten men, in varying stages of their flesh decaying, knew they were doomed to die a horrible death! They pleaded with me—the only one in the universe that had the power to heal them. Just as I had compassionately healed the multitudes of all manner of disease, I cured these men as well. As they went their way, their flesh was soft and new; they were given a complete new lease on life.

Without me, the Messiah, you were eternally doomed. You, like the ten, have cried out to me, the great Physician. You begged forgiveness for your sins, which were corrupting and decaying your life, like the lepers. You are now perfectly whole—born again by the Holy Spirit; all things have been made new. Like the one healed leper—who returned and threw himself at my feet and thanked me profusely from the heart—come close to me in thanksgiving for the everlasting love that I have for you, and for the awesome miracle of eternal life (more wondrous than being healed of leprosy), which I have blessed you with.

Luke 17:12-19 • Psalm 107:19-22

November 9 *Jesus Talks to You*

It was a glorious time of fellowship with Peter, James, and John on the day that I took them with me on the Mount of Transfiguration. They heard my Father speak of his love for me, and they encountered me enrobed with a garment of glory. I desire for you to come with me at times to a "mount of fellowship and transformation" for you. It's a holy place where you will "see and hear" of my wondrous love and power. Come up from the "valley of trial and turmoil". Cast your cares upon me. Open your heart and mouth and offer praise, which I inhabit and am enthroned on. I will talk to you and transform you by the Holy Spirit—encouragement, strength, hope, and love will fill your soul.

Matthew 17:1-8 • 2 Corinthians 3:18 • Romans 15:13 • Romans 8:29-32

November 10 *Jesus Talks to You*

I gave a glorious revelation to John. He saw the new heavens and the new earth, and the holy city, new Jerusalem, coming down out of heaven. He heard a loud voice from my throne saying that the dwelling of God is with men, and that God will live with them.

It is so easy to become focused on the world around you. Events described daily in the media and circumstances of your personal life tend to draw your mind and anxieties to your temporal dwelling. But soon, I will shake the heavens, the earth, and all nations. I will remove what can be shaken (created things), so that what cannot be shaken may remain. I am the Creator of all things, the eternal God. Look to me, the author and finisher of your faith. Since you are receiving a kingdom that cannot be shaken, be filled with thanksgiving and rejoice—my eternal kingdom is real. I am the hope of the world, and I shall return soon.

Revelation 21:1-3 • Colossians 3:1-17 • Hebrews 12:28-29

November 11 *Jesus Talks to You*

David often traveled through the deep valleys; the valley of the shadow of death is often lonely and dark. But my love and presence reaches deeper than the deepest valley. Place your hope in me and allow me to guide you at these times. I will answer your cries, and I will send forth my light and truth to guide you to my holy mountain—to the place where I dwell. You will then be filled with thanksgiving, for I am your Savior and your God.

When the sorrows of death compass you, when troubles and pains come upon you, do as David often did; he called upon the name of the Lord. Do what Peter did when he began to sink while walking on the waves; he cried out, "Lord, save me." After I deliver you, then will your song echo the sweet chords of David's harp and song—"Be at rest once more, O my soul, for the Lord God has been so very good to you."

Psalm 23 • Psalm 42:11 • Matthew 14:24-33 • Psalm 116:1-9

November 12

Jesus Talks to You

Most would consider it a unique and valued honor to be friends with a king, famous artist, prominent physician, well-loved religious leader, extremely wealthy tycoon, world-renowned musician, or a Nobel Prize winning diplomat. I am all of these and incomparably more. As King of kings, I have power over the nations since time began and will reign as Ruler of all forever. As artist, I daily paint a thousand glorious sunsets for mankind to enjoy. As the great Physician, I healed thousands of every disease, including death (I am also a broken-heart specialist). Hundreds of millions have worshiped me as the only true Head of the church; I am the eternal great High Priest. As far as riches, I created and own all the gold, silver, and precious gems on earth. I created music; wait till you hear what awaits you in my kingdom above. As Ambassador of heaven, I have won over millions, who through my blood covenant have received citizenship to my Father's kingdom. As the Prince of Peace, I have brought peace that passes understanding to millions.

You who love me will be loved by my Father, and I also will love you and manifest myself to you—I will be a friend that is closer than a brother.

John 14:21 • Philippians 2:9-11 • Isaiah 57:15

November 13

Jesus Talks to You

Paul considered everything a loss compared to the surpassing greatness of knowing me, his Lord. He also considered the sufferings of this present time not worthy to be compared with the glory that would be revealed in him. As you give your heart more and more to me, a transformation occurs; though you are going through fiery trials and sufferings for my sake, my Spirit is actually changing your inner self to be more and more to be in my likeness. You are gaining me, the Christ, though you may be losing your old life. Follow me to the end, and you will know the power of my resurrection. I will raise you up in glory, and you will reign with me and enjoy the riches of my love and grace forever!

Philippians 3:7-14 • Romans 8:14-18

November 14

Jesus Talks to You

I love you in a most wondrous way. I knew everything about you before you were born—all you would ever think, say, or do. I loved you then, and I will love you forever. I treasure you so much that I came into this world as a man, that you might know me; I died for you—shedding my blood—that you might have forgiveness of all your sins; and I gave you the assurance of eternal life through my resurrection from the dead.

You are a priceless jewel of my heart. I desire for you to get to know me in a very rich way. I will talk to you daily, as you take time to listen. I cherish you and desire to comfort your heart, give you hope, and guide you on my path of life.

Psalm 139:1-18, 23-24

November 15

Jesus Talks to You

Fear and discouragement will come into your life at times; it did even for my prophet Elijah. On one such day, I captured his attention when I sent a mighty wind that tore the mountains apart and shattered the rocks; I was not in the wind. I then sent an earthquake; I was not in the earthquake. Then came a fire; I was not in the fire. After the fire, I spoke in a still small voice—giving him guidance and encouragement.

Beloved child, I am reigning gloriously from Mt. Zion throughout eternity, but with the deepest compassion will I walk close to you when you are in the "valley of the shadow of death". When you cry out, I will hear you; I will deliver you from your troubles. I am close to you when you are brokenhearted and crushed in spirit. Quiet your heart before me; allow my Word to bring you comfort. Listen to my still small voice; let me remind you of my special promises to you. Remember, I am the hope of glory and live in you—that is how close I am to you. I love you and will never leave you or forsake you. I will take your hand and walk with you every day on earth, until the very moment that you enter glory.

1 Kings 19:1-13 • Psalm 34:15-19 • Psalm 32:5-8

November 16 — *Jesus Talks to You*

I am a sun and shield. I bestow favor and honor; no good thing will I withhold from those who walk with integrity. As vital as the sun is for all life on earth physically, so am I needed for all life spiritually. I am the Sun of Righteousness, and I will continually guide you with my light and truth. I commanded the light to shine out of darkness and have shined in your heart, to give you the light of the knowledge of the glory of God as found in me. This light and my perfect righteousness now reside in your heart by faith.

My rays of blessing will favor you who trust in me; abundant life with everlasting fruit will be yours. My Spirit will guide you continually, guard you from evil, and preserve you blameless until the day you are presented before my glorious presence with unspeakable joy.

Psalm 84:11 • 2 Corinthians 4:6-7 • Jude 1:24-25

November 17 — *Jesus Talks to You*

No temptation has seized you except what is common to humanity. I am faithful; I will not allow you be tempted beyond what you can bear. When you are tempted, I will provide a way out so that you can endure it. I am the pioneer of your faith. I was led by the Spirit into the wilderness to be tempted by the devil for forty days; I overcame. I am the author of your salvation, as well as the finisher of your daily struggles against temptation and sin. I was in all points tempted as you are, yet I never sinned. I will give you the wisdom and power to overcome.

Be filled and led by my Spirit, and you will not fulfill the lust of the flesh. In the days of my flesh, I offered up prayers with tears at times. Wholeheartedly seek me in your times of temptation. Remember, you are dead to your old life, crucified with me, yet raised in the newness of life by the glory of the Father. I live in you, and will make all grace to abound to you and will provide you my strength.

1 Corinthians 10:13 • Galatians 2:20 • Galatians 5:16-25

November 18 *Jesus Talks to You*

When the windstorm arose and the waves beat into the ship—so that it was almost swamped—my disciples woke me and asked if I cared that they were perishing. It is very easy to be moved by the winds of circumstance. I created man so that he is weak in relation to the elements of this world. The waves of persecution, sickness, and contrary events can be very overwhelming to your fragile heart and mind. And how ready are some of my children to believe that I do not care or even that I am against them.

The disciples on the Sea of Galilee were greatly amazed when I calmed the storm. When the waves are breaking over your life and you are nearly swamped, look to me, your Savior. I not only command the winds and the sea, but every circumstance and element in all creation. Deliverance and comfort are always close at hand when you walk with me.

Naomi, in her time of sorrow and trial felt that the Almighty was against her. Naomi was not able to see that I was soon to renew her life and sustain her. I would give Ruth, her daughter-in-law, and Naomi, a very honored place in my kingdom. David the king, and me, the Messiah, would be born in Ruth and Boaz's (Ruth's husband) ancestral line.

Mark 4:36-41 • Psalm 107:21-31

November 19 *Jesus Talks to You*

By faith you may come any time into my presence, where there is fullness of joy, comfort, and assurance of love. You are seated together with me in heavenly places. Live today under the shadow of the Almighty. Incline your heart to my Word of comfort, and allow my Spirit to guide you into green pastures and beside still waters. I always welcome you to come into my sanctuary. I will protect you from the enemy and restore your soul. I am truly your refuge and your fortress; trust fully in me. I rejoice to spend time with you in sweet fellowship.

Psalm 91:1-16 • Ephesians 2:6-7 • Hebrews 4:16

November 20 *Jesus Talks to You*

Life will be distressing and perplexing. Brokenheartedness and tears will be your lot at times. You will also suffer persecution as you live a godly life in me, Christ Jesus. When you are overwhelmed with sorrow or confusion regarding a relationship, come to me. I have submitted my heart to feel the pain of my children; I was a man of sorrows and fully understand your heartache. Welcome me to comfort you.

In the midst of your suffering, it may not be clear how I can work this pain for your good, but I promise that I will. Trust me with your heart and soul. Do not give up or despair. I have all power over heaven and earth. I have allowed these circumstances, that you might grow in faith as I do my mighty will; have patience, I will work on your behalf, and you will receive my rich blessing. Let my love rule your heart, actions, and words. You honor me and others when you do.

Philippians 1:29 • 2 Timothy 2:7-12 • Romans 8:28 • Romans 5:3-5

November 21 *Jesus Talks to You*

At times you will suffer emotional grief in your relationships. Sometimes your deepest pain is felt as you pursue deeper bonds with family or friends. This apparent paradox does afford much hope though; you have the golden opportunity to allow me and my love to be more fully formed within you. You can change; you can grow in love!

Banish all bitterness, wrath, resentment, quarreling, and slander from your life. Be kind and compassionate to others, forgiving others, just as I have forgiven you. Bitterness, rage, and similar emotions never help nurture better relationships. Why be a slave to these emotions? Humble yourself and ask me to forgive you for any sin that is hurting your relationships; I will forgive you and transform your heart. Yielding to my Spirit, you will find that loving is more rewarding. Loving will bring healing to your relationships. Honor your family, your friends, and me; allow my love to warm the world around you.

Ephesians 4:31-32 • 1 John 1:7-9

November 22 *Jesus Talks to You*

Give praise to your Father and rejoice greatly in me, your King. Offer thanks for all my spiritual blessings from above. I forgive all your sins and heal your diseases. I have redeemed your life from the pit, and I have crowned you with everlasting love and mercy. I satisfy you with good things so that your youth is renewed like the eagle's. I have blessed you with all spiritual blessings in heavenly places. My thoughts toward you each day are innumerable, and as a cascading waterfall I continually pour my blessings out upon you.

As far as the east is from the west, that is how far I have removed your sins from you. I took you up out of the pit from which there was no escape, and have gloriously brought you into my everlasting kingdom. I have clothed you with my perfect righteousness, a gift you could never earn. I have miraculously given you a new heart of love and compassion; my Holy Spirit imparts to you the power to walk in the newness of life—the same power that raised me from the dead.

Psalm 103:1-5 • Ephesians 1:3-14

November 23 *Jesus Talks to You*

My Father who did not spare me, his own Son, but gave me up for you, will he not also graciously give you all things that relate to life and godliness? He will. You are so precious to my Father, that he sacrificed me to win your heart and soul forever. As freely as he gave you forgiveness and eternal life through me, he shall surely provide all your needs by my riches in glory. You have been given magnificent and precious promises by my Word; I will fulfill them all. I called you and justified you, and I will soon glorify you. Then you will inherit all things and reign with us forever.

Our joy and love toward you is infinite, and our heart is warmed with your thanksgiving—we inhabit and are enthroned in your praise.

Romans 8:32 • Ephesians 5:20

November 24 *Jesus Talks to You*

I, the Lord your God am infinite in wisdom and might, yet I enjoy living with you and in you. I actually rejoice over you with gladness. I desire for you and me to rest in our love together. I exult over you with singing. Let your heart be quieted, and you will hear the joyful song of my love to you. Blessed are you that know the joyful sound.

Let your heart sing of your love to me, the God who created you. I take pleasure in you, and I will crown you with my grace and glory. Rejoice in me, for I have saved you gloriously from sin and death—from a miry pit that you could never climb out of. I have set you upon a rock, established your goings, and have put a new song in your mouth. Sing your song, for others will hear it and see what I have done for you; great shall be the blessings you bring them, as they trust in me for their salvation.

Many are the wonderful works that I have done for you and in you; if you were to proclaim and share them, they are more than can be numbered.

Zephaniah 3:17 • Psalm 149:1-5 • Psalm 40:1-5

November 25 *Jesus Talks to You*

You have been chosen and called; I have loved you with an infinite love. You are kept by my perfect care. I will give peace, mercy and every rich blessing to you, as you abide in me. As you abide in my love, I will keep you and guard you, for I am the great Shepherd. You are an eternally loved and cherished lamb; trust in me, I will shield you from the enemy.

I am rich in mercy and will always give you freely of my compassion and forgiveness. I am the Prince of Peace, and I will fill you with the peace that passes understanding. I am the God of love, and I will cause you to overflow with the love that passes knowledge.

Jude 1:1-2 • Ephesians 2:4-10 • Philippians 4:6-7 • Ephesians 3:14-21

November 26 *Jesus Talks to You*

Do not be anxious about anything, but in everything, by prayer and supplication, with thanksgiving, present your requests to the Father in my name. And my peace, which surpasses all understanding, will guard your heart and your mind as you abide in me, Jesus, the Messiah.

The elements of this world, the forces of the enemy, and your frail, doubting human nature all work against my desire of true peace for your heart and mind. It doesn't take much to cause one of my children to worry and fret. I treasure you and listen to your every prayer and know your every need. I promise to provide for you out of my infinite riches in glory. Bring to remembrance how I fed the five thousand and healed the multitudes of every disease. I even paid the debt for all your sins, when I died on the cross; I conquered death once and for all, and have given you the greatest gift—eternal life. I will provide and will do abundantly above all that you can think or ask. Do you desire the peace that passes understanding? Cast your cares upon me; I deeply care for you.

Philippians 4:6-7, 19 • 1 Peter 5:7

November 27 *Jesus Talks to You*

The fruit of the Holy Spirit is love, joy, peace, patience, kindness, goodness, faithfulness, gentleness, and self-control. These were richly manifested in me, the Son of God, when I walked on earth. My human nature, though tempted just like any man, never won a battle against me.

Your sinful nature desires what is contrary to the Holy Spirit. The Spirit desires to lead you from victory to victory in this area. Your sinful nature has been crucified on the cross with me. I now live in you, and you can do all things through me, and the Spirit who dwells in you. When you are tempted, call on me to strengthen you. Seek my Word and my promises. Give your whole heart to me, and I will lead you by my Spirit. The fruit of the Spirit will abound more and more in your life.

Galatians 5:22-25 • Galatians 2:20 • Philippians 4:13

November 28

Jesus Talks to You

I am the one who created you, O Jacob, the one who formed you, O Israel. Fear not, for I have redeemed you. I have called you by name; you are my treasure. When you pass through the waters, I will be with you, and when you pass through the rivers, you will not be overwhelmed. When you walk through the fire, the flames will not burn you. For I am the Lord your God, the Holy One of Israel, your Savior.

I knew you before time began. From the day you were conceived in the womb until the day you received me as Savior, I loved you. I loved you when you were Jacob (supplanter). But I redeemed you through my blood sacrifice, and a new life is now formed in you. You are now Israel (one who has prevailed and has power, as a prince, with God). I know you, I love you, and I have called you by name. I have a wonderful plan for your life. Through the trials by water and fire, I will be with you. By my Spirit's help, you will overcome and endure to the end; everlasting glory in my kingdom of heaven will be yours.

Isaiah 43:1-3

November 29

Jesus Talks to You

Since you have flesh and blood, I too shared in your humanity, so that by my death I would destroy the devil who holds the power of death, and free you who were held in slavery by your fear of death. Death, with its terrible sting, has hovered over every man, woman, and child. As the Lamb of God, I allowed myself to take the full onslaught of this massive sting. I died! But three days later, I arose in the newness of life! I am the resurrection and the life. The sting of death had been vanquished. The power of the grave had been nullified. You are more than a conqueror with me living in you! Remember, to be absent from the body means to be present with me. Death? As soon as your eyes close in death in your perishable body, you will open them in my kingdom of glory—rejoicing in a new incorruptible body forever with me and the heavenly family.

Hebrews 2:14-15 • 2 Timothy 1:10 • Isaiah 25:8-9

Prodigal Son Returns and is Embraced by His Father—*Luke 15*

November 30 *Jesus Talks to You*

From my first day in a wooden manger to my last day on a wooden cross, I was to fulfill my Father's foreordained plan. I was born to die! I would bear my cross unto death, so that all of man's sins would be washed away through my blood sacrifice. I came to earth as a servant; I fulfilled your needs. But it led me through a cross of extreme suffering and cost me my very life. But as the suffering abounded, so did my Father's glory and honor that was bestowed upon me abound—throughout all eternity it exceedingly surpasses the suffering I had to endure. For the wondrous joy that was set before me, I endured the cross. For you and all of my children are my eternal crown of joy on that day of glory.

If you desire to be my disciple, you must deny yourself and take up your cross and follow me. For if you want to save your life, you will lose it, but if you lose your life for my sake, you will certainly find it.

Matthew 16:24-25 • Romans 8:17-18

December 1 *Jesus Talks to You*

Do not be ashamed of the testimony of your salvation and life that is in me, Jesus, the Messiah. I have saved you and called you to a holy life, not because of anything you have done, but because of my own purpose and grace, planned for you since before the beginning of time. When you suffer for my sake and the gospel, I will give you the grace and strength to continue on. I am the Savior, who has destroyed death and has brought life and immortality to you who believe.

Paul suffered much in his service to me. He denied himself daily and picked up the cross that I gave him. Yet my grace was exceedingly abundant in Paul's life. He was a vessel of my love and was used as my pen to write much of my Word. You can be assured of this: for all eternity Paul is rejoicing in the joy, honor, and glory of my kingdom—absolutely knowing it was worth having picked up the cross, even as I taught him.

2 Timothy 1:8-10 • Romans 5:1-5 • 1 Peter 5:10-11

December 2 *Jesus Talks to You*

You are of infinite value to me. I have called you to be a treasured member of my holy kingdom—a priest of the living God, offering spiritual sacrifices that will glorify your Father in heaven. I will refine and purify you like gold and silver. I came to baptize you with the Holy Spirit and with fire. I will consume the dross of self through my fiery refining process. You will be changed from glory to glory into my image. You will never be made perfect (in the flesh) while here on earth, but over time, you will be amazed at the changes that I have wrought in your life.

I am actually honoring you when I allow you to go through a fiery trial; I trust that you will be faithful as I bring you through the refining process. Rejoice by faith, though the flames rise about you; though your outward self is perishing, the inward self is being renewed to be more in my likeness. I am the hope of glory who lives in you.

Malachi 3:3 • James 1:2-12 • 1 Peter 1:7-9

December 3 *Jesus Talks to You*

You are the light of the world. I have chosen you and all of my brothers and sisters on earth to be like a city that is set on top of a hill. Let your light so shine that the world may see your good works and give praise to your Father in heaven. The early disciples richly experienced my working with them. Empowered by my Holy Spirit, they preached the Word with boldness, and I performed many miraculous signs by their hand—many thousands became members of my eternal family through them.

I am the same today as I was two thousand years ago. Through the power of the Holy Spirit, I will anoint you to fulfill my calling in your life. I will pour forth rivers of living water to a thirsty world through you. Through your work and by your words, let those around you know that I am the Way, the Truth, and the Life. Let my light shine brightly from your life—that those in darkness might live.

Matthew 5:14-16

December 4 *Jesus Talks to You*

I take pleasure in those who honor me, in those who put their hope in my steadfast love. I will crown the humble with victory and fill their heart with joy from above. My delight in you is deeper than the deepest ocean and higher than the highest mountains. As the stars are so high above the earth, so high is my care for and joy in you. My thoughts toward you are more in number than the sand by the sea. I am now preparing a place for you in my heavenly kingdom, and I rejoice as you allow me to prepare you for this place.

In all of my creation what I value most is my relationship with my children and their love one to another. You shall be mine in the day when I make up my treasured possession. I will have compassion on you, just as my Father had mercy and compassion on me when I walked the earth and served him.

Psalm 147:11 • Malachi 3:16-17

December 5 *Jesus Talks to You*

You are a member of my body, and you are members one of another. Picture a most precious, priceless, and glorious gem. As the light shines upon it, the many facets each sparkle their distinctive gleam and particular color of the rainbow. I am this gem of glory, treasured eternally by my Father—each of my children are as facets in the gem. You are that much a part of me! I am in you and you are in me. As a facet of this glorious gem, the only thing between you and your brother or sister (another facet) is me, Jesus, the gem of glory. Rejoice that you are found so richly and intimately in me and partakers with one another. Seek to be polished and washed with the Word. Judge not your brother but seek to bring glory to the gem in your relationships with one another; strengthen and polish your brethren, that they may best represent the gem. May the world see the love and wonders of this gem of glory, as they view you, your words, and deeds. Let my love shine through you.

Ephesians 5:30 • Ephesians 4:1-16 • 1 Corinthians 12:12

December 6

Jesus Talks to You

You are my beloved child now, but what you will be has not yet been made known to you; now you see indistinctly, but soon you will see with perfect clarity. Now you know imperfectly; soon you shall know perfectly, even as I fully know you. When I appear, you shall be like me, for you shall see me as I am; while you possess this hope in me, you purify yourself, even as I am pure.

In the twinkling of an eye, you shall be changed from corruptible into incorruptible; when I appear, you shall appear with me in glory. Creation itself proclaims my love and wondrous plan for you. A seed is planted and awakens to the rain and sunshine; it is changed into a bush filled with beautiful roses. A caterpillar is asleep, wrapped in its cocoon; the metamorphosis occurs and behold, a majestic butterfly.

You shall not die, but live and arise in a new image. All things will be made new. You shall know no sin, death, crying, or pain. Look up for your redemption is drawing near. I am coming soon.

1 John 3:1-3 • 1 Corinthians 13:12 • 1 Corinthians 15:42-58

December 7

Jesus Talks to You

I spoke the universe into existence; it is held together by my Word. I know every star by name. I knew the rise and fall of all the kingdoms of man even before Creation—and I have all power over everything on earth and in heaven. My immeasurable love for you and mankind parallels my infinite power; I died for your sins on the cross and conquered death.

Multitudes in heaven will proclaim that my deeds are great and marvelous, and my ways are just and true. They wonder who will not fear me and bring glory to my name. All nations will come and worship before me. My glory is infinite, and my love for you is unfathomable, my beloved one. I will command my blessings of love upon you richly.

Revelation 15:2-4 • Philippians 2:6-11

December 8 *Jesus Talks to You*

If you believe, you will see the glory of God. Shortly after I said this to Martha, I raised Lazarus, her brother, from the dead. Even four days in the grave cannot stop my power from bringing life to the dead. I am the resurrection and the life; whoever believes in me, though he were dead, yet shall he live.

You believe in me and you too will see the glory of God; you are soon to behold my heavenly kingdom and the holy city, new Jerusalem. But even while on earth, you will see my glory—experiencing the glorious transforming power of the Holy Spirit as you abide in me. Where there once was hate, love will reign; indifference and discouragement will flee as caring and hope flourish in their place.

You will see the glory of God as you go forth in the power of my might. I have promised that you will do the same works that I did. Do not be faithless like those at Lazarus' tomb. Rejoice in the hope of the glory of God. You will see the glory of God as you share my precious and powerful Word with those that are spiritually dead around you. Be bold! My Word never comes back void. You can turn many to righteousness; my Father in heaven will be glorified!

John 11:25-26, 39-45 • John 14:12-21

December 9 *Jesus Talks to You*

Job knew that his Redeemer lives, and would stand upon the earth in the end. Job knew that he would see his Redeemer (me) face to face. This strong confidence of Job in the resurrection was echoed through the centuries by the faithful such as Moses, David, Isaiah, and Paul. I redeemed you from the clutches of death, and have given you the assurance of this victory by rising from the dead. I continue to live not only in heaven, but also within your heart. When my everlasting kingdom is ushered in with glory, you will see your Redeemer face to face.

Job 19:25-27 • 1 John 4:1-3

December 10 *Jesus Talks to You*

Wise Solomon said that whatever you set your hand to, do it with all your might, for there is neither work, planning, or wisdom in the grave. Your life is but a vapor; appearing for a short time, it then vanishes. Your life will soon be past; only what you have done in me, the Christ, will last. You are my workmanship, born again by my Spirit and created in me for good works, which I have ordained for you to walk in—according to my own purpose and grace, given to you before time began.

Yield to my Holy Spirit's leading in your life; as the master builder, I will establish you as a special part of my spiritual building. Kingdoms come and go, but you that do the will of God will abide forever. Moses asked me to teach him to number his days that he might gain a heart of wisdom. He desired that my works be shown to him, that my favor and blessing might rest upon him, and that I would establish the work of his hands; dear child, this I will also do for you.

Ecclesiastes 9:10 • Ephesians 2:10 • 2 Timothy 1:9 • Psalm 90:12, 16-17

December 11 *Jesus Talks to You*

As naturally as sweet songs of the birds rise to the Father each day, as fragrant as the scent of millions of splendorous flowers ascending heavenward, as glorious a proclamation that a rainbow makes of the Father's faithfulness and beauty; so should you offer praise and thanksgiving for his magnificent love to you. With a humble heart and thanksgiving, make your requests known to the Father, expecting him to provide all of your need by his glorious riches in me, Christ Jesus.

Allow my peace to rule in your heart. Let my Word dwell in you richly, teaching and admonishing others in all wisdom, through psalms and songs inspired by my Spirit, with gratitude in your heart to your Father in heaven.

Ephesians 5:19-20 • Philippians 4:6-7 • Colossians 3:15-17, 23-24

December 12 *Jesus Talks to You*

I raise the poor from the dust and lift the needy from the trash heap; I seat them with princes and have them inherit the throne of glory. I created the earth by my spoken Word. I formed man from the dust of the ground, breathing the breath of life into him. Thus the natural man was created. Through my Word, my death and blood sacrifice, and the resurrection power of the Holy Spirit, a new and glorious creation has been conceived—you. Once you were a natural creation, now you are a spiritual one; born again from above. Now you are daily being conformed to my image—the Son of the living God. I am preparing you to reign with me forever. You, who were raised up from the dust, lifted from the miry clay of sin, will soon inherit a throne of honor in my everlasting kingdom!

1 Samuel 2:8 • 1 Peter 1:2-5 • Revelation 21:7

December 13 *Jesus Talks to You*

Beloved child, my love for you is infinite; it will take the endless ages of eternity to reveal the depth of my love for you. Today, please receive the full assurance of my everlasting love. You are greatly treasured—though the world has often taught you otherwise. I care for you so deeply; I desire to be involved in your everyday decisions. Seek me first and yield to my Spirit's leading—my written Word will help you do just that—and I will be strong on your behalf. Though you will need to endure trials of various kinds, trust me through them. I am with you, living in you, and I will surely rain down my blessings upon you in due season. I will open doors for you that no man can close. Your joy, peace, and love of life will be wondrously increased as you allow me to reign in your heart and life. The same resurrection power that raised me from the dead is now working in you; I will transform and fashion anew your lowly body to be conformed to the likeness of my glorious and majestic body. These are just a few of my many great and precious promises that I will fulfill for you. I love you exceedingly beyond what words can say!

Jeremiah 31:3 • Ephesians 3:16-21 • 2 Peter 1:2-4

December 14

Jesus Talks to You

I know you perfectly and completely; I know your joys and sorrows, victories and sins, strengths and weaknesses. I also love you perfectly and completely with an infinitely glorious love. I see you from my eternal perspective and know how you will be when you reign with me forever; I know your love and devotion to me forever.

When you fall short of my glory and sin, I still love you with the same infinite love; please do not condemn yourself. Repent of the sin and confess it to me; know that I fully forgive you, and will cleanse you from all unrighteousness. When I appear, you will be changed in a twinkling of an eye to be like me. Always remember that I am working all things for your good as I fulfill my purpose for your life.

1 John 1:7-9 • Romans 8:28-34

December 15

Jesus Talks to You

I continually make intercession to my Father for you. I desire that you would be strengthened with all power, according to my glorious might, so that you would possess great endurance and patience with joy while always giving thanks to the Father, who has qualified you to be a partaker in the inheritance of my holy people in the kingdom of light.

I am the resurrection and the life; I will give life by my Spirit to your mortal body, that you might excel in doing the will of my Father. I have strengthened the faithful through centuries past and will likewise send grace and power, by my Spirit, at your time of need. Through the gift of faith, saints of old subdued kingdoms, worked righteousness, performed miracles from my hand, obtained promises, stopped the mouths of lions, from weakness grew strong, became mighty in battle, and women received back their loved ones from the dead. Through endurance and patience, these saints who believed in me, the Mighty God of Israel, changed the course of history in wondrous ways.

Hebrews 7:25 • Colossians 1:11-12 • Hebrews 11

December 16 *Jesus Talks to You*

My dear child, I have called you to a life of joy; I have blessed you with all spiritual blessings in heavenly places as you abide in me. I have given you a living hope by my resurrection from the dead; I have conquered death for you. I live in you now and will give you strength to do my will. You are a co-heir with me of all the riches of the kingdom of heaven. Rejoice greatly! This is the truth, this is very real. The elements of this world will pass away, but you are my child forever and will reign with me in the new heavens and new earth—a perfect world without end.

I love you continually and my thoughts toward you each day are more than can be numbered. By being thankful—there is so much for you to be thankful for—you enter a deeper communion with me. I inhabit your praises and we have a union in my boundless love for you.

Ephesians 1:3-7 • Galatians 2:20 • 1 Peter 1:3-4 • Psalm 100:1-5

December 17 *Jesus Talks to You*

Come unto me, and I will give you rest. I desire for you to be filled and guided by my Holy Spirit that you might cease from your own works, walk in my works, and find rest to your soul. Be zealous and strive diligently to enter this wondrous rest in me.

Oh, the glorious rest that awaits your entrance into my eternal habitation! You will soon be clothed with immortality and view the magnificence of the holy city, new Jerusalem—as you behold me, the King of kings, on my throne with ten thousand times ten thousand angels in attendance. You will hear the splendor and majesty of the heavenly music. You will rejoice beyond rejoicing for you and all the glorious family of God have been changed to be in my likeness. As you meet those who are in the kingdom of heaven because you shared my love with them, and take in the beyond-awesome glory of the kingdom, then you will know that you have entered my eternal Sabbath-rest.

Matthew 11:28-30 • Hebrews 4:9-11 • Revelation 22:1-5

December 18 *Jesus Talks to You*

For centuries man wondered, as he looked up at the stars at night, "Who is this God of creation?" Those who read the scriptures of the prophets only possessed a vague understanding of the God of heaven and earth, and they viewed mere shadows of the Messiah who was to come. When Philip asked me to show him the Father, I asked him how is it that he did not know me after being with me for so long; for he who has seen me has seen the Father. Wonder of wonders, I became a man that you might know me. You beheld my glory, full of grace and truth.

Though I am God, I call you my friend. I desire to be your refuge from the storm, your comfort in times of sorrow, and one to rejoice with in victories and in celebrating life. Share some quiet time with me today and every day. Throughout the centuries, the Scriptures speak of men and women who knew me and listened to my voice. I am the good Shepherd and I speak today. Take the time to listen with an open heart. Come experience the deepest and most fulfilling relationship that may be known to man—friendship with the risen Savior and King of kings.

John 14:1-14 • John 1:14 • John 15:9-17

December 19 *Jesus Talks to You*

The greatest love ever shown in the universe is that of my Father loving the world so much that he gave his only begotten Son. I shared this everlasting love when I cleansed the lepers, gave sight to the blind, comforted the brokenhearted, blessed the children, and laid down my life—bearing all of mankind's sin. Though I was spit upon, whipped, mocked, beaten, nailed to a tree, and died an agonizing death, my love for you did not change. I still love you with an everlasting love and always will! I am the same yesterday, today, and forever. I will lead you by this same love, from glory to glory both now and forever!

John 3:16 • John 15:13 • Hebrews 13:8

December 20 *Jesus Talks to You*

Consider it all joy when you face trials and temptations, knowing that the testing of your faith produces perseverance. But let this perseverance and patience have its full effect in your life, that you may be mature and complete in me, lacking nothing. Blessed are you who remain steadfast under trial, because when you have stood the test, you will receive the crown of life that I have promised to those who love me.

Within your human nature, dwell the lust of the flesh, the lust of the eyes, and the pride of life; Satan will use the allurements of the world to entice any of these three where you might be weak—desiring to destroy your walk in the Spirit. Regard your former life and its sins to have been crucified with me. Walk in the newness of life; I raised you from the dead, and I now live in you. Temptation and sin are both subtle and deceptive. Put my Word first in your life, and you will become stronger in me. Avoid situations where you know that you will be exposed to temptations, especially where you know you are weak. Seek me diligently; pray wholeheartedly that you might continually be led by my Spirit.

James 1:1-12 • Galatians 5:16-25 • Galatians 2:20

December 21 *Jesus Talks to You*

You are a treasured member of my holy nation, my royal priesthood, now declaring the praises of your King. I called you out of darkness into my glorious light. Once a slave to sin, you have been washed and sanctified by my atoning blood sacrifice; therefore I am not ashamed to call you my friend. You are now called to be one of my ambassadors; as my Father sent me, so send I you.

Dear beloved child, rest in my finished work on the cross. You have my perfect righteousness in you by faith—it is a gift—you cannot add to it by your own works. Rejoice in the miracle of love that I have wrought in your life.

Revelation 1:5-6 • 1 Peter 2:9

December 22

Jesus Talks to You

It is my Father's good pleasure to give you the kingdom. You need not fear or be anxious over your daily provision. Shall not he who gave his only begotten Son for you also richly provide all things for you? I, who spoke the very worlds into existence and have full possession of all the treasures of heaven and earth, know your every need. My everlasting love, that led me to the cross, is ever caring for you, my dear child. As I miraculously fed the five thousand with five loaves and two fish, or cared for the Israelites for forty years in many wondrous ways, I will always provide for you.

Though the clouds may shadow the sun's rays, its glorious beams shall shortly fall upon your shoulders again. I am the Sun of Righteousness; my steadfast love never ceases, my mercies are new every morning, and great is my faithfulness. So when trials test your faith, you should not trust in yourself, but in me who can even raise the dead. Be thankful for all I have done in the past, and trust me for today and tomorrow.

Luke 12:22-32 • Philippians 4:19 • Lamentations 3:22-26

December 23

Jesus Talks to You

Beloved child, I am your God and love you so deeply and infinitely. I live inside you and am always so close to you—just a prayer away. I will fulfill your heart's desires as you delight yourself in me. My blessings will flow so richly upon you that there will not be room enough to hold them. Your praises shall be joyful and abundant, even reaching to your Father's throne in heaven.

Rest in my love and let my peace reign in your heart today. Know assuredly that I will lead you beside still waters and into green valleys. When storms arise, come under the shadow of my wings. I shall bring a calm for you as I did for the disciples when waves were flooding our ship. Look to me, the author and finisher of your faith; I will guide you through the trials of this world and bring you to your desired haven—my kingdom of glory.

December 24

Jesus Talks to You

Though I am the eternal God, Creator of heaven and earth, I became a baby; I clothed myself in the likeness of sinful flesh. I put on mortality with all its pain, sorrow, hunger, and thirst. I was welcomed to earth in a Bethlehem stable and given the unique privilege of getting to sleep in a feeding box for animals. Though I am the King of kings, I only received a reception that day from lowly shepherds. That's OK. I wanted it that way. I didn't come to reign as King on earth, but that you, my child, might soon reign with me in my kingdom above. I only came here to love you; I came to be a sacrifice for your sins. For those who wait for me, the Son from heaven, I will appear a second time, not as the sacrificial Lamb of God, but as the triumphant Lion of the tribe of Judah. I come as the reigning King of kings and Lord of lords. I come to bring you salvation. I am coming the second time to bring you to my kingdom of glory. I just want to bring you home!

Hebrews 9:28 • Titus 2:11-14 • Revelation 21:1-7

December 25

Jesus Talks to You

I spanned the great gulf between man and God by being born into this world as a human—a tiny baby. While lying in a feeding trough, wrapped in swaddling clothes, and comforted by the loving gaze of my parents, Mary and Joseph, the glory of the Lord was shining around shepherds in the field, with an angel proclaiming the good news of great joy; the Savior is born this day in the city of David. Then suddenly a multitude of the heavenly host also appeared to the shepherds proclaiming to all mankind—glory to God in the highest heaven and on earth peace to all men on whom his favor rests. As soon as the angels had returned to heaven, the shepherds hurried through the fields and found Mary, Joseph, and me, just as it was told them. The shepherds glorified and praised God as they spread the news.

The ancient prophecies of Isaiah had come to pass—a child was born, a son was given. I was that child who would soon be called Wonderful Counselor, Mighty God, Everlasting Father, and Prince of Peace.

Luke 2:1-20 • Isaiah 9:6-7

December 26

Jesus Talks to You

My disciples and I were invited to celebrate a marriage at Cana in Galilee during which they ran out of wine. I instructed the servants to fill six large stone waterpots with water. I revealed my glory that day when I turned the water into wine; the wedding was a success.

When I direct you to cast the net on the right side of the boat, and you have already fished all night and caught nothing—just do it. When I bid you to fill the jars with water because the wedding celebration ran out of wine—just do it. My power transcends the laws of nature. If you have faith and obey, you will see the glory of God.

May the turning of the water into wine, my first working miracle, encourage you to trust me as my first disciples did. And someday you shall sit down with them at the marriage supper of the Lamb; I personally will serve you. And when you drink the wine of the grapes of heaven, you shall rejoice beyond measure saying, "Truly, you have saved the best wine until now!"

John 2:1-11

December 27

Jesus Talks to You

Once you were a little stone covered with dirt, stuck in the miry clay, in the mountain of sin. I pulled you out of the depths; I washed you and purified you. I am the God of power and miracles; I am transforming you into a precious gem fit for my royal kingdom.

My Word is living and powerful, sharper than any two-edged sword, piercing to the dividing of soul and spirit; it judges thoughts and intents of the heart. You, who were conformed to this present evil world, need daily to be transformed by the renewing of your mind. As you enter the domain of my Word, and allow me to work deeply, my Spirit will transform you more and more into my likeness—Jesus, the eternal Son of God.

Hebrews 4:12-16 • Psalm 40:2-3 • 1 Thessalonians 5:23-24

December 28

Jesus Talks to You

I, the living God, have called you out of the darkness into my marvelous light. You are now a royal priest unto me—offering praise continually as you bring glory to my name. I am holy; you are called to depart from sin, walk with me, and be filled with my Holy Spirit. My Father chooses to glorify me, his eternal Son, by acts of the Holy Spirit, working through men and women who love and worship their God with their whole hearts; these are truly priests of the Most High God. As a priest, your earnest and continual prayer as an intercessor is powerful and effective. I highly value your love and service as you call upon my name. I will work mightily on your behalf in blessing the church and bringing my Word of life to a dying world.

Revelation 1:5-6 • 1 Peter 2:9-11 • Acts 14:3 • Hebrews 2:4

December 29

Jesus Talks to You

I desire that you learn from me by taking upon yourself my yoke. I will personally guide you in loving others and doing the will of your Father in heaven. I have chosen to work alongside you as you plow through everyday life. I will bring true rest to your soul.

The early disciples forsook all to follow me—considering everything as loss compared to the honor of being sons and daughters of the living God. Their faith honored me and I honored their faith; I endued them with power from on high. By faith the disciples laid hands on the sick and they were healed. By faith they loved the unlovely. By faith they brought hope and salvation to millions through the centuries, by their written words and their Spirit-led deeds of love. By faith they overcame the world. You can too; I live in you and will give you strength daily. Let my faith and love blossom and flourish in your heart and life; allow the Holy Spirit to fill you daily, that you might know my love and touch lives by its power.

Matthew 11:28-30 • Philippians 3:7-15 • Acts 1:8 • Romans 15:13

December 30 *Jesus Talks to You*

My beloved child, I greatly humbled myself by becoming a man and dwelt on earth, that you might behold my glory, love, and righteousness. I, who was rich—the possessor of all the riches of the eternal kingdom of heaven—became poor for your sake, that you might become rich through my poverty.

My life was further humbled, as I went to the cross to give my life as a ransom for many. My Father made me, who knew no sin, to be sin for you—that you might become the righteousness of God in me. Therefore, my Father has exalted me to the highest place, and he has given me a name that is above every name; every tongue will acknowledge that I am Lord, to the glory of God my Father.

Philippians 2:6-11 • John 1:1-14 • Matthew 20:28 • Hebrews 9:28

December 31 *Jesus Talks to You*

With a violent earthquake, a lightning-bright angel, with clothing as white as snow, had rolled away the stone and sat upon it. The guards shook with fear and well they should; they neither believed in me nor were they looking for me. But the angel comforted the believing women for they were true seekers of their Messiah; he told them to not be afraid, and stated that I had risen from the dead, just like I promised; I would be going ahead of them into Galilee; there shall they see me.

Look for me in times of sorrow and trial; I will comfort you and remind you of my great promises. The women thought that I was dead and buried in the tomb. Yet, I was risen! At their darkest hour, the "Sonrise" gave them a new dawn—the brightest and most glorious day of their lives. In your darkest hour, keep looking to me, the author and finisher of your faith. I am the Sun of Righteousness and will bring to you a new dawn. I also will be going ahead of you with my love, grace, and power each day. There you will see me.

Matthew 28:1-9 • Psalm 42:5 • Romans 15:13 • 2 Thessalonians 2:16-17

You Were Made to Know GOD

Deep down, there is a void in every one of us that is made for one thing—a relationship with God. Through Jesus Christ, the Messiah, you can have a true relationship with your heavenly Father. God is love, and knowing him is the only way to have fulfillment in life and a peace that passes understanding.

Sin has separated you from God. But he loved you so much, that he gave his only begotten Son, so that if you would believe in him, you would not perish but have everlasting life. You don't need to put off receiving his great gift of salvation. Come as you are. He loves you with an infinite love and is ready to receive you right now.

I encourage you to pray, "Lord Jesus, I believe you are the Son of God, that you died for me, and rose again from the dead. I have sinned against you in my words, deeds, and thoughts. Forgive me please of all of my wrongdoing. I desire to enter into a relationship with you. I place my trust in you as my Savior and Lord. I accept the atoning work you accomplished on the cross, shedding your blood, and forgiving me of all my sins. Please come live in my heart and life. Thank you that I am now born again and now possess the gift of eternal life. Help me to live for you each day. Amen."

God will now begin to transform you daily, by the Holy Spirit, which is now in you. Thank him for all of his blessings each day; trust him when times are tough. He is with you always; great is his faithfulness.

Read the Word of God (the Bible) every day, talk to God through prayer, and attend a Bible-based church where you will get encouraged by true friends who care for you. Jesus promises to bring you into an abundant life as you follow him.

May our God richly bless you!
Your brother in Christ,
Robert Barry

Help Others Embark on a Life-Changing Journey with

Jesus Talks to You

• Give this book as a gift. As you have discovered, the rich treasures of wisdom and the words of love from the risen Savior in this book have strengthened you in your faith and comforted you much as you walk daily with him. We invite you to share *Jesus Talks to You*—a unique inspirational devotional—with others who will benefit greatly by it.

• Reach out to others who are in need of encouragement and the love of God. Provide copies of *Jesus Talks to You* to people in retirement homes, hospitals, nursing homes, jails and prisons.

• Consider setting up a book study group. *Jesus Talks to You* provides messages of hope and godly living. The daily messages, coupled with the study of the Scripture references that are provided, will offer you and your church family the opportunity for great fellowship and growth in Christ and His Word. Invite your neighbors, friends, or co-workers—lives may be changed, eternally.

Jesus Talks to You

Paperback is available at:
amazon.com
JesusTalksToYou.com

eBook is available at:
amazon.com (Kindle)
barnesandnoble.com (Nook)

Special Sales
Paperback is available at special quantity discounts when purchased in bulk by churches, organizations, schools, corporations, and non-profits.

For information, please send Email: JesusTalksToYou@aol.com

17947301R00139

Printed in Great Britain
by Amazon